Looking for a Job?

Proven Resumes
and Confidence Builders

Is Your Solution:

This book contains strategies for every job hunter whether employed or unemployed. Innovative, cutting edge techniques to get hired in the '90s.

• • • • • •

"These strategies landed me a job that pays $17,000 more."

• • • • • •

"I received 7 job offers using these techniques."

• • • • • •

"You'll discover hiring secrets that only professionals have known."

• • • • • •

"Regina trained 40 of our career development and computer instructors. Her techniques have increased our success in placing hundreds of students."

Published by Abrams & Smith Publishing, PO Box 52901, Bellevue, WA 98015-2901. To order call 1-206-820-9779 or 1-800-957-1209.

Copyright © 1997, 1996, 1995, 1994, 1992 Regina Pontow. Cover Design by Regina Pontow.

ISBN: 1-884668-05-4 Manufactured in the United States of America.

About The Author

In 1983, I began a wordprocessing and resume writing business having several years of secretarial experience; a degree in marketing; and an award for non-fiction writing. By 1985 I had become a college instructor recognized for helping clients market themselves and cut the length of their job searches while increasing their confidence levels. After 5 years I left my resume business, entered the personnel field and gained experience interviewing and placing hundreds of applicants in permanent and temporary positions. Having succeeded in this industry I opened a personnel agency but missed teaching. Re-entering the job market I became a career development instructor for a local business college. Over the last ten years I have spent more than 4,000 hours interviewing and counseling job seekers. During this time I have written over 1,500 resumes for clients with incomes ranging from $10,000 to $200,000 annually.

Why I Wrote This Book

Working with hundreds of job seekers I have developed proven strategies which have helped my clients increase their confidence and generate more interviews; I hope to share these methods with you. Having interviewed thousands of job seekers, I know that most people experience some degree of fear or self-doubt when changing jobs. These feelings can keep people in unsatisfying jobs, cause them to put off writing a resume, and can erode their confidence. Our feelings and confidence level are the most important factors in determining how easy or how hard it is for us to secure a better job, write a resume, or interview successfully.

Working with clients from all walks of life I continually see how feelings of self-doubt keep many people from achieving their career goals. Self-doubt can cause them to procrastinate and undermine their success. Many clients come into my office feeling dejected and say things like:

"If I can't feel confident about myself, how will I ever get an employer to feel confident about hiring me?"

"I've never had to look for a job before, it's really scary."

"I was fired from my last job. I'm not sure anyone will hire me."

"I feel so defeated each time I try to write a resume. It seems like I don't have any 'real' skills."

I feel compelled to write this book because feelings such as these affect job search success. The impact that self-confidence has upon career achievement goes unaddressed in current career and resume books. No matter how good a career or resume book is, if you are feeling a lot of self-doubt and the book does not show you how to deal with these feelings, it is likely you will fail to attain your goals. It won't matter if you have the best or the most expensive resume money can buy. If you aren't feeling confident, this will come across in interviews and sabotage your success.

The Importance of Self-Confidence

If your self-confidence isn't boosted before resume writing begins, what do you get? A weak, understated resume that reinforces self-doubt, doesn't work, or generates job offers below your abilities. Helping people deal with their feelings and boost their confidence is the main reason I've been so successful in writing resumes. I spend at least two hours with each of my clients as they share their hopes and fears with me. This allows me to reflect back to clients their feelings and give them new input about their skills and abilities. A large part of my role as a resume consultant is being both a counselor and cheerleader. Chapter 1 and Chapter 12 provide a variety of methods I've developed as a career counselor and motivator. These chapters show you how to change any doubts you may be feeling into feelings of confidence. The rest of the book deals with "nuts and bolts" information that teaches you how to create a great resume and conduct a successful job search. Sprinkled throughout these sections are anecdotes to inspire you and help you achieve your goals. *Good luck on your journey!*

I want to thank Melissa and Jay for all the support and love they have given me. Special thanks to Janet Anderson for her expertise in helping me to edit this book.

Table of Contents

1 ————————————————————————

The Importance
Of Your Self-Image——————————

A few years ago I worked with Ted, a man who had patented a product which generated over $4 million for his company. He also managed major accounts with annual sales of $50 million. When I asked him what salary he would negotiate for he said, *"Somewhere between $100,000 to $125,000."* Those of us who have made less money tend to think Ted would be very confident of his abilities. Yet, when we completed his resume Ted said, *"This sounds great, but I don't know, what if an employer expects me to be able to do all these things? It's kind of scary."*

I use Ted as an example because many people think Ted would have no reason to doubt his abilities when he makes so much money. When I told Linda, a personnel manager, about Ted she said, *"I can't believe he'd have any trouble looking for a job."* On the flip side, many of us think Linda should have no problem writing a resume because she's a personnel manager. Yet, she said, *"I write resumes for all my friends and employees but I can't write one for myself. Here I am managing personnel operations for a staff of 250 with a salary of $45,000. It's embarrassing that I can't write my own resume."* When Ted returned to pick up his resume he mentioned how glad he was to have it completed. He felt silly that he had so much trouble putting it together. I told him Linda's story. He couldn't believe she'd have any trouble writing her resume since she was a personnel manager. The point is: We all tend to doubt our abilities when writing a resume. Don't let self-doubt lead you to create a weak resume or to undersell yourself in an interview and ultimately limit your job possibilities.

Self-Doubt Can Result In Weak Resumes——————————

Recently, I worked with Pam who made much less than Ted or Linda. She experienced similar doubts. Pam had over 7 years experience in reception, general office, and customer service but felt her experience wasn't important. She said, *"I'm really a hard worker and have accomplished any task I've been given, but I can't write a resume that shows my capabilities. The more I read about resume writing, the more confused I become. Every book recommends something different. It's been at least 2 months since I even worked on my resume and I need a new job now!"* Her voice revealed the self-doubt and fear she was experiencing. As we talked I asked her to describe her work history to me and what she had been responsible for. Once I got a good idea of her background I told her she had very good skills and could make at least $400 more per month. She said, *"Boy I don't know, it seems like I don't have any skills, my salary has only been $1,100 a month."*

1 ♦ ————————————————————————

Do Not Copy or Make Handouts

By summarizing her strongest skills I knew her resume would convince employers to interview her and would result in higher salary offers. It was obvious she doubted what I was saying. To her surprise, Pam's confidence increased as she read her new resume. She said, "*I can hardly believe it's me. I would have never described my background like this. I really thought a lot of these things were too trivial to mention.*" About 2 weeks after we completed her resume, she dropped into my office to say she had just accepted a job starting at $1,500 a month. She said the person who had hired her had kept shaking his head yes as he read her resume. Then she said, "*He thinks I can do a lot. I'm scared, but I'm really going to work at it!*" It looks like both the employer and I believed Pam could accomplish a lot, she's the only one who doubted it.

Negative Situations Can Damage Your Self-Image

If you've had a bad experience with an employer you may discount your skills. For example, Judy managed a sales office, yet her boss treated her with little respect. Judy handled all customer complaints, sales processing, and emergency problem solving. She literally ran the office because the staff was in the field 95% of the time. When I recommended she label her experience as office management and customer service she felt uncomfortable. She said her boss never acknowledged that she performed work at that level and treated her as if her work was menial. She said, "*Oh, I can't use office management or customer service as titles. My boss would never say I was an office manager or customer service person. He always called me a secretary. In fact, when I asked for a raise last year he denied it because I hadn't taken on any new responsibilities. In his mind I was still just a secretary.*"

I told her we wouldn't say she was an office manager or customer service manager. We would instead substitute functional headings to describe her experience as office management and customer service. Even if her boss told a prospective employer she hadn't managed the office, Judy had every right to accurately describe her responsibilities in her resume. To help Judy maximize her experience, yet feel she was being truthful, we included her title as secretary at the end of her job description. Here's what it looked like:

OFFICE MANAGEMENT / CUSTOMER SERVICE

Managed all office and customer service functions including:

♦ Sales quoting, order processing, and problem solving to support a staff of 10 Sales Representatives (as a Secretary for XYZ Company).

Reading the sample above, Judy said, "*Written that way it sounds great. If they call my employer they'll see my title was Secretary. So I guess that's not lying. Let's do it!*" I have helped many people who perform work beyond their job titles to describe their experience in stronger ways. Situations such as Judy's cause people to doubt their abilities and feel they are lying even when they truthfully describe their job duties. It is important to be on the lookout and avoid employers who build themselves up by knocking others down.

This was the situation Judy had been in. If she had written her resume without a "pep talk," how do you think it would have turned out? If you have had a similar experience it's easy to understand the mixed emotions you may feel as you write your resume. Feelings of self-doubt and memories of an employer's negative attitude can cloud your judgement and result in a weak resume. Generally, I spend as much time boosting a person's confidence as writing the resume. Since I'm not there to work with you I want to boost your confidence with success stories throughout this book. Take them to heart as they will help you.

Your Comfort Zone

The issues we've discussed show how resume writing can cause us to feel uncomfortable or "out of our comfort zone." We each have a professional comfort zone that includes areas of work we feel confident performing. On the other hand, we are "out of our comfort zone" when we don't feel confident performing them. Ted's statement, *"This really sounds great, but what if an employer expects me to do all this, it's kinda scary,"* clearly showed that he felt "out of his comfort zone." He worried about whether he could live up to his resume. What made Ted doubt his abilities? I believe he felt that way because his new resume focused on his strongest accomplishments. These were not tasks that he did every day with ease. Obtaining the patent had been hard work and he had often doubted himself in the process.

Ted also discounted the skills he used to manage his accounts. He saw himself as merely someone dealing with friends and helping them solve their problems. He had never estimated the sales from his accounts. Stating that he managed key accounts with annual revenues of $50 million did not match the image he had of himself. Describing the money his patent had generated along with the million dollar accounts he managed pushed Ted way out of his comfort zone. Ted was not used to *"tooting his own horn."* These statements made him feel phony and like he was exaggerating his skills. Ted wanted to minimize his accomplishments and exclude these figures from his resume. He knew he would feel more comfortable with his resume if he downplayed these achievements.

I asked Ted, *"Did you really do these things, can you do them again, and are the figures you've given me correct?"* His answer to each question was, *"Yes!"* By proving to Ted that the statements on his resume were accurate and not exaggerated he realized that his fear of failure was motivating him to minimize his accomplishments. Clarifying his feelings helped him accept that he could do these things and there was no reason to feel scared or dishonest about this information. Ted wisely chose to include in his resume the information about his patent and the revenues generated from the accounts he managed. He realized these accomplishments would help him obtain a higher position with an increased income and better advancement opportunities. Once Ted sorted out his feelings and understood them he felt very comfortable with his new resume. Most of us experience being "out of our comfort zone" when writing resumes. We're not used to describing our best achievements let alone having others read about them. Maximizing our strengths is critical in creating a great resume, generating more interviews, getting more job offers, and making more money.

3 ♦

Even I feel a little "out of my comfort zone" when I write my resume. As I describe my accomplishments I get a little scared. So, I ask myself, *If you did those things once, can you do them again? And, are the estimates of your achievements correct?"* My answer is always, *"Yes."* I still feel "out of my comfort zone," but I know how important it is to have a strong resume so I include this information.

Working with clients like Judy, Linda, and Ted, I'm constantly aware of how self-doubt affects the way people describe themselves. Having worked with over 1,500 clients I'm convinced that most of us do not want to exaggerate or overstate our qualifications. In fact, we do just the opposite. We downplay or negate our skills. Why is this? I believe it is because most of us suffer from "low self-image" to one degree or another. Low self-image and self-doubt go hand in hand. When you doubt your abilities you become very concerned about failing. You may worry that you'll be offered a job that's over your head. To prevent this from happening you may be motivated to tone down your resume. However, your goal is to generate as many interviews as possible which requires a strong resume. If you are offered a position that is over your head then you can always turn it down. This puts you in control. If you create a weak resume that generates few interviews, you will have less control of your job search. You may then feel you have to take whatever you can get.

Self-Image & Resume Development

Our society reinforces the negative much more than the positive when it comes to our feelings about ourselves. We've all been told not to brag or act boastful. Before reading further, I'd like you to write 10 positive and 10 negative things about yourself. Don't spend a lot of time thinking. Quickly jot down ideas as they come to you.

10 Positive Things About Myself

_____

_____

_____

_____

_____

_____

_____

_____

_____

_____

10 Negative Things About Myself

_____

_____

_____

_____

_____

_____

_____

_____

_____

_____

What did you write about first? Something positive or negative? Did you end up with more positive or negative statements? Many people find it easier to describe their negative traits rather than their positive ones. Because most of us are used to identifying our negative attributes we often feel phony and uncomfortable describing our positive ones. This conditioning makes it hard for us to accept and appreciate our best accomplishments let alone tell anyone else about them.

Did You Really Do It?

To create a strong resume focus on your true responsibilities and accomplishments. Highlight your strongest qualifications and learn to feel comfortable with them. Be aware of the tendency to present a weak version of your skills and experience as you write your resume. If you write a strong statement that makes you feel uncomfortable ask yourself:

> *"Did I perform this task - even if my job title doesn't sound like it?"*
> *"Could I do this again on another job?"*
> *"Are the estimates of my achievements accurate?"*

If your answers are all "*Yes*," you are not overstating your skills. You may feel phony, but it's only because you're not used to talking positively about yourself. Don't let fear of failure and the feeling of being "out of your comfort zone" cause you to minimize or eliminate your best accomplishments from your resume.

What Shape Is Your Self-Image In?

Take a moment to answer these questions before you continue reading. Be extremely honest with yourself. Rate your answers on the graphs below from one to ten. One indicates that you experience little or no doubt or worry in relation to each question. Ten indicates you experience a lot of doubt or worry in relation to each question.

Have you worried about writing your resume?

1	2	3	4	5	6	7	8	9	10

Have you felt anxious as you read this book?

1	2	3	4	5	6	7	8	9	10

Do you have nagging doubts about your abilities?

1	2	3	4	5	6	7	8	9	10

Do you worry you won't get a better job?

1	2	3	4	5	6	7	8	9	10

Do you worry that you'll do badly in an interview?

1	2	3	4	5	6	7	8	9	10

Do you worry that you won't do well on your next job?

1	2	3	4	5	6	7	8	9	10

If you rated yourself higher than three on any of the graphs I urge you to read Chapter 12 before writing your resume. If your answers were two or below - congratulations! You have a lot of confidence in yourself and a strong self-image. Remember Ted? I think his self-image was very good. He had only a few areas where he experienced discomfort and self-doubt. By gaining new information about himself and creating a strong resume he improved his self-image.

On the other hand, Judy's self-image was low. She needed to spend more time learning about her abilities and building her self-confidence. Having been in a negative, demeaning work environment her self-confidence had been damaged and needed repair. Helping her and others to increase their confidence and improve their self-image is what this chapter and Chapter 12 are about. If you are in this category take the time to read and ponder these chapters. It will help you tremendously. Then move on to Chapter 2. If you feel like Judy did, you'll have a hard time writing a strong resume and conducting a job search until you mend your self-confidence. Take the time to take care of yourself. Beyond higher pay and better jobs your reward will be increased happiness and satisfaction with yourself.

How Does Your Self-Image Affect Your Goals?

You may have purchased this book because your confidence needs a boost. To increase your confidence it is important that you understand how your self-image determines your confidence level and controls your behavior. Your self-image also determines the level of success you achieve in all areas of your career and personal life. It determines how easy or hard it is for you to accomplish any task whether it's learning new skills, looking for a job, or writing a resume. Your self-image also determines how confident and comfortable you feel in any given situation. You tend to move toward goals that match your self-image and move away from goals that don't match your self-image. When you feel you can reach a goal then you tend to move toward the goal because it matches your self-image. You believe you are capable of reaching the goal and feel good when you contemplate working on it. Such a goal is easy and motivating to pursue. When you're not sure you can reach a goal then you tend to move away from that goal because it doesn't match your self-image. When you contemplate working on the goal you may experience anxiety and doubt, which you do not enjoy feeling. You find such a goal hard to work on and may put it off as long as possible. You move away from the goal so you can maintain feelings of comfort. This moving toward or away from goals determines the level of success you reach in all areas of your life.

When Your Self-Image Doesn't Match Your Goals

As you can see, problems occur when your self-image doesn't match your goals. When this happens you must learn how to bring your self-image in line with your goals. To do this you must understand how your self-image was created, how you maintain it, and how you can change it.

As a resume consultant I have seen how this issue affects many people to one degree or another. It has been a big issue for me. Bringing my self-image in line with my goals has been the most challenging thing I've ever done. Having come from a dysfunctional background I didn't begin to feel confident about myself until I was 24 years old. My family was very poor. Most of my clothes were second-hand and we lived on the "wrong" side of town. By the time I was 13 we had moved over 30 times. This alone wasn't enough to damage my self-image but when combined with the rest of my family's background I grew up feeling everyone else was better than me. My parents and older siblings suffered from alcoholism. Physical violence and verbal abuse were typical in my family's daily life. I was often told, *"You're dumb. You'll never amount to anything. You can't do anything right!"*

My background caused me to be timid and shy. I dreaded trying anything new because I was always ridiculed by my parents if I made any mistakes. As an adult on my first job I struggled continuously with feelings of stupidity. My thoughts were so negative about myself that I found it hard to function. Thankfully, I began to question if I was really stupid. I had always made straight A's in school. Intellectually I knew I wasn't stupid, but emotionally I still felt like a timid little girl. It has been hard work to improve my self-image but well worth the time and effort. I hope to share with you the techniques I've learned and have used to help others improve their self-image.

Originally I hadn't included this information because I wasn't sure how relevant it would be to readers. However, a friend of mine who has an extensive background in personnel felt that by sharing my life I could help others feel motivated in improving their self-confidence. When I reveal my history in career classes many students share their backgrounds with me. People discuss how they have been influenced by a negative environment and how they have worked to improve their lives. By sharing my past I have been able to separate my actions and self-image from my family's. Talking about these things has helped me to no longer feel ashamed of myself and has given me an opportunity to receive positive feedback and support from others. I hope to help you in a similar way.

Do You Set Goals?

We are all born with the ability to grow and to set goals for ourselves. Every toddler has the goal to walk. Given a nourishing environment, a toddler continues to get up and try walking after every fall. However, in an oppressive environment where a child is hit or ridiculed he may withdraw into himself. In these instances, physicians use the term "failure to thrive" in describing children who are behind in their ability to walk, talk, or communicate with others. I think we can also apply the term "failure to thrive" to ourselves as adults when we don't set goals and accomplish them. In this instance, we often lose the will and determination needed to "keep getting up." We've lost the excitement and wonder that children have as they explore and learn. Our actions show this when we dread going to work every day but remain in jobs that aren't stimulating or challenging. We're not happy, but we don't have the drive or enthusiasm to make a change. I believe it's important to feel satisfied and fulfilled in our daily work life. If we don't, then it's time to reassess our careers and see how we can improve them.

By exploring how we feel about ourselves and learning how to be our best - we can be like a toddler again. We can explore life with excitement and develop the drive to keep trying and improving. As you read and apply information throughout this book you will be happy with the new career and job search goals you set for yourself.

Your Feelings

This section explores some of the feelings you may experience when changing jobs, asking for a raise, writing a resume, or interviewing. It explores how self-doubt and fear can cause you to procrastinate or accept lower career goals. Several years ago I experienced a lot of self-doubt when I read a book titled, "*Go Hire Yourself an Employer*." Did that idea ever intimidate me! The mere thought of applying directly to an employer, telling him why he should hire me, and boldly presenting my qualifications to him scared me so much that I put the book away and never used it. I now know that it contained excellent information and described effective job hunting methods. Yet, it did not tell me how to feel and believe that I could do those things. It seemed scary and impossible. So, I disregarded and pushed aside the information. I continued to do the least frightening thing, which was to answer want ads. It did not matter to me that the methods in "*Go Hire Yourself An Employer*" were effective because I couldn't see myself doing them. My fear and lack of confidence held me back. The methods were there but I couldn't use them.

Writing resumes, I continually hear and see these same feelings manifested in my clients. When I inform clients of effective resume writing and job hunting methods their eyes often glaze over and they tune out what I am saying. Many clients have a hard time believing they can do these things. They react just as I reacted when I read, "*Go Hire Yourself an Employer*." When I recommend such things as using stronger words in a resume or researching employers, clients frequently say things like:

"*Oh, I wouldn't use that word - my skills aren't that strong.*" (I can see that they doubt their abilities.)

"*Oh, I couldn't talk to my friends and ask them about jobs.*" (I can see that they think it will be embarrassing or an imposition to their friends to ask them about jobs.)

"*I don't want to research employers, it's easier to answer want ads.*" (I can see they are scared of contacting employers.)

You, too, may experience similar feelings as you read this book. Discomfort may motivate you to ignore information that intimidates you or scares you. If this happens you have two options to consider. You can:

Avoid discomfort by not using the information in this book.

Or,

Identify and replace any feelings of discomfort with feelings of confidence so you can fully use this book.

If you avoid using the information in this book you may be unable to move toward your goals. You may want to avoid situations you may fail at or make mistakes doing. Yet, most of us learn by making mistakes not by succeeding. That's how I've learned most of my life. Not all areas of my businesses were successful. However, those areas that didn't work provided me with an excellent opportunity to analyze and improve them. I asked myself, *"Why isn't this working? How can I make it better? What am I not seeing that I need to see?"* To be successful, you need to approach your job search in the same way. You may send out a batch of cover letters and resumes that don't generate the response you'd like. Instead of seeing this as a failure and quitting it helps to see it as a valuable lesson. You may realize you have targeted the wrong industry or selected an industry that is being hit with cutbacks. You may find no one is hiring and realize you must be more creative in making job contacts. Or, you may realize that you need to try an industry that is growing. You then have an opportunity to discover how your skills "transfer" to an unexplored industry. The strategies in this book will teach you how to be flexible and creative in your job search. If you ignore and discard these strategies it's likely you won't move ahead in your career and you may stay "stuck" where you are.

You Must Be Comfortable With Your Goals

When you are comfortable with your goals and believe they are achievable then you will achieve them. By ridding yourself of crippling self-doubt you will free up a tremendous amount of energy which you can devote to success. You can stop expending the energy it takes to avoid scary possibilities or unhappy employment situations. Your feelings are what motivate you and inspire you to either achieve or not achieve your goals. *Mere information does not.*

For example, my husband and I attended several real estate seminars and became excited about purchasing foreclosure homes. We learned good information and felt like we could go through all the necessary steps while we were at the seminars. Yet, we both experienced a lot of doubt when the seminars ended. We couldn't see ourselves approaching people in foreclosure and negotiating to buy their homes. It didn't matter that many people would be grateful for our financial assistance. What mattered was how uncomfortable we would feel making a good deal off of someone in foreclosure. It made us feel like swindlers or slick salespeople making a buck from someone else's misfortune. We had *good information* about buying foreclosure homes but we couldn't use it. Our feelings got in the way and kept us from approaching even one homeowner. What we needed was a step by step process to help us stop feeling like swindlers and help us feel like we were helping homeowners in tight financial situations. This concept was not clear to us at the time and we let go of our dream because it caused us too much anxiety. Understanding this concept will allow you to recognize and deal effectively with feelings of self-doubt you may experience while reading this book. This awareness combined with confidence building techniques sprinkled throughout the book will help you apply the new information and techniques presented. You will learn how to identify your strongest skills, increase your confidence and reach your career goals. By combining the information in this book with your new found confidence you can succeed.

Changing Jobs Can Be Frustrating

Changing jobs, conducting a job search, or writing a resume can be scary and frustrating, causing even the most confident person to experience self-doubt. Self-doubt can immobilize you and cause you to put off your goals. Therefore, it's critical that you be aware of these feelings and deal with them effectively. When changing jobs you may worry about:

- *Whether you will succeed in a better position*
- *How well you will get along with a new employer*
- *If you are making the right move*
- *Or, if your new salary will relieve financial pressures.*

You may also have hopes or dreams you wish to accomplish such as:

- *A better job*
- *A career change*
- *To make more money*
- *Or, to achieve a higher level of job satisfaction.*

If you doubt your ability to get a better job then you may find it difficult to identify your skills because you don't think you have any. If you have had a bad experience with a past employer it may be hard for you to describe your qualifications accurately and strongly. Hopes and fears such as the ones above affect your confidence, motivation, and energy level to varying degrees. One hour you may feel very confident and the next you may feel like no one would hire you. When you feel up, you may feel very motivated to work on your resume or look for a job. But when you feel down, you may procrastinate and put off working on your resume. Dealing with these emotional fluctuations drains your physical and mental energy which makes it hard to maintain momentum in your job hunting efforts. When you examine this process it's easy to understand why it can be frustrating and time consuming. This is why many people put off looking for a job for months and even years. The demand for resume writers and career counselors proves that many people need assistance marketing themselves and dealing with these feelings. If you have kicked yourself for not writing the perfect resume or eagerly pursuing your job search then know you are not alone. Give yourself credit for what you have accomplished. Pat yourself on the back for having the courage to start now.

Your Self-Image Affects Your Career Growth

Your self-image is an accumulation of feelings and thoughts you have about yourself based on events and memories from your childhood to the present day. These feelings and thoughts influence all aspects of your life. If you have many positive feelings about yourself you probably find it easy to achieve your goals. If you have many negative feelings about yourself you probably find it hard to achieve your goals. Consider these examples of how positive and negative self-images were formed:

Ann has many positive memories of her childhood like the time she wrote a poem for her grandma who said, *"My! This poem is beautiful! I believe you'll be a writer when you grow up!"*

Ann was only six and loved writing poems. She believed what her grandma told her. Growing up Ann always dreamed of being a writer. Although it hurt her feelings when her elementary school teacher made fun of her writing she clung to her dream. On her first job, Ann enjoyed writing and editing correspondence for her bosses. They noted her writing abilities and made her the editor of the company magazine. She now manages its publication. As an adult, Ann submitted many of her poems for publication and received rejection after rejection. Taking them in stride, she continued to believe she would be published. After 36 rejections she is now a published poet.

On the other hand:

Pat has many negative memories of her school years when her family moved from a small town to a big city. Pat had always known everyone in her small classes back home and had a hard time making new friends. She found the big classes overwhelming. She was teased because her clothes were different from the other kids. Making matters worse, her science teacher berated her because she didn't maintain an A average. Soon after moving, Pat began to believe she couldn't make friends, that people didn't like her, and that she was a slow learner. On the positive side, Pat's family and art teacher felt she was talented and gave her glowing compliments, but Pat did not believe them. Pat now works as a wordprocessor and deals with other people very little. She has turned down several promotions because she fears criticism and worries that co-workers in a new department might reject her.

Your Beliefs Determine Your Self-Image

Ann and Pat received both positive and negative messages about themselves. Ann chose to believe the positive while Pat chose to believe the negative. The messages Ann and Pat received didn't determine their self-images; rather what they believed and internalized about themselves did. Consider another example about three boys who grew up with parents who told the boys they would never amount to anything. One boy became an alcoholic, another went to prison, and the third built a corporate empire. When we hear stories like this we wonder how children from the same family can turn out so differently. In this instance, two of the boys grew up believing what their parents told them. Each time they failed they told themselves:

> *"Gee, I guess I will never amount to anything. Mom and dad are right - I'll never graduate high school. I'll never have anything more than I have right now."*

But, the third child refused to believe his parents. He always felt he could be more. When he thought about his life he told himself:

> *"I might not be the smartest person in the world, but I know if I try I can usually do what I set out to do. Mom and Dad are so busy seeing all the horrible things in the world they can never see the good."*

This child adopted a much healthier view of life than his brothers. He realized his mom and dad weren't always right. He learned at an early age to question what they told him, especially when they made negative statements about him. The power of what you believe about yourself cannot be overstated. It affects how you advance in your career, how easily you learn new things, how much money you make, how well your romantic and family relationships work, what kind of car you drive, what kind of clothes you wear, and so on from the most important things in your life to the most trivial. To the degree that you believe you cannot succeed, to that same degree you may choose not to believe any new information or programming that tells you, *"You can succeed."* No matter how good the information in this book is, you may reject it if it does not match the belief system you have about yourself. That's why a positive self-image is so critical to your success in using this book.

The Power Of Negative Programming

Many of us grow up hearing negative comments about ourselves. Some of them might seem minor, such as being told we're shy, we're not good with math, or we'd better let someone else do our writing for us. These statements don't seem like they'd influence us too much. However, if we take any one of them to heart it can have a dramatic impact on our lives. For the rest of our lives we might feel we are shy. We might avoid parties, public speaking, or taking on new projects. We might decide we're no good in math and avoid entire careers in engineering or science. If we had ever dreamed of writing, all hopes for this dream might be crushed and discarded.

Such programming teaches us to feel badly about ourselves which, in turn, causes us to talk negatively to ourselves. The more we think and feel negatively about ourselves the more our actions become negative. For example, the more you say to yourself, *"I'll never get a better job,"* the more you'll believe it's true. Each time you say to yourself, *"I'll never get a better job,"* you feel fright, disillusionment, and resignation. If you think and feel this repeatedly, you come to believe it. When you consider changing jobs you may think:

"I hate this job, but I'm afraid I can't get anything better."

"The only jobs I can get are just like this one. So why bother?"

"I don't even have a decent resume so how can I change jobs?"

"I can't write and I hate writing resumes."

"Sure, I've gotten 3 promotions over the last 4 years - but that's only because everyone else is so incompetent. That's the only reason I've made it."

"How can I be sure it won't be worse at the next company I go to?"

"It's been a long time since I interviewed for a job. I don't even know what to say."

Thinking such thoughts do you increase or decrease your confidence? Do you motivate or de-motivate yourself? Do these thoughts make you want to jump into your job search or put it off? Let's look at what you have focused on with these thoughts:

Hating your job.

Doubting if there's anything better out there.

Not being able to write well.

Hating the thought of writing a resume.

Negating your abilities.

Worrying about interviewing badly.

One of my friends proofread this section and said, *"Just reading this page makes me feel depressed. You need to follow this section with a positive one and show people how to deal with these feelings."* She was currently looking for a job so I took her comments seriously. It is amazing that reading so few negative statements could trigger off such a strong response. This really drives home the degree to which negative thoughts affect us. Let's look at how we can turn these negative thoughts into positive ones:

"I've really accomplished a lot on this job. It will be great to find another company where I can continue to grow."

"I enjoy certain parts of my job and know I'm good at them. I need to find companies where I can use these skills all the time."

"It's exciting and fun to put my best accomplishments down on paper. I've really done more than I realized."

"I've gotten 3 promotions over the last 4 years because I've done an excellent job. I am proud of myself."

"I know that I am an honest and hardworking employee and that by seeking out employers who respect their employees I will enjoy a happy and satisfying career."

"I know when I practice for an interview I do really well. I enjoy talking to prospective employers when I know what to say and know how I'm going to market myself."

It's amazing how much our thoughts alter our feelings and motivation. Answer this question honestly, *"How often each day do you have negative thoughts about yourself?"* Now multiply that number by 365. This is how many negative suggestions you give yourself and store in your memory over a year's time. Remember, the more you think something about yourself or a situation the more you will believe it.

We Process Up To 60,000 Thoughts A Day

Current studies estimate that we process up to 60,000 thoughts per day. If you are confident and have high self-esteem you may feel you have few negative thoughts about yourself. However, even if you think negative thoughts only 5% of the time that is over 3,000 negative thoughts each day. In one year that's over 1 million negative thoughts or feelings.

People are always surprised at these numbers. Most of us have never calculated how many negative thoughts we think in a day. Many people have told me that they think negatively at least 75% of the time. This results in thinking 45,000 negative thoughts each day or 15 million negative thoughts each year.

At this rate, a 20 year old could have already stored over 300 million negative messages in his or her memory. And many of us wonder why it's so hard to change how we feel about ourselves. We go to a motivational seminar and get pumped up. For a few hours we feel we can conquer the world. But within a few days or maybe even hours, we've lost that feeling and experience disillusionment in our ability to change.

Using these calculations it's easy to understand why so many motivational seminars don't work. We may receive several thousand positive messages during the seminar, but can't expect a few thousand positive messages to wipe out millions of negative thoughts stored in our brains. It just doesn't happen. The only method that does work is constant repetition of new, positive thoughts. As we become aware of negative thoughts it's important to focus on something positive about ourselves and the goals we want to achieve. Otherwise we seal our fate with negativity.

I hope this has been dramatic and convincing and that you see how important it is to replace negative thoughts with positive ones. In this way you can create a new, positive self-image and believe you are a capable, successful and worthy person. I urge you to read Chapter 12 and learn how to use SUCCESS IMAGERY before you begin writing your resume or looking for a job. If you feel any self-doubt or fear about your job search it is important to increase your confidence before starting your job search.

2

Are Resumes Really That Important?

Yes, they are! Many employers receive from 100 to 400 resumes for each position they advertise. Out of hundreds of resumes, only 10 to 15 people may be selected for an interview. With competition like this your resume must stand out and get an employer's attention. It must highlight skills an employer is looking for, and be arranged in a style or format that makes these skills easy to spot. Your resume is a verbal picture of you and must make an employer want to see you.

Employers that receive hundreds of resumes must sort them quickly. If an employer spends 30 seconds scanning each resume, it will take over an hour and a half to sort 200 resumes. Most personnel managers and recruiters are busy with job duties other than resume reading. Faced with a hectic schedule, many interviewers feel resume reading is an interruption in their work day. Therefore, your resume must attract and hold an employer's attention before he moves on to complete other tasks.

Studies show that employers spend as little as 10 seconds glancing at resumes before discarding them or saving them to look at further.

It's imperative that your resume highlight your best qualifications so that it is not discarded. It must land in the stack that will be kept and read again. To do this your resume must standout from hundreds of other resumes. Employers quickly scan all resumes they've received for a position. As they find resumes that match the skills or experience they need they put these resumes in a stack to be looked at further. After all resumes have been screened, employers then have a smaller stack of 20 to 30 resumes. Employers then read each of these resumes more thoroughly. Even if an employer spends only one more minute reading each resume it will require another 20 to 30 minutes out of his schedule, and this is something most employers want to finish as quickly as possible. This final screening then narrows the last group to approximately 5 to 12 resumes. These are the individuals who will be called for an interview. Therefore, your goal is to create a resume that "passes inspection" and lands, time after time, in that last pile of resumes that get interviews.

The Best Preparation for an Interview

Writing a resume makes you identify and verbalize your strongest skills and helps you be aware of your weaknesses. This is great preparation for an interview since most employers ask you to describe both your strengths and weaknesses.

15 ♦

Do Not Copy or Make Handouts

Getting your skills on paper and presenting them in an effective eye catching format also increases your confidence. Organizing your thoughts makes you better prepared to discuss how your skills match the position you are interviewing for. This process normally takes hours of self-appraisal and will pay off big when you have only a few minutes to "sell" yourself in an interview.

It Takes Time To Create A Great Resume

You may feel impatient putting a resume together and want to speed up the process perhaps taking only an hour or two to complete it. However, it takes time to remember skills and abilities that you have developed over several years of time. You may not remember some of your most important achievements until a day or so after beginning your resume. If you've already prepared your resume you may be tempted to leave out any new information you remember. This data could be what catches an employer's eye and gets you an interview.

It often takes my clients several hours before they remember significant achievements. For example, I worked with Sandra for about two hours and we were almost done when I asked her if she received compliments on the job. She said, *"Yes, I'm complimented all the time on how quickly I serve customers and how well I know their accounts."* So I asked Sandra what her responsibility was in handling the accounts. She said, *"Well, I deal with about 50 key accounts each day. In fact, I once reviewed the charge account for a major client and caught a $4,500 error. We should have charged the customer $5,000 but a typo was made and he was charged $500. I went to my boss and let him know about the mistake. That's when he promoted me to oversee client accounts in our front office."*

Before this discussion Sandra had described herself as "merely a secretary." This new information presented her as an account manager which is an entirely different image than that of "merely a secretary." As we talked I asked Sandra how she liked this type of duty. She said she loved dealing with customers and processing their accounts. As a result, we emphasized these skills in her resume. About five weeks later Sandra dropped in to tell me about her new "Account Representative" position. She was no longer a secretary and had made an impressive career move. Sandra beamed as she gave me her business card and pointed to her new title. This story shows how important it is to thoroughly explore your skills and abilities in order to create a strong resume.

Because each interview lasts only 15 to 30 minutes you must be familiar with your qualifications before the interview begins. You must be well prepared to sell yourself. You won't have time in an interview to assess your abilities or fumble around trying to express them. Most interviewers don't have the time nor the skill to identify and pull this information from you. Your resume must do this for them, quickly and efficiently. A strong resume will also guide the interviewer in asking you questions. After initial introductions, most employers will read your resume while you sit at their desk. Many will refer to back to it in order to ask you questions about your work history and experience. In this way, a strong resume continually reinforces your best qualifications throughout the interview.

If you have a weak resume the interviewer will ask you questions based on weak information. If you have a strong resume the interviewer will ask you questions based on strong information which provides a solid base of information about you. This automatically puts you ahead of the majority of applicants who have weak resumes.

Your Resume is a Marketing Tool

How often have you been in a grocery store, picked up a product with torn or damaged packaging and put it back on the shelf? The product inside may have been in perfect condition but the damaged packaging caused you not to buy it. The same principle applies to your resume. It represents you. If it is too long, too wordy or has spelling errors, it can cause an employer to "put you back on the shelf" and never interview you. Make sure you're not put back on the shelf and have several people proofread your resume. Make sure it is perfect before you print it. If you think that a "minor" typing, spelling, or grammatical error won't make any difference - you're wrong. It can cause an employer to discard your resume within seconds.

Who Gets Hired?

It's often not the best technically qualified applicant who receives a job offer. It's the person who develops an effective resume and interviews well that convinces employers he is the most qualified. In one study, the Bureau of Census surveyed 10 million job seekers to identify successful job hunting tactics and released the following quotation:

> **"The skills that make a person employable are not so much the ones needed on the job as the ones needed to get the job, skills like the ability to find a job opening, complete an application, prepare a resume, and survive an interview."**

Many qualified applicants look for jobs but can't find them. The real problem, as the quotation above explains, is that most people don't know where to look for jobs and don't know how to market themselves. Highly qualified applicants often lose job opportunities to lesser qualified applicants because the lesser qualified applicants know how to write effective resumes and market themselves.

Rewards of an Effective Resume

The time and careful consideration you put into creating an effective resume will result in:
- *Putting You Ahead Of The Competition*
- *Increased Confidence*
- *Organizing Your Thoughts and Phrasing for The Interview*
- *Guiding the Interviewer in Asking you Questions*
- *More Interviews and Better Job Offers*

As you can see, a resume can be a powerful tool in generating and increasing the success of your interviews and job offers.

Identifying Skills Increases Confidence

As you write your resume, it is very important that you think broadly about your skills. Many people have "tunnel vision" when it comes to their skills. They are used to describing their experience with terminology used in their industry. This often limits their ability to see how these skills can be "transferred" or applied in other jobs or careers. For example, I worked with Todd, a construction worker who wanted to move into an office setting. Todd felt stumped everytime he thought about his job as a "laborer." He knew this title didn't present him well as a potential office worker. He also worried that he had no transferrable skills that would be valuable in an office setting.

My goal was to help Todd realize that many of the skills he used as a construction worker were transferrable to office positions. Todd said his supervisor came to the worksite each morning for about thirty minutes. During this time he gave Todd instructions for projects to complete each day. Later each day, he came back and inspected the work. If anything was to be changed he gave Todd instructions on how to complete the task and re-inspected it the next morning. To capitalize on Todd's experience, we substituted a functional heading for his job title and wrote sentences to match the image of an office worker. We avoided labor and construction oriented descriptions. Instead we kept in mind that Todd wanted to work in an office environment and created descriptions that are "transferrable" to an office setting. Here's what we came up with:

PROJECT IMPLEMENTATION

Completed projects on properties valued to $3/4 million, working independently over 90% of the time.
- ◆ Followed superintendent's work orders to meet contract specifications.
- ◆ Worked as part of a 4-person team completing rush projects.
- ◆ Position required attention to detail, accurate completion of work orders and governmental reporting forms.

The sentences above match the duties of many office workers who work independently, yet follow the instructions of others. They often process detailed paperwork and work as a team member in completing projects. Compare Todd's old description, below, to the one you just read. Which one creates an image in your mind of someone who would fit into an office environment?

LABORER

Completed labor projects on-site including concrete pouring and laying of foundations, digging of ditches and laying of drainage pipes. Understand a wide range of construction terms and building requirements.

Why couldn't Todd come up with the first description on his own? Because he got stuck, like many people do, viewing his job as he had always heard and seen it described. This also happens because we may experience negative feelings about ourselves and our jobs as we try to describe them. When Todd imagined changing careers he felt overwhelmed and worried he would never be more than just a laborer, or a grunt as he was often called. That was his self-image. He'd get to thinking this way and notice how dirty and beat up his hands were. Then he'd feel like he would never fit into an office environment. He knew people in offices didn't look like they'd just worked on a dirty construction site. He might then look at his clothes and think he would never do well in an interview for an office job. Pretty soon he'd feel overwhelmed, thinking he could never make a job move.

Thinking negatively, his body became tense and his mind came to a grinding halt. He couldn't seem to "view" his job or himself differently. Trying to write a resume was a discouraging experience for him. Todd took a courageous step and found the help he needed to deal with his feelings and to change careers. You are doing the same, by reading this book.

Just like Todd, many of my clients feel they have no "valuable skills." However, when I show them other clients' resumes with similar backgrounds they say things like:

"Hey, this resume could be mine!"
"I didn't know the work I did was this important."
"I'd never have thought to describe it that way."
"Gee, I already feel better."
"I guess I've got more skills and experience than I thought!"

Most people don't realize how many marketable and transferrable skills they possess. Patrick is another example of this. He had experience running a department which produced commercial mixers. In his industry these products were called agitators. His job title was Agitator Manager. Here's a section of his before resume:

AGITATOR MANAGER

Oversaw agitator production. Maintained agitator inventory and schedules. Supervised warehouse and production employees.

Most of us have no idea what an Agitator Manager does. Therefore, Patrick had to make sure that anyone reading his resume would understand his skills and abilities. In questioning Patrick, I learned that he had managed a department which generated sales of $1/2 million annually. He supervised a staff of 15 and managed his department's production. Because the title Agitator Manager doesn't sound transferrable to an office environment we labeled this experience Departmental Administration. A section of his new resume appears on the next page:

DEPARTMENTAL ADMINISTRATION

Managed department generating sales of $1/2 million annually.

♦ Oversaw 15 employees, successfully leading the department to meet or exceed all quotas.

♦ Maintained an in-house inventory of $100,000.

♦ Coordinated and expedited delivery schedules with the engineering department.

♦ Administered all departmental paperwork including payroll approval, purchase orders, invoicing, production and shipping logs.

Compare the before description to this one. Are the images created in your mind about Patrick's skills and abilities different? Which description creates a feeling of Patrick having the ability to supervise employees, manage a department and administer its paperwork? Patrick wanted to move into an office setting and out of a production environment. Notice that his after description doesn't emphasize production. It creates an image of someone who has experience in an office setting, who can handle office paperwork, and who can communicate in a corporate setting.

Patrick was thrilled with his new resume. It gave him a new way of viewing his experience and how his skills were transferrable to an office environment. His new resume worked very well. Within a month he was hired to work in the records department of a major corporation. Patrick went through three interviews before being hired. Each person that interviewed him used his resume to ask him questions. He felt he wouldn't have been hired without his new resume because the old way he described his experience wouldn't have related to his new job.

Patrick's new resume served as a strong foundation and gave him confidence throughout his interviews. He feels he wouldn't have gotten his first interview, let alone second and third interviews, with his old resume. By identifying and re-labeling your experience as Todd and Patrick did, you too, can identify your transferrable skills, increase your confidence and generate more interviews.

3

*Become a Detective*_____

The most important way I help clients to develop effective resumes is by acting like a detective. Webster's dictionary defines detective as:

**"One employed or engaged in getting information
that is not readily accessible"**

I ask a lot of questions to uncover information about a client's skills and experience - information that is not readily accessible to that person. Because we often use many diverse skills on the job it is easy to forget some of them, or to feel they are unimportant. It's surprising how much more capable and qualified we appear on paper when these skills are written out. Most of us also tend to negate or downplay our skills, experience, and accomplishments. To create a successful resume we need overcome these feelings and learn how to "toot our own horn." Ralph was struggling with similar feelings when we met. This is how he described his job: *"I supervise 35 people who install and test avionics equipment on airplanes. But, the job I'm applying for requires someone with experience managing multi-million dollar operations, so I don't think I'm qualified."* I then asked Ralph how much each plane that his crew worked on was worth. He replied, *"Over $35 million."* My next question was if he oversaw the work on more than one plane at a time and he said, *"Yes, sometimes I'm responsible for up to 8 planes at a time, all at different stages of production."* Using this information we wrote the following sentence: *"Managed production projects valued up to $280 million while supervising 35 technical staff."* As a detective, I asked questions to gather important information for Ralph's resume. To develop an effective resume, you too, need to act like a detective. This chapter includes several tools which will help you uncover important information about your skills and abilities.

Your Rough Draft Worksheets_____

Complete the rough-draft worksheets on pages 23 and 24 as you read this chapter. Photocopy each worksheet so that you will have one sheet for each paid or volunteer position that you have held. Describe one job at a time, going step by step through this chapter. When you're done describing your first job then go back to the beginning of this chapter and start another worksheet for your second job. As you identify skills that support your objective, insert this information into the appropriate worksheet. As you describe each job ask yourself, *"What image does this description project?"* Then ask several people what assumptions they make about your skills and abilities as they read your descriptions. If several people tell you that the image you present is too weak, too strong, or doesn't match your objective then you need to re-write your descriptions.

An Important Tip

It's critical that you ask only those people who are supportive of your goals to read your resume. If you think your friend, father, husband, or wife may be intimidated or made to feel insecure by your resume then do not ask them to read it. Unintentionally, friends and family often want to keep us in our existing pattern or relationship. If they feel this is threatened they may belittle us. One of my clients came in crying because her husband said her resume was all lies. Of course it wasn't, but he was going through a rough time. He'd been laid off and wasn't working. He admitted later that he was afraid she'd get a good office job, make more money than he did, and meet other men. Once he admitted his real concerns to her (and himself) he was able to support her job search. He also let her know, honestly, that her resume was accurate and that she possessed all the skills described in it.

Remember to add as much detail to your descriptions as Ralph did. Think about all your skills and expand the descriptions of your experience. Don't worry about writing perfectly. You don't even have to write complete sentences at this point. Right now concentrate on developing a thorough outline of your skills and accomplishments. It's better to start with a lot of information in your rough draft and then go back and edit this information when you reach Chapter 6.

#1 - Seeing Yourself at Work

If you feel overwhelmed when you try to write your resume then pretend that you are doing the job you want to describe. Imagine walking in the door and remember what normally happened each day. If you performed certain tasks on a special project, even if it was only for a few days, include this information. If you completed certain duties on a weekly or monthly basis remember to include them. Make short notes on your rough draft worksheets about each task you performed. When you finish, put check marks next to those skills that most strongly relate to and support your objective.

The sample list, below, may help you remember your skills and responsibilities. Feel free to use these entries and/or add to them. Remember to describe all skills relevant to your objective. Don't worry about writing perfect sentences! If you try to write perfectly your progress will be much slower.

1. Went to the office and turned on all the lights and equipment.
2. Answered the phone before other staff came in.
3. During day talked with customers by phone and helped them with problems.
4. Helped Bob with writing and editing of the company newsletter (did most of it myself).
5. Was very good at dealing with customers who were irate or difficult.
6. Matched and verified invoices. If there was a problem researched and solved it.
7. Caught an invoicing error that saved the company $10,000.
8. Took in the daily cash, balanced it and completed the necessary bookkeeping.
9. Ordered all the office supplies and tracked the costs.

Rough Draft Worksheet

Instructions: Make a copy of this worksheet for each full-time, part-time or volunteer position you have held.

Your Objective:

Describe the position you want or the skills you wish to use:

_____

_____

_____

Keep this information in mind as you think about your background. Slant the wording of your descriptions to support this objective.

Employer / Organization:_____

Dates of Employment:_____

Title:_____ **Heading to Replace Title:**_____

Skill Group(s) for Functional/Combination Resumes:_____

_____

_____

Responsibilities & Achievements In This Job:

_____

_____

_____

_____

_____

_____

_____

_____

23 ◆ _____

Do Not Copy or Make Handouts

Skills Used In This Job:

_____
_____
_____
_____
_____
_____
_____
_____
_____
_____
_____
_____
_____
_____
_____
_____

Education / Awards / Memberships:

_____
_____
_____
_____
_____
_____
_____
_____

Tool #2 - Getting Your Thoughts onto Paper

Somewhere between verbally stating a thought and writing that thought down we sometimes become confused, frustrated, and overwhelmed. It's often easier to say things out loud than to write them. If this is true for you then have a friend help you. Tell him what duties you performed for each job and have him write down what you say without editing it. You can also talk into a tape recorder, then play it back and write down the information that supports your objective. This has helped many of my clients overcome writer's block and create a great resume. Once you've gotten something on paper, it may be too long winded or not quite right, but it's a start. Once you've written these descriptions you can then prioritize and edit them. Tom wanted to move into an Executive Assistant position. He gave me this verbal description of his past duties:

> *"I was responsible for <u>researching travel arrangements and obtaining rates</u> for hotel, airfare and car rentals. This was detailed work because some executives made 3 to 4 trips a week. I had to compare all airfare, hotel, and car rental rates to <u>select the fastest and most economical reservations</u>. I <u>scheduled reservations for a staff of 50 that included the President, V.P. and upper management</u>."*

> *"My ability to negotiate good rates was really important because the company spends over $200,000 in annual airfares. Through careful planning and advance booking I <u>reduced costs by about 15%</u>."*

In the example above, I underlined those duties that are most important and promote the image of an Executive Assistant. Take a look at how we used these duties to create Tom's resume:

- Scheduled reservations for a staff of 50 that included the President, Vice President, and upper management.

- Reduced airfare costs approximately $30,000 and assisted in managing an annual budget of $200,000.

- Researched and selected hotel, airfare, and car rental accommodations maintaining contact with over 30 vendors.

Get information down on your worksheets by saying it out loud if you have a hard time writing it. Your goal at this point is to get as much data down as possible. You can then edit and improve it in Chapter 6.

Tool #3 - Identifying Repetitive Skills

Creating resumes with clients, I often see repetitive skills and strengths in each person's background. I'm always amazed when people are unaware of these patterns. Read the following example on the facing page and notice what skills Virginia uses repeatedly:

- Developed effective clerical procedures and retrained a pool of 20 secretaries, which increased departmental output.

- Decreased labor requirements by converting to a computerized system.

- Reduced paperflow by updating and eliminating obsolete reporting forms.

- Cut student registration time 20% by streamlining registration procedures.

It's obvious from this that Virginia enjoys and excels at improving operations. When I mentioned this, Virginia blushed and said, "*I really do enjoy making everything work as efficiently as possible. I've done all these things but they were never part of my job description so I wasn't sure they should be included in my resume.*" By grouping these accomplishments together Virginia saw the consistent pattern she had of increasing efficiency and productivity. Like most of us she had tended to negate and downplay these skills. Seeing the strength and consistency of these skills gave her confidence a huge boost. I asked her, "*If you were an employer would you want to know these things about an employee?*" She said, "*Well sure, I'd find ways to have that person help me improve operations.*" I then replied, "*Well, that's exactly how any employer will feel - so it's important to include this information in your resume.*" Look for repetitive skills in your background. Understanding the type of duties you like to perform, and perform well, gives you further direction in selecting a position that you will enjoy and be successful in.

Functional Headings & Skill Groups

Look at the rough draft worksheet on page 23. You'll notice that space is provided for you to list one employer; your dates of employment; and your job title. Next to your job title, space is provided to list a functional heading to replace your job title if it is weak or doesn't support your objective. On the next line, space is provided to list the skill group(s) you will use to describe your job if you select a functional or combination resume format. To refresh your memory on how to use functional headings take a look at page 18. You'll notice that we used the functional heading of "Project Implementation" to replace Todd's job title of "laborer." Now look ahead to page 120, which is a combination resume. You'll notice that this format uses skill groups to categorize job duties rather than listing each job chronologically. A list of functional skill headings is provided on the next page.

Tool #4 - Questions To Uncover Your Skills

Read through the questions that begin on page 28 to help you uncover more information for expanding your job descriptions. As you think of things that you should include in your resume make notes on the empty lines I've provided below each question. When you're done with each question transfer your notes to your rough draft worksheets.

Functional Skill Headings

Account Management
Accounting
Acquisitions
Administrative Skills
Advertising
Auditing
Aviation
Banking
Boating
Bookkeeping
Budget Control
Carpentry
Cash Accountability
Cashiering
Chemistry
Claims Adjustment
Claims Processing
Communications
Community Affairs
Construction
Cost Savings
Counseling
Credit Management
Culinary
Customer Service
Data Entry
Data Processing
Dental Office Management
Departmental Liaison
Design
Drafting
Electronics
Engineering
Estimating/Bidding
Fabrication
Finance
Financial Management
Food Service Management
Front Office Administration
Fund Raising
General Management
Graphic Design
Human Resources
Inspection
Interviewing
Investigation
Investments
Labor Relations
Layout & Design
Legal Experience
Liaison
Loan Processing
Management
Management Information Systems
Manufacturing

Market Research
Marketing
Materials Handling
Mechanical Design
Mechanical Skills
Medical Knowledge
Medical Office Operations
Merchandising
Mortgage Banking
Mortgage Brokerage
Navigation
Office Administration
Office Management
Operational Analysis
Organizational Skills
Outside Sales
Personnel Administration
Pipe Fitting
Planning
Plumbing
Printing
Problem Solving
Product Development
Production Control
Production Management
Program Development
Programming
Project Management
Promotion
Public Relations
Public Speaking
Publicity
Purchasing
Quality Control
Real Estate
Reception
Recruitment
Remodeling
Research
Retailing
Sales
Scheduling
Secretarial Skills
Shipping & Receiving
Shop Mechanic
Social Work
Statistical Analysis
Stock Brokerage
Supervision
Systems & Procedures
Systems Management
Teaching
Telemarketing
Wordprocessing
Writing & Editing

Whom did you work for and with?

Your Notes:_____

_____

_____

Will defining your relationship to whomever you worked for create or expand the image you want to project? By answering this question Lisa's and Tim's resumes were dramatically improved. Read the following before and after descriptions:

_____Lisa's Resume_____

Before:
- ◆ Handled multi-line phones, typed correspondence, and resolved customer problems.

After:
- ◆ Provided departmental support to the <u>President, Vice President</u> and management staff.
- ◆ Managed a multi-line reception center.
- ◆ Communicated with <u>major clients such as IBM and U.S. Bank</u> resolving customer service problems.

_____Tim's Resume_____

Before:
- ◆ Sold individual computer systems valued in excess of $100,000. Supervised installation of systems and provided troubleshooting.

After:
- ◆ Marketed individual computer systems valued in excess of $100,000 to <u>corporate accounts such as Microsoft, Hewlett Packard, Boeing Aerospace, and Weyerhaeuser</u>.
- ◆ Negotiated contracts, designed and supervised installation of systems to meet client specifications.

Notice that the after examples are more impressive. In Lisa's after example, it reflects well on Lisa that she dealt with executives. This promotes the image of her working in a prominent position as a secretary/receptionist. The first description is much weaker because it doesn't mention whom she worked for. The same goes for Tim's before example which doesn't give much of a feel for the level of sales he's doing. His after example promotes a strong image of his corporate sales experience and his ability to work at that level.

Will describing the size of the company or department you worked for expand your image?

Your Notes:_____

_____

_____

For example, here's a before and after sample from Bill's resume:

_____Bill's Accounting Resume_____

Before: ♦ Assisted with all accounting duties from general ledger to financial statements.

After: ♦ Worked directly with Vice President of Accounting for this $40 million corporation.
♦ Performed all accounting duties through financial statements for over 2,000 corporate A/R and A/P accounts.

Which one of Bill's descriptions is stronger? Which one do you think will generate Bill more interviews and better pay? Reading the before statement what assumptions do you make about Bill's skills and abilities? You probably assume he knows something about accounting duties and financial statements, but there's not enough information to make other assessments about him.

Reading the after sample, what assumptions do you make about Bill's skills and abilities? Did your image of his skills and abilities expand? Now you may assume he can handle a high level accounting position and that he is able to deal with top management. You may also assume he can manage corporate accounts. Which sample causes you to imagine someone in a suit, dressed appropriately for a corporate setting? Which one makes you think Bill is more responsible and able to work independently? Stating that Bill worked for a $40 million corporation reflects well on him and expands his professional image. Adding that he handles 2,000 corporate accounts also strengthens his image. Since these attributes strongly support the image Bill wants to project, the after description will generate more and better job offers for Bill.

Will using numbers to describe your responsibilities project an image that supports your objective?

Your Notes:_____

_____

_____

Melissa worked as an Accounts Receivable and Payable Clerk but wanted to move into purchasing. She knew she would have heavy competition and wanted to maximize the purchasing experience she had gained as an A/R and A/P clerk. Here's a section from her resume:

_____Melissa's Resume_____

Before: **Accounts Receivable / Payable**

- Process accounts receivables and payables.
- Purchase office supplies and capital equipment.

After: **Purchasing / Accounting**

- Purchased up to $250,000 annually in capital equipment and office supplies.
- Dealt with over 50 vendors, negotiating pricing and payment schedules.
- Approved all purchase orders and invoicing.
- Maintained accounts receivable and payable for over 1,250 accounts and payroll for up to 200 employees.

Notice, in Melissa's after sample, that the initial emphasis is placed on Melissa's purchasing background by describing that experience first. I listed her accounts receivable and payable experience last to draw attention away from it. This helped to keep the focus on Melissa's purchasing background.

As you describe each position you've held ask yourself, "*What have I done that I can quantify or put into numbers?*" Specific descriptions are always more convincing than general descriptions. Specific descriptions that quantify and use numbers create a much stronger image in the reader's mind. The before statements above aren't as strong as the after statements because they describe job duties in general terms.

Question #4

Did you create, reorganize, conceive, or establish any procedures or systems?

Your Notes:_____

_____

_____

People forget how often throughout their careers they have created, reorganized, or established new procedures. Don't downplay or negate your achievements. Jennifer worked for a major retail chain as a Floor Manager for over 8 years. During this time she implemented many new systems in her department but hadn't gotten recognition from her supervisors for her accomplishments. Therefore, she didn't feel she should put them on her resume. Compare her before and after descriptions:

=============================Jennifer's Resume=============================

Before:
- As Floor Manager oversaw retailing space, displays, and use of schematics.
- Supervised and scheduled employees. Hired and trained new recruits.
- Utilized computer to communicate with other stores.

After: **Departmental Management**

- Managed floor operations for 100,000 square foot facility, with sales in excess of $24 million annually.
- Supervised a staff of up to 15 sales associates and cashiers.
- Increased departmental sales up to 15% by maximizing shelf and design space.
- Designed new schematic system which was implemented by corporate office and utilized in 15 outlets.
- Reduced labor requirements by 200 hours per month resulting in savings of $20,000 annually.

In Jennifer's after sample I underlined those areas in which she improved or established new systems. Which example do you think will generate Jennifer more interviews? Almost every client I work with has developed a new system or idea that they're proud of. Including your achievements will generate more interviews and make you proud of your resume.

Did you increase productivity, streamline paperflow, save money, or reduce labor?

Your Notes:_____

_____

_____

Doug worked as a Word Processor for an engineering firm. When hired, Doug found the filing system had not been purged in over five years. The old system had also been set up numerically by job number. This meant that each job had to be cross-referenced, written in a log, and filed by that number. The only way you could find something was by looking at the log. It sometimes took hours to find files because the system was archaic.

Doug streamlined and updated the firm's entire filing system. He also made several changes in the Word Processing Department. Doug wanted to apply for a city Departmental Administration position, so this is what we wrote:

Doug's Resume

Before: **Word Processor**

- Provided word processing support to staff of 12 engineers.
- Oversaw filing and document tracking system for all engineering documents.

After: **Departmental Administration**

- Created and implemented new filing system to track over 10,000 documents each month.
- New system decreased daily labor requirements by 20%, a cost savings of over $5,000 annually.
- Increased word processing productivity by 30% and shortened engineers' editing time by developing over 50 boiler-plate documents.

Question #6

Did you have responsibility for special projects?

Your Notes:_____

_____

_____

Mark, an Administrative Assistant, had managed a special project in which he oversaw the implementation of a new computer system. He wanted to apply for an Office Management position which required these skills.

Mark's Resume

Before: **Administrative Assistant**
- As Administrative Assistant, worked with the President researching, purchasing and implementing a computer network.
- Researched equipment, bids and vendors.

After: **Computer System Implementation**
- <u>Purchased and oversaw implementation</u> of a $200,000 computer system installed in 10 corporate offices.
- Consulted vendors in system set-up, negotiated pricing, and coordinated installation in all sites.

Which description is stronger? Why? The after description puts direct responsibility on Mark for what he accomplished. We left out that he *worked with the President*. While he consulted the President, Mark was actually the person doing the research and overseeing the project. We emphasized Mark's responsibility in achieving these tasks, rather than the President's. To reflect back on Mark's capabilities we included the cost of the system and that it was installed in 10 corporate offices. We also labeled his experience as "Computer Implementation."

You may have been responsible for organizing a variety of special projects. Be sure to include this information if it supports your objective. You might describe such information like this:

- Managed and coordinated the annual Christmas party and company picnic for 250 employees.
- Coordinated and delegated assignments to 30 committee members.
- Managed the annual expense budget of $6,000.
- Purchased all supplies and selected sites for events.

A few more projects might include preparing the company newsletter; helping purchase office equipment; or coordinating equipment repair. Remember, you won't see how your experience stacks up and creates an impressive image until you've written it down. Don't leave anything out.

Are you complimented for special talents?

Your Notes:_____

_____

_____

This question helps many people recognize their special skills and abilities. Many of us are complimented for things that we do well, but we don't necessarily remember to include them in our resumes.

For example, Jessica had been promoted to Night Manager at a McDonald's restaurant. She felt working at McDonald's was embarrassing because her mother is a teacher and her father is a dentist. She didn't feel what she did had much value.

When I asked if customers complimented her, Jessica smiled and said, *"Yes, for a lot of things."* Here's her after descriptions with her compliments thrown in.

Jessica's Resume

- Managed nightly operations, generating monthly sales in excess of $40,000.
- Supervised a staff of 10 and coordinated all work schedules.
- Recognized by management for increasing store sales by 5% and reducing employee turnover.
- Complimented by customers for improving customer service and speed of operations.

When we completed Jessica's resume she turned to me and said, *"You know I really do have good skills. I never realized that my relationships with customers helped increase our sales to almost $1.5 million a year. I guess I am management material after all."*

Do you have technical or special skills relevant to your objective?

Your Notes:_____

_____

_____

If you have technical or specialized skills that support your objective, be sure to include them. Tammy had used WANG computers to process correspondence and run programs in the past. However, WANG systems aren't as common as they used to be and Tammy's WANG knowledge was out of date. To update her computer knowledge she took classes at a local computer college. We focused on Tammy's current knowledge of MS Word, WordPerfect and Lotus 1-2-3. We then backed it up with her experience as a WANG Operator. Tammy's WANG experience coupled with her knowledge of current software programs gave her excellent qualifications as a word processor.

_____Tammy's Resume_____

Computer Training, XYZ Computers

♦ Utilized MS Word, WordPerfect and Lotus 1-2-3 to prepare correspondence, formletters, mailing lists, newsletters, and spreadsheets on IBM compatible systems.
♦ Operated peripheral equipment including - laser, dot matrix and daisy wheel printers (1992 - 1993).

Computer Operator, WANG, Inc.

♦ Utilized mainframe system to process correspondence and reports, and run programs to support a staff of 20 executives.
♦ Complimented on ability to manage fast-paced and stressful projects (1980 - 1986).

We used a unique strategy to describe Tammy's computer training. Her training required that she type and prepare correspondence just as she would on the job. Therefore we described her training in the same way we would describe real, on the job experience. Notice we didn't say, *"Learned how to prepare correspondence...,"* we gave Tammy credit for preparing it just as we gave her credit for using the equipment.

Do you have experience hiring, training, or supervising personnel?

Your Notes:_____

_____

_____

Many people forget how often they have trained new employees. People also tend to leave out that they have supervised volunteers, part-time workers or high school students. When I asked Anna, a Secretary for a food bank, if she had supervised or trained employees she said, *"No,"* and then added, *"But, I have trained and supervised groups of 40 volunteers on the weekend. I coordinated time schedules and assigned them to work sites. I didn't get paid for this so I thought I shouldn't include it on my resume. Should I?"* Do you think Anna should include this information? Her goal is to become an office manager or supervisor. This experience certainly demonstrates that Anna has the ability to work with people as well as train and supervise them.

When I asked Randy, an Assistant Manager for a fast food restaurant, if he trained employees he said, *"Yeah, but I only train one person at a time. That doesn't sound like anything."* I then asked him how long he had been an Assistant Manager. He replied, *"Over two and a half years."* Because fast food restaurants have high turnover and many run three shifts per day I knew he had probably trained a lot of employees so I then asked him how many employees he had trained during this time.

His whole demeanor changed as he said, *"Gee, I must have trained at least 5 new people a month. In a year's time I trained at least 60 people. Gosh, I've trained over 120 people! That's amazing!"* I then asked if Randy had been successful as a trainer. He said that new employees always complimented him because he helped them feel comfortable while learning in a stressful, fast-paced situation. Randy was very pleased with his new job description:

ASSISTANT MANAGER, XYZ Burgers

♦ Trained over 120 employees and management staff in cashiering, food production, and customer service.
♦ Recognized for increasing employee morale and significantly cutting production time.

Question #10

Have you received promotions that demonstrate achievement which supports your objective?

Your Notes:_____

_____

_____

Many people receive promotions within a short period of employment with a new company. Rapid advancement demonstrates the ability to learn quickly. It also presents an individual as self-motivated and company oriented. Therefore, it can be a real asset to show how quickly you've progressed.

For example my daughter, Melissa, was hired to prepare the Salad Bar at a Rax Restaurant. Because she learns quickly and handles pressure well she was promoted to Coordinator/Head Cashier within two weeks of being hired. Here's what we put on her resume:

COORDINATOR / HEAD CASHIER

- Supervised sales and customer service operations generating $60,000 monthly.
- Within 2 weeks of employment was promoted to coordinate and supervise cashiering and drive-up functions.

This sounds very impressive, especially since this was Melissa's first job and she was only 16 years old. This shows how important it is to include your achievements and promotions.

Have you received any awards or certificates that relate to and support your objective?

Your Notes:_____

_____

_____

For example, Denise had received a certificate for completing a management training program. Because it wasn't a college certificate or diploma, she wasn't sure she should put it in her resume. However, this is what we came up with:

Executive Management Certificate - IBM

- ◆ Received an Outstanding Management Candidate award.
- ◆ Selected as 1 of 5, out of a staff of 40, to complete the corporate management program.

Even if you're not sure an award or certificate should be in your resume still put it on your rough draft worksheet. You can always leave it out if you decide you don't need it. The risk is not putting it on your rough draft worksheet. If you don't write it down then you may forget it. When you complete your final draft you can decide how well it supports your objective, and whether or not to include it.

Have you identified the top five skill requirements
for the position you want?

Andy wanted to apply for a position as a computer instructor. The top five requirements for that job were: six months experience as a computer instructor; a four year degree; experience creating instructional materials; background leading groups of 30 or more; and good administrative skills. Each of these requirements is listed in the left hand column below. In the right hand column, we described how Andy's background matches each requirement. Andy's only weakness in applying for this position was that he had received an A.A.S. Degree in Marketing, which is a two year degree rather than a four year degree. To minimize this weakness, we merely said that he had a Degree in Marketing.

Top Five Skill Requirements	How Andy's Background Matches
6+ Months Experience	Over 1 Year's Experience
Four Year Degree	Degree in Marketing, Highline College
Creating Instructional Materials	Created over 32 lesson plans
Leading groups of 30+	Trained groups of up to 45
Good administrative skills	Compiled grades for 3 classes each month

In the left hand column below I'd like you to list five of the top skill requirements for the position(s) you want to apply for. In the right hand column describe how your qualifications match each requirement. Review what you've written in your rough draft worksheets to make sure that you've shown how your experience and skills match these requirements.

Top Five Skill Requirements	How Your Background Matches
_____	_____
_____	_____
_____	_____
_____	_____
_____	_____

Use Help-Wanted Ads to Identify Your Skills

Another way to identify your skills is to read help-wanted ads and gather job descriptions for positions that you are interested in. Underline or highlight any skills you possess that are requested in the ads and notice how employers describe these skills. You may want to use the same wording for your resume. As you find information that fits your background add it to your rough-draft worksheets.

I used this method to create the skill lists you'll use in the next chapter. I cut apart each job section of the want-ads and then compiled a list of the skills required for each job category. Within a few hours I had developed skill lists for over 20 job categories. If your particular skills aren't listed, do the same thing. Read the want-ads and compile your own list of skills to match the industry you want to work in. Be creative and use any tool that helps you identify and describe your skills.

If You Feel Overwhelmed

You may have read this section and thought, *"Gee, my resume can never be this good. I just don't have those kind of skills."* I'm here to tell you that you do. Remember, I've helped write over 1,500 resumes for people with incomes from $10,000 to $200,000. It doesn't matter what type of job you've had because you can make it sound very good and you will be very proud of yourself. Don't let feelings of being overwhelmed or discouraged keep you from working on your resume. JUST DO IT! Even if you spend only 15 minutes a day working on your resume, but do it consistently, within a week you'll have most of your resume done. Remember, no matter how good the information is that I give you, if you let your feelings cause you to procrastinate you'll be stuck where you are. You can do it.

The Skill Lists and Sample Sentences in the next chapter will make creating your resume even easier. I put that chapter after this one to make you pull information out about yourself first. If you use the Skill Lists and Sample Sentences alone you might miss identifying a skill that could land you a job. Get going and good luck!

Sample Dialogue

The dialogue below illustrates how I work with clients asking the questions we've just discussed. This dialogue was with a secretary although the process can be applied to any position whether it's for a laborer or a top executive.

As you read these questions and responses, be aware of how Angelica remembers more information; reveals information she thought was unimportant; and how we word her sentences for maximum impact. Below is what we started with:

Angelica's Before Resume

- As a Secretary typed documents; maintained filing; organized records; took messages and screened calls.
- Implemented a computerized system.

Dialogue with Angelica

Q: Were you the only secretary for this company?

A: *"Yes."*

Q: How many people did you work for, and what were their titles?

A: *"Eighteen business executives, the President and Vice President."*

Q: Can you say you managed or directed all administrative functions to support the President, Vice-President, and a staff of 18 business executives?

A: *"Yes, but we did have a Division Manager. However, I was responsible for getting all the work out. I think directed would be better than managed."*

Q: What were the most important things you did for them?

A: *"Screening their calls; scheduling the calendar; and making travel arrangements for staff and clients throughout the U.S., Canada, Hong Kong, and Thailand."*

Q: Did you deal with customers?

A: *"Oh, yes! I solved client problems, looked up shipments, and quoted prices. I also had to make travel arrangements for visiting dignitaries."*

Q: Which is most important - scheduling the calendar, making travel arrangements or dealing with the customers?

A: *"Dealing with the customers because I was often the only one there to help them. In an emergency it was really critical."*

Q: Did you manage any special projects?

41 ♦

Do Not Copy or Make Handouts

A: *"Yes, I researched and prepared a detailed presentation recommending that we purchase a $50,000 computer system. I also worked with the programmer to create programs to track sales by executive, product, and account."*

Q: **Has this system been successful and if so, can you estimate how much it increased productivity or reduced costs?**

A: *"I know for sure it reduced labor. We had been hiring between 2 and 3 temporaries each month."*

Q: **How many hours did the temporaries work each month? Do you know how much it cost per hour for each temporary?**

A: *"All of them together was about 75 hours each month, at $10.50 per hour."*

Q: **So that figures out to be about $787 per month or just under $10,000 per year. Does that sound right?**

A: *"Yes."*

Q: **Can we say you achieved an annual cost savings of $10,000?**

A: *"Yes, because we had even more temporaries than that during our peak seasons."*

Q: **You mentioned that you worked with temporaries - did you hire and train them?**

A: *"Oh, yes! I forgot all about that. That does give me some supervisory experience. I hired and trained them, and assigned work to them each day."*

Q: **Can you think of anything else important about this position?**

A: *"I can't think of anything else. It sounds great!"*

_____Angelica's After Resume_____

OFFICE ADMINISTRATION

Directed administrative functions to support President, Vice President and staff of 18 business executives.
- Worked with clients solving problems; quoting prices; and verifying shipments.
- Controlled and maintained the corporate calendar.
- Scheduled national and overseas travel arrangements for staff and visiting dignitaries.
- Implemented a computer system which achieved an annual labor savings of $10,000.
- Worked with programmers to create a sales tracking system.
- Hired, trained and supervised clerical personnel.

Compare Angelica's after description to her before description on the facing page. You can see how answering a few questions added a tremendous amount of detail to her resume.

4

Skill Lists
*and Sample Sentences*_____

To help you brainstorm, read the index below to find the skill lists and sample sentences that match your background. Go to those pages and check off any skills or sentences that describe your experience. Once you've finished reading the lists, transfer the skills and sentences you have checked off onto your rough draft worksheets.

Index of Skill Lists:

As you read these lists you may recall other skills or responsibilities that are not listed. Transfer these skills, or the thoughts you have about them, onto your rough draft worksheets. It's a good idea to skim each list even if it doesn't seem to match your background. You may be surprised to find that you have skills listed in an entirely different skill category than the one you originally looked for. For example, a secretary often performs a variety of bookkeeping functions. A construction worker might perform warehouse or shipping functions.

These lists are by no means exhaustive. They are meant to assist you in compiling your skills rather than being the only source for creating your resume. Be sure to answer the questions in Chapter 3 to ensure that you describe all of your skills and abilities. Most of the Sample Sentences are written in the past tense but some are written in the present tense. When describing a position that you are currently employed in, use present tense verbs. When describing a position you are no longer employed in, use past tense verbs. Edit the sentences as needed to match your background.

Some of the sentences are written to be used in the Objective & Qualifications section of your resume. Take a look at page 70. You'll notice that the sentences in the Objective and Qualifications section are written to summarize areas of experience.

While preparing this section I read hundreds of help-wanted ads and job descriptions. The ads and job descriptions were very specific in describing hard skills required for each industry. You'll find that some hard skills are transferrable to other industries.

Employers Look For Transferrable Skills

In contrast, soft skills are transferrable to all industries. For example, strong time management and organizational skills were requested for secretaries as well as construction workers. The ability to prioritize projects and meet deadlines is also an important skill in any position or industry. Read the sample sentences on page 63 that describe transferrable skills used in all jobs and industries. Ask yourself how you've used these skills in each of your jobs and mark those that match your experience.

If you are changing careers identify the transferrable, or soft skills, required for the position you want to move to and determine how your background matches those skills. For example, Carmen wants to become an inside sales trainee. Her past experience has been as a sales secretary with customer service responsibility. She might describe her background in this way:

SALES SUPPORT / CUSTOMER SERVICE

♦ Dealt with key accounts including: Key Bank, Nordstrom, Hewlett Packard and IBM.
♦ Increased repeat business by developing strong rapport with major accounts and solving problems.

Notice that we labeled Carmen's experience as *Sales Support / Customer Service* versus *Secretary*. In describing Carmen's background we focused on her customer service skills and emphasized her customer rapport and problem solving skills. She developed these skills as a secretary but they are transferrable to an inside sales position. By focusing on these skills Carmen's experience matches an inside sales position much better than if she had focused on her secretarial skills.

Always keep in mind the image that you want to project with your resume. Describe your background so that it matches the transferrable skills employers look for in the industry you want to move to. By doing so you will dramatically increase the success of your resume and your job search.

Accounting / Bookkeeping Skill List

_____**Full-Charge Bookkeeping**
____General Ledger
____Subsidiary Journals
____Accounts Payable
____Accounts Receivable
____Sales Journals
____Expense Journals
____Cash Management
____Cash Accountability
____Cash Receipts
____Cash Disbursements
____Corporate Bank Accounts
____Bank Reconciliations
____Bank Deposits
____Bank Drafts
____Petty Cash

_____**Analysis & Preparation**
____Financial Statements
____Trial Balance
____Balance Sheets
____Business Plans
____Budgets & Forecasting
____Expense Allocations
____Interest Calculations
____Fixed Asset Reports
____Depreciation Reports
____Inventory Valuation Methods
____Gross Margin Analysis
____Internal Finance Controls
____Trust Accounts
____Tenant Accounts
____Portfolio Management
____Loan Applications

_____**Taxes**
____Quarterly Reports
____State & Federal Taxes
____Profit Sharing Records

_____**Personnel Administration**
____Payroll Preparation & Taxes
____Time Card Tracking
____Benefits Implementation
____Insurance Records
____Employee Orientation
____Knowledge of EEO Guidelines
____Union Negotiation
____Contract Administration

_____**Purchasing/Buying**
____Inventory Tracking
____Invoice Verification
____Purchase Orders
____Supply Budgeting
____Vendor Contact

_____**Credit Management**
____Set Credit Limits
____Application Approval
____Negotiated Payments
____Traced Bad Debts
____Skip Tracing
____Manual Billing
____Automated Billing

_____**Miscellaneous**
____Job Costing
____Inventory Control
____Auditing
____Work with Auditors
____Maintained Confidentiality
____Problem Solving

_____**Supervision / Training**
____Clerical Personnel
____Accounting Staff
____Work Delegation
____Departmental Coordination
____Performance Evaluations

_____**Computerized Accounting**
____Automated Conversion
____Lotus 1-2-3
____Excel
____Peachtree

Accounting / Bookkeeping Sample Sentences

Bookkeeping

___Managed general office, reception and bookkeeping functions to support staff of _____ .

___Managed general ledger and subsidiary journals for firm with sales of $_____ annually.

___Oversaw all bookkeeping functions through financial statements.

___Tracked cash receipts and disbursements for corporation with sales of $_____ annually.

___Maintained A/R, A/P, and billing for over _____ accounts.

___Processed biweekly payroll and calculated salesmen's commissions for staff of _____ .

___Consulted management in budgeting, forecasting, portfolio and fixed asset analysis.

___Prepared and filed quarterly reports, state and federal taxes.

___Oversaw personnel administration, benefits and union contracts for _____ employees.

___Worked with auditors verifying all accounting records.

Purchasing

___Purchased $_____ annually in capital equipment and inventory.

___Negotiated and managed purchase agreements valued up to $_____ per contract.

___Developed and maintained database for over _____ vendors.

___Tracked purchase orders for department with sales of $_____ annually.

___Approved invoicing for _____ departments with sales in excess of $_____ monthly.

Credit Management

___Managed credit application and approval for client base of over _____ customers.

___Authorized to set up new accounts or extend credit to $_____ .

___Increased bad debt collections by $_____ annually.

___Oversaw billing for _____ accounts with sales in excess of $_____ annually.

Supervision

___Supervised and trained staff of _____ accounting and clerical personnel.

___Coordinated workflow for _____ departments comprised of _____ employees.

Computer Conversion

___Implemented conversion of manual system to _____ automated system.

___Utilized Lotus and Excel to prepare financial and forecasting reports.

Administrative Assistant Skill List

_____**Administration**
____Office Management
____Front Office Administration
____Order Administration
____Project Management
____File & Records Control
____Contract Administration
____Coordinating Meetings
and Conferences
____Purchasing - Supplies
and Equipment
____Petty Cash Control
____Budget Forecasting
____Expense Control
____Appointment Scheduling
____Sales/Contract Coordination

_____**Secretarial**
____Typing_____wpm
____Transcription/Dictaphone
____Shorthand
____Minute-Taking for
Departmental/Board Meetings
____Proofreading
____Preparation of Proposals,
Reports, Contracts,
Newsletters, Price Lists
____Support to Executive Staff

_____**Reception/Customer Service**
____Multi-Line Phones
____Customer Service
____Account Verification
____Problem Resolution

_____**Supervision/Training**
____Clerical Personnel
____Accounting Staff
____Work Delegation
____Departmental Coordination

_____**Purchasing/Buying**
____Inventory Tracking
____Invoice Verification
____Purchase Orders
____Supply Budgeting
____Vendor Contact

_____**Credit Management**
____Set Credit Limits
____Application Approval
____Traced Bad Debts
____Negotiated Payments
____Skip Tracing
____Manual Billing
____Automated Billing

_____**Miscellaneous**
____Job Costing
____Inventory Control
____Auditing
____Work with Auditors
____Maintained Confidentiality
____Problem Solving

_____**Computer**
____Data Entry
____CRT
____Formletters/Mail Merge
____Wordprocessing
____Spreadsheets
____Database Input
____Billing/10-key
____Lotus 1-2-3
____Excel
____MS Word
____WordPerfect
____MS Works
____MS DOS
____dBase
____IBM Compatible Systems
____MacIntosh Systems

Administrative Assistant Sample Sentences

Bookkeeping

___ Managed office, reception and bookkeeping functions to support staff of _____ .

___ Coordinated order administration for department with sales of $_____ annually.

___ Managed marketing and administrative projects to support President and sales staff.

___ Oversaw administration of department producing _____ documents annually.

___ Developed forecasts and expense reports to track annual budget of $_____ .

___ Oversaw personnel administration, benefits and contracts for _____ employees.

Secretarial

___ Provided administrative support to executive staff, for this $_____ corporation.

___ Prepared proposals and contracts for projects valued in excess of $_____ .

___ Coordinated conferences, reservations, and luncheons for up to _____ attendees.

___ Purchased $_____ annually in capital equipment and inventory.

___ Recorded confidential meeting minutes for the President and Board Members.

Reception/Customer Service

___ Managed front office administration to support _____ departments.

___ Processed over _____ calls daily, while managing _____ incoming lines.

___ Handled _____-line phone system, transferring calls to _____ extensions.

___ Processed work orders for department with sales of $_____ annually.

___ Utilized computerized system to maintain database of _____ customer accounts.

___ Dealt with ___ customers daily, resolving problems and promoting public relations.

Computer

___ Utilized MS Word and Lotus to process correspondence, reports and spreadsheets.

___ Processed computerized billing for _____ customers.

Supervision/Training

___ Trained clerical and temporary staff in office procedures and computer applications.

___ Supervised and delegated workflow to staff of _____ office and accounting clerks.

Cashiering/Customer Service/Retail Sales Skill List_____

_____Cashiering
____Manual/Computerized Systems
____Cash Accountability
____Balancing of Tills
____Bank Deposits
____Safe Drops
____Posting of Cash Receipts
____Approval of Checks/Charges
____Corporate Accounts
____Credit Approval
____Front Counter Sales
____Multi-Line Phones
____Order Processing
____Bulk Orders

_____Merchandising
____Inventory Control
____Stocking
____Pricing
____Invoice Verification
____Receiving/Warehouse
____Purchasing/Ordering
____Vendor Contact
____Displays
____Floor Set-up
____Product Promotions
____Market Analysis & Trends
____Stock Rotation

_____Facility Management
____Opening/Closing
____Authorization to Keys & Safes
____Building Security
____Set-Up of Equipment &
Inventory for Next Shift
____Implementation of
Emergency Procedures
____Theft Control

_____Supervision / Training
____Crew Supervision
____Lead Trainer
____Cross-Training Coordinator
____Hiring & Supervision
____Employee Orientation
____Performance Evaluations
____Salary Recommendations
____Benefits Administration
____Shift Scheduling & Tracking
____Employee Scheduling
____Workflow Delegation
____Shift Management

_____Sales / Customer Service
____Set Credit Limits
____Application Approval
____Sales Presentations
____High Closing Ratio
____Contract Negotiation
____Catalog / Product
Demonstrations
____Purchase Order
Administration
____Order Follow-Up
____Expediting Orders
____Coordination with
Manufacturers/Vendors
____Cold Calling
____Territory Development
____Telemarketing
____Corporate Marketing
____Appointment Scheduling
____Key Account Management
____Repeat Sales & Referrals

Cashiering/Customer Service/Retail Sales Sentences_____

Cashiering

___ Over ____ years experience utilizing manual and computerized cashiering systems.

___ Handled up to $_____ monthly, consistently balancing till to the penny.

___ Dealt with up to _____ customers daily, handling over $_____ per month.

___ Accounted for up to $_____ per day, making all safe drops and bank deposits.

___ Approved checks and charges for up to _____ accounts daily.

___ Managed front counter sales generating revenues in excess of $_____ annually.

___ Handled multi-line phones, taking and processing _____ orders daily.

Merchandising

___ Managed inventory for _____ square foot department.

___ Stocked and priced merchandise for _____ departments.

___ Verified and approved invoicing; and signed for orders.

___ Purchased up to $_____ in merchandise on a monthly basis.

___ Increased sales approximately $_____ by setting up innovative displays.

___ Developed good rapport with approximately _____ vendors.

___ Analyzed sales and marketing trends to purchase seasonal merchandise.

Facility Management

___ Opened and closed facility with sales in excess of $_____.

___ Authorized to carry all keys with access to safes and personnel records.

___ Maintained building security and implemented safety procedures.

___ Managed set-up of equipment and inventory for each shift.

___ Reduced losses by _____% through implementation of theft control measures.

Supervision

___ Hired and supervised staff of up to _____.

___ Trained employees in cashiering, customer service, and inventory procedures.

___ Served as Lead Trainer to crew of _____.

___ Conducted performance evaluations and recommended salary levels.

___ Coordinated workflow for _____ departments.

___ Scheduled _____ rotating shifts and hours for _____ employees.

Clerical/General Office/Reception/Secretarial Skill List_____

_____**Office Management**
____Front Office Administration
____Order Administration
____Project Management
____File & Records Control
____Contract Administration
____Coordinating Meetings
and Conferences
____Petty Cash Control
____Budget Preparation &
Forecasting
____Expense Control
____Appointment Scheduling
____Sales/Contract Coordination

_____**Secretarial**
____Typing_____wpm
____Transcription/Dictaphone
____Shorthand
____Minute-Taking for
Department/Board Meetings
____Typing/Editing Correspondence
____Proofreading
____Preparation of Proposals,
Reports, Contracts,
Newsletters, Price Lists
____Support to Executive Staff

_____**Clerical/General Office**
____File Maintenance
____Document Control
____Light Typing
____Copying/Duplication
____Data Entry
____Bulk Mail Preparation
____Mail Distribution

_____**Reception/Customer Service**
____Account Verification
____Multi-Line Phones
____Transferring/Screening Calls
____Message Taking
____Appointment Scheduling
____CRT/Data Input

_____**Personnel Administration**
____Payroll Preparation & Taxes
____Time Card Tracking
____Benefits Implementation
____Insurance Records
____Employee Orientations

_____**Purchasing/Buying**
____Inventory Tracking
____Invoice Verification
____Purchase Orders
____Supply Budgeting
____Vendor Contact

_____**Credit Management**
____Set Credit Limits
____Application Approval
____Traced Bad Debts
____Negotiated Payments
____Manual Billing
____Automated Billing

_____**Supervision/Training**
____Clerical Personnel
____Accounting Staff
____Work Delegation
____Departmental
Liaison

_____**Computer**
____Data Entry
____CRT
____Wordprocessing
____Spreadsheets
____Database Input
____Formletters/Mail Merge
____Correspondence
____Reports
____Newsletters
____Mailing Lists
____Pricing Lists
____Catalogs

Clerical/General Office/Reception/Secretarial Sentences

Administration

___ Managed front office and bookkeeping functions to support staff of _____ .

___ Coordinated order administration for department with sales of $_____ annually.

___ Managed marketing and administrative projects to support President and sales staff.

___ Oversaw administration of department producing _____ documents.

___ Developed forecasts and expense reports to track budget in excess of $_____ .

___ Oversaw personnel administration, benefits and contracts for _____ employees.

Secretarial

___ Provided administrative support to executive staff, for this $_____ corporation.

___ Prepared proposals and contracts for projects valued in excess of _____ .

___ Coordinated conferences and luncheons for up to _____ attendees.

___ Purchased $_____ annually in capital equipment and inventory.

___ Recorded confidential meeting minutes for the President and Board Members.

Clerical / General Office

___ Maintained files and documents to support _____ departments.

___ Opened and distributed mail to support staff of _____ employees.

Reception / Customer Service

___ Managed front office administration to support _____ departments.

___ Handled _____-line phone system, transferring calls to _____ extensions.

___ Processed work orders for department with sales of $_____ annually.

___ Utilized computerized system to maintain database of _____ customer accounts.

___ Dealt with _____ customers daily, resolving problems.

Computer

___ Utilized MS Word and Lotus to process correspondence, reports, and spreadsheets.

___ Processed computerized billing for _____ customers.

Supervision / Training

___ Trained clerical and temporary staff in office procedures and computer applications.

___ Supervised and delegated workflow to staff of _____ office and accounting clerks.

Computer Programs / Equipment Skill List

_____ **Wordprocessing**
____MS Word, MS Works
____WordPerfect
____WordStar
____Lotus Word Pro
____AmiPro

_____ **Wordprocessing Functions**
____Editing/Revision
____Mail Merge
____Mailing Lists / Labels
____Split Windows
____Footnotes
____Page Numbering
____Graphics
____Spell/Grammar Check
____Business Letter Formatting
____Macros
____Newspaper Columns

_____ **Desktop Publishing**
____Pagemaker, MS Publish
____Ventura
____Corel Draw
____Paradox
____FrameMaker
____Quark

_____ **Accounting/Bookkeeping**
____Peachtree
____Quicken
____Quick Books
____TurboTax
____MYOB
____OneWrite
____DacEasy

_____ **Spreadsheets**
____Excel
____Lotus 1-2-3
____AsEasyAs
____QuatroPro

_____ **Database Management**
____dBase, RBase
____Fox Pro
____Microsoft Access

_____ **Operating Systems**
____Windows NT
____Netware
____MS DOS
____OS2
____UNIX

_____ **Programming Languages**
____COBOL, MVS, CICS, VB
____Fortran, C/C ++, Oracle
____RPG 400, SYNON, OSI
____SNMP, TCP, IP, SQL, C
____Visual Basic, Assembler
____Access, Sybase, Windows NT
____Assembler, Pascal
____Powerbuilder, Lotus Notes

_____ **Internet/World Wide Web**
____HTML Home Page Set Up
____Web Site Administration
____E-Mail Administration

_____ **Hardware**
____IBM Compatibles
____MacIntosh
____Microcomputers
____Mini Computers
____Mainframe Systems
____Lap Top Computers

_____ **Peripheral Equipment**
____Laser, Dot Matrix and
____Daisy Wheel Printers
____Plotters
____Scanners
____Modems
____Network Servers
____Tape Backup Systems

Computer Programs / Equipment Sample Sentences_____

Wordprocessing

___   Utilized _____ and _____ programs to process reports and spreadsheets.

___   Skilled in advanced editing, mail merge, and list management applications.

Desktop Publishing

___   Created ___ page corporate newsletter distributed to _____ employees.

___   Designed flyers, brochures and company stationery utilizing _____ program.

Accounting / Bookkeeping

___   Converted manual system to computerized _____ accounting system.

___   Utilized _____ program to process over _____ A/R and A/P accounts.

___   Processed payroll for over _____ employees using _____ program.

Spreadsheets

___   Performed statistical analysis of hazardous waste materials using _____ program.

___   Utilized _____ to create and produce monthly payroll and timecard tracking system.

___   Created annual budget for corporation with sales in excess of $_____.

Database Management

___   Compiled and updated database for over _____ customers and accounts.

___   Produced mailing lists for over _____ accounts utilizing database software.

Disk Operating Systems

___   Experienced in basic functions of _____ and _____ operating systems.

___   Managed files and hard disk storage utilizing _____.

Programming Languages

___   Programmed database and accounting software utilizing _____.

___   Over _____ years programming experience includes _____, _____ and _____.

Hardware & Peripheral Equipment

___   Utilized _____, _____, and _____ to prepare documents.

___   Managed daily back-up of ___ megabyte system processing _____ transactions.

Construction Skill List

_____On-Site Construction
____Tools (Specify)
____Valid Driver's License
____Reliable Transportation
____Good References

_____Areas of Experience
____Residential
____Commercial
____Interior/Exterior Trim
____Cabinets
____Stairs
____Flooring
____Finish Work
____Finish Carpentry
____Concrete & Wood Framing
____Sheetrock
____Concrete Tilt-Up
____Concrete Finishing
____Industrial Foundations
____Formsetting
____Vinyl Siding Application
____Pipe Laying
____Roofing & Repairs
____Interior/Exterior
      Painting
____Site Cleanup/Maintenance
____General Labor
____Excavation
____Heavy Equipment Operation
      (Specify Type/Tonnage)
____Windows & Doors
____Truck Driving
      (Specify License/Tonnage)
____Decks/Patios
____Electrical/Lighting
____Plumbing
____Heating/Ventilating
____Brick Laying
____Spackling/Finish Work
____Curbing/Asphalt Repair
____Underground Utilities

_____Technical Skills
____Blueprint Reading
____Analyze Building Plans
      to Determine Materials
____Knowledge of Building
      Codes
____Material Takeoffs
____Bidding/Estimating
____Coordination/Supervision
      of Subcontractors &
      Tradesmen
____Coordination with
      Architects, Engineers,
      and Building Officials
____Permit Application &
      Approval
____Safety Regulations
____Strong Math Skills
____Computer Skills

_____Hiring / Supervision
____On-Site Inspection
____Daily Work Delegation
____Crew Foreman
____Site Lead
____Project Management
____Employee Training
____Employee Termination
____Contract Negotiation &
      Administration
____Budgeting
____Scheduling to Meet
      Contract Requirements
      and Deadlines

Construction Sample Sentences

On-Site Construction

___ Own all tools necessary for interior/exterior work as a _____ worker.

___ Possess valid Washington Driver's License (specify type) - expiration date _____.

___ Maintain an excellent driving record with current comprehensive insurance.

___ Can provide excellent references from last _____ employers.

Areas of Experience

___ Over ____ years experience includes all phases of construction valued to $_____.

___ Worked independently completing _____ projects valued up to $_____.

___ Areas of experience include: _____, _____, _____.

Technical Skills

___ Able to read blueprints and building plans.

___ Developed material take-offs for projects valued to $_____.

___ Prepared bids and estimates for commercial/residential projects up to $_____.

___ Coordinated and supervised all trades and subcontractors.

___ Possess thorough knowledge of building codes and permit process.

___ Completed permit applications and followed through to approval.

___ Background demonstrates strong math, analytical and computer skills.

Hiring / Supervision

___ Supervised crew of up to _____ laborers, finish workers and equipment operators.

___ Managed on-site projects valued to $_____.

___ Hired and trained workers in all areas of _____.

___ Managed and enforced contracts with subcontractors and vendors.

___ Controlled schedules, consistently bringing projects in on time - at or below budget.

Restaurant / Food Service Skill List

_____**Hostess / Cashiering**
    ____Manual/Computerized Systems
    ____Cash Accountability
    ____Bank Deposits / Safe Drops
    ____Scheduling of Reservations
    ____Seating/Service Coordination
    ____Problem Solving
    ____Multi-Line Phones
    ____Staff/Work Delegation

_____**Waiting Tables**
    ____Order Processing
    ____Work Prioritization
    ____Organizational Skills
    ____Time Management
    ____Departmental Coordination

_____**Cooking**
    ____Order Processing
    ____Inventory Control
    ____Purchasing
    ____Work Coordination
    ____Order Delegation
    ____Work Prioritization

_____**Restaurant / Bar Management**
    ____Displays/Promotions
    ____Advertising
    ____Implementation of
    Customer Service
    Programs
    ____Purchasing
    ____Inventory Control
    ____Vendor Contact
    ____Marketing/Sales
    Analysis
    ____Contract Administration
    ____Bookkeeping
    ____Posting of Daily Receipts
    ____Health Inspection
    Requirements
    ____Balancing of all Tills
    ____Theft Control
    ____Security Procedures
    ____Budgeting
    ____Cost Control
    ____Price Negotiation
    ____Invoice Verification

_____**Hiring / Supervision**
    ____Interviewing/Reference
    Verification
    ____Employee Training
    ____Cross-Training
    ____Departmental Coordination
    ____Work Flow Delegation
    ____Quality Control
    ____Performance Evaluations
    ____Benefit Administration
    ____Salary Reviews
    ____Time Card Control

Restaurant / Food Service Sample Sentences

Hostessing / Cashiering

___   Handled up to $_____ monthly, providing service to _____ customers daily.

___   Consistently balanced till to the penny.

___   Prepared daily bank deposits and safe drops to $_____.

___   Managed multi-line phones, reservations and seating for capacity of _____.

Waiting Tables / Bussing

___   Served up to _____ customers daily, with sales in excess of $_____ monthly.

___   Generated highest tips of _____ service staff.

___   Processed over _____ orders on a monthly basis.

___   Coordinated service requirements with _____ departments.

Cooking

___   Prepared orders for up to _____ customers on a monthly basis.

___   Verified invoicing, stocked and maintained all inventory.

___   Purchased up to $_____ monthly, and coordinated with _____ vendors.

___   Organized and prioritized orders to maximize efficiency and service.

Restaurant / Bar Management

___   Managed operations generating sales in excess of $_____ annually.

___   Increased sales ____% by designing and advertising a new product line.

___   Implemented customer service program which increased repeat business ____%.

___   Purchased up to $_____ in inventory.

___   Successfully negotiated up to ____% off major purchases.

___   Analyzed sales trends and strengthened sales of selected products by ____%.

___   Maintained daily bookkeeping and posting of cash receipts.

___   Implemented a theft control program which decreased losses by ____%.

Hiring / Supervision

___   Supervised up to _____ employees in _____ departments.

___   Delegated and reassigned duties to maximize sales and efficiency.

___   Conducted performance evaluations and salary reviews.

___   Recognized for increasing morale and reducing staff turnover.

Inside / Outside Sales Skill List

_____**Inside Sales**

____Customer Service
____Bidding/Estimating
____Materials Calculation
____Production Planning /
    Scheduling
____Proposal Development /
    Submittal
____Price Quoting
____Order Processing
____Purchase Orders
____Invoice Verification
____Materials Verification
____Parts Requisition
____Knowledge of Freight
    Forwarding Methods
____Freight Pricing
____Profit Margin Analysis
____Add-On Sales
____Coordination with Factory,
    Design Dept., Engineers,
    Production, Sales,
    Billing and Shipping
    Departments
____Catalog Management
____Records Control
____Creativity/Problem Solving
    in Design/Sales Solutions
____Strong Math Skills
____Blueprint Reading
____Blueprint Production
____Design/Ordering of Dies
    and Fabrication Equipment
____Project Management
____Contract Negotiation
____Contract Administration
____Material TakeOffs
____Use of Computerized
    Parts Tracking/Scheduling
    Systems

_____**Outside Sales**

____Territory Development/
    Management
____Key Account Management
____Proposal Development/
    Submittal
____Cold Calling
____Telemarketing
____Networking for Leads &
    Referrals
____Appointment Scheduling
____Lead Follow-Up
____List Management
____Corporate Sales
    Presentations
____Project Management
____Order Follow-up
____Implementation of
    Customer Service Programs
____Group Presentations
____Public Speaking
____Customer Training
    Seminars
____Product Demonstrations
    and Training
____Creation of Sales
    Literature, Brochures,
    and Flyers
____High Closing Ratio
____Setting/Meeting/Exceeding
    Quotas
____Servicing of Technical
    Products
____Quality Control of
    Finished Product
____Knowledge of
    Competitive Marketing
    Methods and Pricing
____Knowledge of Industry
    R & D Methods

Inside / Outside Sales Sample Sentences

Inside Sales

___ Handled up to _____ calls daily, generating sales in excess of $_____ monthly.

___ Managed / developed key accounts including: _____, _____, _____, and _____.

___ Negotiated individual sales in excess of $_____.

___ Calculated material requirements and verified delivery dates.

___ Expedited orders with manufacturers and production department.

___ Developed proposals for projects in excess of $_____.

___ Processed orders for over _____ monthly sales transactions.

___ Position required strong mathematical, problem solving and negotiation skills.

___ Possess extensive knowledge of freight forwarding methods and pricing.

___ Increased sales by ____% by maintaining projected profit margins.

___ Coordinated order requirements with _____ departments.

___ Maintained current catalog and pricing information from over _____ vendors.

___ Increased repeat sales through creative design and scheduling solutions.

___ Managed projects in excess of $_____ annually.

___ Utilized computerized parts tracking system to schedule and coordinate work orders.

Outside Sales

___ Developed _____ territory covering ___ states and generating $_____ annually.

___ Managed key accounts including: _____, _____, _____, _____, and _____.

___ Developed corporate proposals for individual contracts in excess of $_____.

___ Increased sales by ____% through cold calling, networking and lead development.

___ Increased sales of major accounts up to ____% through add-on sales.

___ Developed client list and direct marketing literature which increased leads by ____%.

___ Provided technical training to groups of up to _____ customers and vendors.

___ Awarded for highest closing ratio competing with ___ Sales Representatives.

___ Selected as Sales Trainer for staff of _____ Sales Representatives.

___ Recognized as "Corporate Sales Leader" for winning company's largest account.

___ Achieved highest percentage in increased sales by utilizing "Value Added Selling."

___ Consistently met and exceeded all sales quotas.

___ Recognized for excellent territory and time management skills.

___ Increased sales by monitoring and improving quality control of finished products.

Shipping/Receiving/Driving/Warehouse Skill List_____

_____**Shipping / Receiving**
____Invoice Verification
____Freight Forwarding
____Postal Requirements
____UPS
____Bills of Lading
____Customer Billing
____Cash Receipts
____Parts Processing
____Product Inspection/
Quality Control
____Invoice Verification
____Parts Requisition
____Freight Pricing

_____**Equipment Operation**
____Forklift
____Forklift Certified
____Pallet Jacks
____Pneumatic Ladders
____Vacuum Sealers
____Vacuum Formers
____Machine Shop Equipment

_____**Truck Driving**
____Commercial License
A or B Rating
____Excellent Driving /
Safety Record
____Excellent Attendance
____Delivery Van
____Truck
____Dump Truck & Pup
____Use of Computerized
Parts Tracking/Scheduling
Systems

_____**Warehouse**
____Quality Control /
Product Inspection
____Parts Requisition
____Inventory Control
____Warehouse Management
____Inventory Design/
Placement
____Order Processing
____Work Prioritization
____Parts Kit Preparation
____Production Scheduling
____Product Testing
____Departmental Coordination
with Assembly, Shipping
and Sales Departments

_____**Assembly / Fabrication**
____Tooling Set-Up
____Die Design / Cutting
____Vacuum Forming
____Vacuum Sealing
____Machining
____Read Blueprints &
Drawings
____Document Control
____Strong Math Skills
____Good Vision
____Proper Handling of
Hazardous Materials
____Knowledge of Safety
Requirements

Shipping/Receiving/Driving/Warehouse Sentences

Shipping & Receiving

___ Process up to _____ orders for department with sales of $_____ annually.

___ Prepare all invoicing, freight forwarding and packing slips.

___ Utilize computerized system to verify and pull inventory.

___ Pull parts and prepare parts kits to support _____ departments.

___ Coordinate with _____ departments to expedite and prioritize orders.

___ Verify invoicing for $_____ worth of products shipped on a monthly basis.

___ Control and track an in-house inventory of $_____.

Truck Driving / Equipment Operation

___ Forklift Certified - 3 years with excellent safety record.

___ Extensive experience operating forklifts, pallet jacks and pneumatic ladders.

___ Over _____ years experience as a Commercial Driver with _____ ratings.

___ Heavy equipment operation includes _____, _____, _____.

___ Deliver up to _____ loads daily throughout the _____ area.

___ Experience delivering loads in excess of $_____, in high-value products.

___ Proven history of accuracy and detail in completion of paperwork.

___ Coordinate with in-house departments and customers to meet delivery deadlines.

Warehouse

___ Purchase up to $_____ in annual inventory and supplies.

___ Maintain contact with approximately _____ vendors.

___ Control quality of $_____ in monthly shipments.

___ Requisition parts and process orders for up to _____ monthly shipments.

___ Manage _____ square foot warehouse and control $_____ of inventory.

___ Coordinate with _____ departments to maintain inventory and process orders.

___ Prepare over _____ customer orders on a daily basis.

Assembly / Fabrication

___ Fabrication experience includes tooling, die cutting, and vacuum forming methods.

___ Perform light machining to trim metal products.

___ Read blueprints and drawings to meet product specifications.

___ Control approximately _____ documents on a monthly basis.

___ Produce blueprints and schematics to support _____ departments.

___ Possess knowledge of proper chemical handling and safety procedures.

Transferrable Skills For Any Position

Communication / Interpersonal Skills

___ Background demonstrates proven organizational and communication skills.

___ Proven history as a Team Player, motivating others to meet corporate objectives.

___ Excellent interpersonal, verbal and written skills.

___ Able to manage projects and support top executive staff.

___ Prepared and edited company newsletters and promotional materials.

___ Strong mathematical, spelling, and grammatical skills.

___ Learn technical information quickly - strong self-learner.

___ Able to teach myself by reading manuals and performing "hands-on" work.

___ Serve as Liaison between management, customers and staff.

Organizational and Problem Solving Skills

___ Able to handle challenges - with proven history of increased productivity.

___ Coordinated a variety of tasks in stressful, and fast-paced environments.

___ History of flexibility - being able to handle constant change and interruptions.

___ Able to prioritize and operate proactively.

___ Self-starter, who learns quickly and applies individual initiative to get the job done.

___ Very detail oriented with excellent analytical and project tracking skills.

___ Recognized for ability to juggle multiple tasks and meet deadlines.

___ Strong problem solver who is resourceful and able to work independently.

Customer Service

___ Deal effectively with a diverse clientele while solving problems.

___ Able to promote public relations while dealing with irate or difficult customers.

___ Dynamic, outgoing individual able to develop strong rapport with customers.

___ Customer service skills have resulted in increased sales and referrals.

Supervision & Training

___ Hired, trained and supervised administrative staff.

___ Cross-trained clerical staff in reception and general office procedures.

___ Conducted performance evaluations and made salary recommendations.

5

What You Should and Shouldn't Tell Employers

Many clients come to me because they've sent out resumes but haven't gotten interviews. Not surprisingly, many of their resumes included irrelevant or damaging information. This chapter will help ensure that you don't end up in a similar predicament. You'll learn how to eliminate any information that will keep you from getting interviews. And, on the flip side, you'll learn what to include and how to word it in order to generate more interviews.

Like my seminar participants you may be wondering, *"What do employers want to see on resumes?"* They want to see and read information that is relevant to the position you are applying for. Employers want to be reassured and feel confident that they are making the right choice in interviewing and ultimately hiring you. Therefore, it's imperative that your resume project an image that you meet their needs. Because your resume is a marketing tool it should include any experience, skills or knowledge that will get you in for an interview. So far you've been asking yourself, *"If I say it this way or that way - which one is better? Which sentence or description makes me sound more qualified? Which presents a stronger picture? Which one will make an employer want to call me for an interview?"*

You'll want to continue this process as you complete your resume. The rest of the data you'll include is not merely a listing of age, marital status, or sex that you obligingly supply. It is information that you carefully analyze. You'll decide what to include and what to exclude in order to maximize your sales success. Supplying the wrong data, or presenting it inadequately, can damage your chance for an interview. Analyze any information that you consider putting into your resume. If it supports your objective include it. If it doesn't then leave it out. Word all information to maximize the image you want to project. Remember, employers must eliminate dozens of applicants as they sort resumes. If employers read anything about you that makes you appear undesirable your resume will be tossed out. The pros and cons of including or excluding certain data and where it should be placed are discussed on the following pages. There are no strict rules in selecting or omitting data. You will need to judge the relevancy of information you provide based on your objective and the image you want to project.

Should You Use An Objective Statement?

An objective statement tells an employer why he or she has received your resume; what position or field you desire; and your qualifications. You can imagine what it would be like to sort through 200 resumes without objective statements on them.

If job titles, areas of experience or skill headings didn't jump out and get your attention you'd have no idea what each person was qualified for. You certainly wouldn't have the time to read each and every resume. If you tried to do that you could spend a whole day just reading resumes and trying to decide what department or job each person fit. And, even if you thought you knew where each person fit - chances are you'd be wrong!

Based on this scenario, it's normally a good idea to include an objective statement to make sure an employer knows what type of position you want. Later, you'll learn some clever ways to write an objective statement whether you have a certain job in mind; only know the industry you want to work in; or merely know the skills you want to use. If you want to leave your objective statement out, your argument may be that you want to pursue several positions in different fields. In this instance, you'll be better off creating a resume with an objective statement for each industry. The other point that supports leaving an objective statement off a resume is running out of space on a one page resume. If you've written great job descriptions and just don't have space for the objective statement then you may decide to leave it out. You'll then need to write individual cover letters for each position. If you don't do this, you run the risk of employers receiving your resume and not knowing what to do with it. If you don't pull your skills together in a cover letter and explain how your background matches each job then you may lose out on interviews. You can't rely on employers to do this thinking for you - they don't have the time and many don't have the skill.

How Will You Transmit Your Resume?

Another point to consider, before you decide to leave out your objective statement, is how you will transmit your resume. If you mail it, you will include a cover letter. In this case, you're almost 100% sure the employer will receive both the resume and cover letter. However, if you give your resume and cover letter to a friend to show an employer then there's no guarantee that the cover letter won't get separated from your resume. This happened to Jerry who gave his resume and cover letter to a friend who worked at Boeing. To his detriment, Jerry's resume didn't have an objective statement on it. In his cover letter he had explained how his experience fit together to make him well qualified as an assembler with Boeing. After a month Jerry still hadn't heard from his friend and called him. The friend asked his Boeing supervisor what he thought of Jerry's resume. The supervisor replied, *"It looked good. I passed it on to the department head that same day. I'm surprised he hasn't called Jerry. Let me call him and see what happened."*

As it turned out, the cover letter and note had gotten separated from the resume. When the department head received the resume he had no idea why he had gotten it or who Jerry was. Because it didn't state that Jerry wanted assembly work he didn't call Jerry and hired someone else. Because Jerry's friend was an excellent worker, his supervisor was willing to gamble that Jerry would be too. When the next position came open the supervisor set up an interview for Jerry and he was hired. But, it took three months. If Jerry's resume had included an objective statement he would have been hired much sooner. As you can see, I think it's a good idea to include an objective statement on your resume.

No matter what your objective is, there's bound to be a way to word it that feels comfortable to you. Over the next few pages, we'll discuss several ways to write an effective objective statement. These recommendations are meant as guidelines. I've found they work very well. However, feel free to change the wording by adding or deleting information as needed. I've included a worksheet that lets you "fill in the blanks." Many people like the worksheet because it's easy and keeps their objective statements focused.

If You Know The Position You Want to Apply For

If you want a specific position it's good to state this in your objective so employers will clearly understand what you want and if they can provide it. For example, Beth wanted a better position as an Executive Secretary. This was the only type of position she would consider. Therefore, our goal was to write an objective statement which projected a strong image of her executive secretarial skills. Here's what we came up with:

OBJECTIVE:

♦ Position as an Executive Secretary utilizing my executive support, project management, and computer expertise.

This description projects a very competent image. It pulls together these aspects of Beth's experience as strong reasons to hire her as an Executive Secretary. Read Beth's original objective statement:

OBJECTIVE:

♦ Seek a secretarial position offering challenge and growth.

Which statement do you prefer? Which one do you feel is the strongest and most likely to get Beth the type of position she wants? As you can see, naming a specific position and then backing it up with your skills makes a very strong statement.

Drawbacks to Stating A Specific Objective

There can be drawbacks to naming a specific position. You may find that openings for the position you want are not as available as you thought. You may decide you want to consider several positions. Or, you may find a position that you qualify for, but it has a different title than the one you named in your objective statement. In these instances you may lose out on interviews if you don't broaden your objective statement.

If you feel strongly about naming the position you want, do so, but consider making a second resume with a broad objective statement. This way you'll have both bases covered, so to speak. This will enable you to apply for the specific position you want with your first resume. With your second resume you'll be able to apply for positions with different job titles. In the next section you'll learn how to write a broad objective statement based on your skills.

Remember, you are packaging yourself to make a sale. Advertisers wouldn't put together a marketing package geared to teenagers - then try to use that same package to market to senior citizens. If they did they'd be doomed for failure. Advertisers know the importance of target marketing and spend billions on packaging. You don't need to spend billions but you must spend the time needed to market yourself effectively. Make the changes. It will be worth it. Generating several different versions of your resume is a snap when you use a wordprocessor. If you don't own a computer you'll learn how to have your resume professionally wordprocessed in Chapter 6. This way you'll have as many versions as you need.

Several Positions Using The Same Skills

If you are interested in several positions that use the same skills don't mention specific job titles. Instead focus on the combination of skills that qualify you for these positions. For example, Randy qualifies for several different positions. He has been an Executive Secretary, Office Manager and Outside Sales Representative. He doesn't know exactly what position he wants - but does know that he wants to use his administrative, customer service and marketing skills. Listing the variety of jobs Randy will accept in his objective statement may cause him to be eliminated as a candidate. If an employer considers Randy for an Office Management position he may be concerned that Randy will get bored because Randy has such a strong sales background. Conversely, if Randy interviews for an Inside Sales position an employer could worry that Randy is more secretarial rather than sales oriented. Here's an example of what he shouldn't do:

OBJECTIVE:

♦   Position as a Secretary, Office Manager, or Inside Sales Representative.

It's easy to see how the job titles above conflict with one another. A more effective objective statement which focuses on Randy's skills is shown below:

OBJECTIVE:

♦   Seek a position utilizing my Administrative, Customer Service and Marketing skills.

This objective statement worked much better for Randy since he could use it to apply for all the positions he was qualified for. Because all three of these skills can be utilized as a secretary, office manager or inside sales representative this objective did not concern employers. Randy ultimately accepted an Office Management position in which he supported a staff of five sales representatives.

Avoid General Statements

Avoid naming general skills in your objective statement. For example, Ed's resume had this statement at the top of it:

OBJECTIVE:

♦   Seek a position utilizing my people skills.

What exactly does "people skills" mean? It could be customer service, sales, nursing, or counseling skills. This statement doesn't tell an employer anything important because it's too general. When I read statements like this I tune out. Just like an employer, I want to be convinced of a person's specific skills and abilities. I want to see how an applicant's skills fit the job being applied for. If I don't get a strong picture or feeling about the applicant's skills I lose interest. Having owned a personnel agency and hired hundreds of employees, I want to know what an employee can do for me.

The objective statement above doesn't tell me anything except that Ed believes he has people skills. It's surprising how often people include statements like this in their resumes, yet when you meet them you don't think they have the skills they described. Ed was a typical example of this. He was very shy and kept his head down the entire time we worked together. He didn't seem people-oriented to me and I wouldn't have thought he would want a job using his people skills. However, Ed did become excited and animated when we talked about his computer experience. You can guess which skill we based his new objective statement on, and it wasn't people skills. Ed admitted he hadn't put any real thought or effort into his resume. He said he had found a resume in a book that looked OK and copied it almost word for word. As a result, Ed's resume was full of general statements that didn't reflect his unique capabilities.

By identifying your own accomplishments you won't need to use general statements. You'll have plenty of specific examples that describe your strengths and abilities. Let's look at a few more examples of what not to do:

What Not To Do:

OBJECTIVE:

♦   Seek a position utilizing my communication and problem solving skills.

Cynthia's resume contained the objective statement you just read, yet her resume provided no descriptions of her communication or problem solving skills. By not backing up or proving this statement with specific examples of her abilities Cynthia's objective statement was weak and unbelievable. I don't put statements like this at the top of a resume unless they are backed up with convincing examples of the person's abilities. I've read so many resumes that I barely glance at a general statement like this. I keep it in mind as I scan the resume. If I read good descriptions in the body of the resume I can be convinced that the person has that skill. However, that rarely happens. Most people never tie their objective statement together with supportive job descriptions. They say they can do something but never give any evidence to prove it.

It's much stronger to put specific information in your objective statement. If you want to add a general statement then include it in one of your job descriptions. Put it as the last entry after you've created a convincing picture of that skill. This gives your resume punch and keeps it interesting. Compare the statements below:

Don't Be Too General:

♦ Seek a position utilizing my communication and people skills in conjunction with my problem solving abilities.

Do Be Specific:

♦ Seek a position utilizing my Supervisory, Budgeting and Departmental Coordination experience.

Which statement is more effective? Which one gives you a solid feeling for that person's experience and abilities? Did the first statement seem weak because it is too general? Did the second statement seem stronger? Did you automatically assume that someone with supervisory, budgeting and departmental coordination experience has good communication, people and problem solving skills? Assumptions such as these will be made about you as employers read your resume. By writing strong statements you can control the assumptions employers make about you. Ask yourself what you want employers to think about you as they read your resume and then be sure to create an objective statement that projects that image. When you've completed your resume ask supportive friends to read it and tell you what assumptions they made about your abilities. If several people describe your abilities in a different way than you want to be viewed then rewrite it. Many of you may be thinking, *"Yuck, I just want to get done with this thing!"* If you have the urge to quickly finish your resume and be done with it, consider this:

If your resume helps you get a better job which is more satisfying, imagine the increase in self-esteem you'll feel. If you receive an increase in pay of even $100 per month, that's $1200 a year. A few minutes or hours of your time can result in high rewards.

Don't Describe What You Want

Every employer wants an employee who is willing to work 100% and do his best. Objectives that mention the desire for challenge, adequate compensation, respect, or growth opportunities come off sounding me-oriented rather than company-oriented. Employers don't want to hire people who are only interested in what they're going to get from a company. Take a look at these examples:

Don't:

♦ Position which will compensate me for my work and provide continuing growth opportunities.

♦ Seek a challenging position with opportunity for advancement.

♦ Seek a position with a major firm that will result in increased responsibility.

Do you feel these statements tell an employer what the applicant is willing or able to do for the company? Do you feel they present a strong image? I think they are me-oriented, project a weak image and waste resume space. Everyone wants these things and if we are good workers we deserve them so these statements lack impact or selling power. You'll be remembered much more readily by stating something unique about yourself. By stating your specific skills and abilities in your objective statement you will project a much stronger image than "give me" statements. Your resume motto should be, *"What can I do for this company?"* Not, *"What can this company do for me?"*

Combine Your Objective & Qualifications

By combining your objective and qualifications together you can often save up to 4 lines of space in your resume. Read the sample below and notice the impact this method has:

OBJECTIVE & QUALIFICATIONS

Seek an Executive Assistant position utilizing the following background:

♦ Over 7 years Office Administration experience.

♦ Providing support to staff of 12, including the President.

♦ Degree in Business Administration, University of Washington.

Within the time it took to read these sentences what type of assumptions did you make about this person? Do you think she is a qualified Executive Assistant? This format is very powerful. I recommend it for anyone who has several significant skill areas that match the position sought and prove an applicant's qualifications.

I have used this format to market hundreds of clients and they have received great responses to their resumes. Phyllis, a friend of mine, went from $18,000 to over $40,000 in her first year. She sent out 2 resumes, went on one interview, and was working at her new job within two weeks. Peggy, my most memorable client, received an increase in her salary from $36,000 to $53,000. She was told by all five people who interviewed her that her resume was great. As you write your objective statement make sure that it is specific and that you provide examples which substantiate and prove your qualifications.

How To Create Dynamite Objective Statements

Step by step, we'll look at how Marilyn created a variety of objective statements. On the facing page is a condensed version of Marilyn's rough draft worksheets.

(1) Marilyn had been a Receptionist, CRT Specialist, and an Accounts Receivable Clerk. Marilyn's goal was to become an Office Manager. While these job titles show diverse office experience they don't project the level of responsibility Marilyn had achieved.

(2) We used functional headings to replace her job titles and show the diversity of her experience.

(3) We then put check marks next to Marilyn's strongest job description statements and used them to complete the Objective Worksheet you'll find on page 74.

Let's look at how Marilyn's job titles compare to the functional headings we selected:

Job Titles	Functional Headings
Receptionist	Front Office Administration and Executive Support
CRT Specialist	Account Management
Accounts Receivable Clerk	Bookkeeping

Objective: Office Manager

Which list most strongly supports Marilyn's goal of becoming an Office Manager? Which list makes you feel she has strong office management experience?

Sample Rough Draft Worksheet

Employer/Organization __Alpha Trucking__   Dates of Employment __10/91 - Present__

(1) Job Title: __Receptionist__

Responsibilities & Achievements:

(3) ✓ Manage front office administration to support staff of 15.

* ✓ Provide secretarial support to President and sales staff.

* Prepare all contract documents for projects to $1 million.

* Set up tracking system which decreased processing time 10%.

(2) Functional Heading: __Front Office Administration & Executive Support__

Employer/Organization __Allen's Insurance__   Dates of Employment __9/88 - 9/91__

Job Title: __CRT Specialist__

Responsibilities & Achievements:

* ✓ Managed 1,500 computerized customer accounts.

* Processed up to 200 claims daily, coordinating with 20 field agents.

* Served as liaison between 5 departments and sales agents.

* Prepared correspondence and claim verifications.

Functional Heading: __Account Management or Customer Service__

Employer/Organization __Smith's Leasing__   Dates of Employment __9/86 - 9/88__

Job Title: __Accounts Receivable Clerk__

Responsibilities & Achievements:

* ✓ Maintained bookkeeping for 1,200 A/R accounts.

* Negotiated payment schedules and authorized credit to $2,500.

* Set-up new accounts and verified credit references.

* Prepared weekly, monthly and quarterly receivables reports.

Functional Heading: __Bookkeeping or Accounts Receivable__

Marilyn's Objective Statements

(1) Naming a Specific Position:

In the first box on the facing page, Marilyn named the position she wanted which was Office Management and then strengthened it with supportive skills.

(2) Naming the Skills You Want To Use:

In the second box, Marilyn named the skills she wanted to use in case she found an interesting position that wasn't titled "Office Manager."

(3) Combining the Objective & Qualifications:

In the third box, Marilyn named the position she wanted. She then transferred the job description statements she had checked on her rough draft worksheet to this section. These statements proved her qualifications as an Office Manager.

Which of these objective statements presents the strongest image of Marilyn as an Office Manager? As you can see, stating specific skills and using functional headings really strengthens a resume. By using targeted skills and functional headings you can determine and control the image you project with your resume. A blank Objective Worksheet appears on page 248. Be sure to make several copies of it so you can write different versions of your objective statements. Reword your objective statement(s) until they are strong and pull together your best qualifications for the positions you'll apply for.

One Page Versus Two Page Resumes

Many employers prefer a one page resume because of the volume of resumes they receive and the time it takes to sort them. However, a two page resume can be effective if you highlight your most important data on the front page. If you put something that is important on the second page and it's not highlighted on the front page it may never be seen. This can cause you to lose interviews and possibly a job. Since employers spend as little as ten seconds glancing at resumes they may never turn to the second page. To maximize the success of a two page resume ask yourself, *"What are my top 4 selling points? Have I drawn attention to them on the front page of my resume? If appropriate, have I included them in my objective?"* Be sure you can answer, *"Yes,"* to each of these questions before you send out a two page resume. Remember to put your phone number on the second page of your resume, like the example on page 140 illustrates. If the employer loses the first page of your resume providing your phone number on the second page will still enable him to contact you.

I generally recommend preparing a one page resume. Getting your background onto one page makes you narrow your focus to your strongest skills. This helps you to be more focused and articulate in an interview. Some people create three and four page resumes that are long, boring and ramble. I always wonder if such people are this long-winded and talkative at work, which is not a good impression to give prospective employers.

① Naming A Specific Position

- Seek an ___Office Management___ position utilizing my ___Executive Support___, ___Customer Service___, and ___Bookkeeping___ skills.

or:

- Seek an ___Office Management___ position utilizing over ___7___ years ___Office Administration, Executive Support and Bookkeeping___ experience.

② Naming Skills

- Seek a position utilizing my ___Office Administration___, ___Executive Support___, and ___Bookkeeping___ skills.

③ Combining Objective & Qualifications

_____**OBJECTIVE & QUALIFICATIONS**_____

Seek an ___Office Management___ position utilizing the following background:

- Managing front office administration to support a staff of 15.
- Providing secretarial support to President and sales staff.
- Managing 1,500 computerized customer accounts.
- Maintaining bookkeeping for 1,200 A/R accounts.

How Far Back To Go In Your Work History_____

Normally you only need to cover ten years of experience on a resume, but there are exceptions to this rule. If you have older experience that strongly supports your objective you may want to include it. However, you'll need to de-emphasize that it is older experience. In the next few sections you'll learn how to do this effectively.

When and How To Use Dates_____

Many clients come to me because they are screened out on paper due to their age. They have listed dates of employment or education which made it easy for employers to calculate their current age. This is a problem when employers can estimate an applicant's current age as being between 45 to 50+ years old. As employers imagine the traits of an ideal candidate they may develop a preconceived image of the candidate's age, education level, and experience. They then screen resumes accordingly.

Your goal is to present yourself so that you are not screened out by these preconceptions. An employer may think that because most of his employees are in a certain age range that everyone else he hires should also be in the same age range. For example, if most of the employees are from 30 to 40 years old then many employers will eliminate candidates who are several years younger or older than this age range. Employers will then eliminate resumes from candidates that don't meet these preconceptions.

However, if a great candidate can land an interview he or she can often get the job regardless of age. Getting in front of an employer and presenting your skills and personality are the key to being hired. Therefore, it's important that you use resume formats that minimize negatives and result in more interviews. The following section will also help you determine how far back to go in describing your work history. Later you'll learn about resume formats that maximize your experience and skills, yet delete or de-emphasize dates of employment.

When To Include Dates_____

Include dates of education and employment when they portray you at an age that fits the image and position you want. If your age may make an employer feel you are a risky candidate because you are either "too young" or "too old" then omit dates completely, de-emphasize them or cut-back your work history. It's easy for employers to guess your age if you have dated information in your resume.

For example, Sue graduated from Junior College in 1965 and got her first job in 1966. If you subtract 1965 from the current date of 1994 you know it's been 29 years since she graduated. You can assume she graduated from college at the age of 22. By adding her age to the length of time that has elapsed since college you can assume she is at least 51 years old. Be sure to calculate your age using this method if you use dates in your employment and education sections. This will help you determine whether to include or exclude dates.

75 ♦ _____

Gaps In Employment

If you need to conceal gaps in employment - use "year to year" versus "month to month" dates.

Month to Month	Year to Year
06/1990 - Present	1990 - Present
12/1987 - 01/1990	1987 - 1990
03/1984 - 12/1986	1984 - 1986

As you can see in the "month to month" example, gaps in employment are easily spotted. Starting from the bottom, there was a full year of unemployment from 12/1986 to 12/1987. There was also a five month gap from 1/1990 to 06/1990. Whereas the "year to year" format concealed these employment gaps. This technique, alone, has helped many of my clients get more interviews. If you feel that this is misleading, don't worry because this technique is widely used in resume writing. In addition, you will provide your full work history when you complete applications. Remember, the name of the game is to get as many interviews as possible and to use whatever marketing techniques that help you get them!

Streamline Several Positions With One Employer

If you have held several positions with one employer you can save space by using this design technique:

ORIAN STORES INC. 1984 - Present

Full-Charge Bookkeeper
- Managed a full-set of books for this outlet with sales in excess of $4 million annually.
- Implemented computerized accounting system and trained management staff in new systems (1988 - Present).

Payroll Assistant
- Prepared daily reports and posting to support Bookkeeper.
- Cross-trained in all bookkeeping and clerical functions.
- Managed office in absence of Bookkeeper (1984 - 1987).

ALLIED MANUFACTURING, 1982 - 1984

Accounts Receivable Clerk
- Maintained over 150 A/R accounts, posting $30,000 in monthly transactions.
- Negotiated payment schedules with clients.

If You've Worked for Only One Employer

If you have worked for only one employer use the design on the next page to maximize your skills. Don't lump your experience into one big paragraph. Break it into functional headings, or skill categories, like this example illustrates. Notice how much better this directs and controls the eye path rather than one big paragraph or job title would.

SMITH & THOMAS PUBLISHING COMPANY 1976 - Present

<u>Office Management</u>

- Managed all office functions to support staff of 45, for this corporation with sales in excess of $2.5 million.
- Maintained cash disbursements and receipts journal, making daily deposits to $10,000.
- Supervised a staff of 5 secretaries.

<u>Computer Conversions</u>

- Managed conversion of manual bookkeeping and wordprocessing systems to computerized system.
- Researched and purchased $120,000 network system.
- Trained management and clerical staff in system operations.

<u>Program Development</u>

- Developed training program and manuals which increased productivity by 15%.
- Created and implemented a cross-training program which increased effectiveness in vacation and sick-leave coverage.
- Awarded for "Outstanding Innovation and Increased Productivity."

If You've Worked For Temporary Agencies

The format below works well if you've worked for several temporary employment agencies. Instead of listing each agency, label the type of work you performed and list the agency you did the most work with. Then give the length of years that you worked as a temp. This keeps your work history looking stable and helps to maximize space for other job descriptions. Read the example below to get some ideas:

OFFICE ADMINISTRATION, Manpower, Inc. 1991 - 1992

- Provided secretarial support to executives and administrative staff as a temporary employee for several agencies during this time.
- Managed front office administration and reception to support a staff of up to 45.
- Demonstrated the ability to learn new tasks quickly and efficiently.
- Due to these abilities many assignments were lengthened and my duties upgraded.

How To Describe Volunteer Experience

If your volunteer experience supports your objective then you may want to include it. When you describe volunteer experience don't label it as "Volunteer Experience." Just because it's not paid experience doesn't mean that it's not as valid as paid experience. List it just like you would any job. State your title or functional heading; the organization; and your dates of volunteerment. Remember, during an interview you can always let an employer know your experience was as a volunteer. It's to your advantage to describe volunteer experience exactly as you do paid employment in order to generate more interviews. I've found that many people downplay their volunteer experience, yet many have had more responsibility as a volunteer than in paid employment. If this is your case, don't downplay your skills. Use your volunteer experience as a stepping stone to a better job with more responsibility. Take a look at the example below:

PROJECT COORDINATOR, Youth Mission 1990 - Present

- ♦ Coordinated fund-raising projects which raised over $75,000.
- ♦ Supervised and delegated work assignments to groups of up to 40 volunteers.

How To Describe Education

If you have completed high school but have not gone to college it is usually better to omit education from your resume. Many employers prefer at least two years of college. Listing high school alone draws attention to the fact that you don't have a college education. This can sometimes prevent you from getting an interview. In our degree conscious society you don't want to focus attention on what could be viewed negatively. Omit the education section entirely if you feel your education is extremely weak when compared to others applying for the position you want.

If you are a recent high school or college graduate with a short or erratic work history the strategy is different. In this case, it is to your advantage to include your education. If you worked while completing high school or college then list the dates you attended school. Employers will see that your employment dates overlap the dates you were in school. Most employers will understand an erratic work history if it's because you worked while completing your education.

Special Areas of Study

If you specialized in a specific area of study, graduated with Honors or participated in extracurricular activities that support your objective then you may want to describe these activities. Ask yourself if it is beneficial to include this information. When describing educational activities first draw attention to the activity and then list what college or high school you attended.

DO:

♦ Business & Office Administration Concentration, Bellevue High School - GPA 3.5

♦ Manager - Supply & Equipment Store, Redmond High School

DON'T:

♦ Bellevue High School
  Business & Office Administration Concentration
  GPA 3.5

♦ Issaquah High School
  Supply & Equipment Store Manager

College With a Degree

If you have a college degree then it's not necessary to list the high school you attended. Generally, it's better to save space by streamlining your education. The exception would be if you specialized in an area which supports your objective or if you received high honors in high school. List your degree or area of study; the college you attended; the date you graduated (unless the date gives away your age in a negative way); and your GPA. You can often get this information on one line.

DO:

♦ B.A. - Business Administration, University of Iowa, 1986 - GPA 3.7

or:

♦ B.A. - English, University of Washington 1982

DON'T:

♦ University of Wisconsin
  Sara Toga, Wisconsin
  B.A. in English
  1982 - 1985

College Without a Degree

If you have taken numerous college courses, group areas of study together that support your objective. Remember to omit irrelevant coursework. For example, a Bookkeeper may have completed the following courses:

DO:

♦ Accounting & Financial Analysis, Bellevue Community College 1981 - 1983

DON'T:

♦ Bellevue Community College 1981 - 1983:
  Accounting I & II   Assertiveness Training
  Financial Statistics   Supervisory Skills for Female Managers
  Business Communications   Pottery

If the years you attended college are recent and span two or three years time then list them. This is a substantial amount of study. Listing them is a good strategy, particularly if you are competing against other applicants with degrees. In this case, your work experience combined with your college education is often considered equivalent to someone with a degree and no experience. If the dates are older and reveal your age in a negative manner then drop them and specify the number of years you studied instead.

DO:

♦ Accounting/Financial Analysis, Bellevue Community College 3 Years

♦ Accounting/Financial Analysis, Bellevue Community College 1990 - 1993

DON'T:

♦ Accounting/Financial Analysis, Bellevue Community College 1960 - 1963

If You Attended Several Colleges

Unless several colleges or universities you attended are prestigious, list only the most recent college you attended. The last college you attended will have a complete transcript of the courses you have taken and where you completed them. If an employer wants to verify your education you can request that a transcript be forwarded to him from your last college.

College Projects

If your college coursework is your strongest qualification then devoting a major portion of your resume to it can often strengthen your resume. This is especially true if you have little experience, or are making a career change. For example, while Sue completed her major in Business Administration she served as a marketing consultant to a video and TV outlet. She wanted to capitalize on this experience and move from being a secretary to a management trainee. Because she wasn't paid for this experience she wasn't sure if she should include it.

MARKETING CONSULTANT, Pacific Video & TV

♦ Increased annual sales 30% by creating and implementing an innovative advertising program.
♦ Identified a specific market which no other competitors were marketing to.
♦ Implemented a marketing plan utilizing products and advertising targeted to this market.
♦ Designed window and in-store displays as well as radio and newspaper copy.

This resume landed Sue a management trainee position with a major telecommunications company. If your coursework supports your objective look through the resume samples in Chapter 8 to get ideas for format and layout.

Including or Not Including Your GPA

Include your cumulative GPA if it is 3.5 or higher. If it is lower than 3.5, but the GPA for your major is 3.5 or higher, include the GPA for your major; don't mention your cumulative grade point average.

DO:

B.A. - Business Administration, University of Kansas - Major GPA 3.5

DON'T:

B.A. - Business Administration, University of Kansas - Cumulative GPA 2.2

Where to Place Your Education

If your education is one of your strongest selling points, consider placing it in the top of your resume. If you combine your Objective & Qualifications, like the sample on page 70, list your education as one of your qualification statements. If it's not a major selling point put it at the bottom of your resume.

Corporate Training

If you have completed several corporate training seminars, streamline and summarize them:

DO:

Corporate Training: Office Administration & Personnel Management

DON'T:

Sylvester Institute, Credit Management, 1 Day 1965. Motivational Center, Personnel Techniques, 2 Days 1978. XYZ Training Center, Sales & Customer Service, 3 Days 1980.

As you write descriptions for your training ask yourself, *"What was the primary focus of this training? How can I label this training so that it sounds supportive of my objective? What areas of my training will help sell me for the position I want?"*

Leave Off Addresses of Employment

Don't list address, city and state for each employer you've worked for. It takes up space and doesn't reveal anything important to an employer. Listing the address, city and state for each employer also makes the eye jump around a lot. Compare the two samples at the top of the next page. Which one do you think is more appealing and has better design?

Harbor Barges Inc., Secretary   1986 - 1990
1515 Harbor Avenue, Seattle, Washington 98051

or:

Secretary, Harbor Barges   1986 - 1990

Personal Information

Personal information is not normally required on a resume. However, some of your personal information may support your objective. While managing my personnel agency we placed electronic assemblers at ATL, a Northwest manufacturer of ultrasound equipment. The department supervisor was always interested in applicants with jewelry making or needle point hobbies. She found that employees with these hobbies had the manual dexterity needed for assembly work. They also had the ability to focus on small, detailed work for long periods. She consistently hired applicants with no experience but who had these hobbies. In this instance, it was a plus to describe my applicants' hobbies in their resumes.

Most of the time, however, you shouldn't list hobbies on your resume. It's more important to use resume space for job and skill descriptions. Below are several bits of information that you shouldn't put on your resume:

Omit the following:

Height & Weight	Citizenship
Birthdate	Marital Status
Social Security Number	Race or Sex

When applying to airlines some request your height and weight. Airlines are one of the few employers who can legally request this information. A Flight Attendant needs to be physically fit and able to handle emergency situations such as lifting sick or wounded passengers. Listing your height and weight would not be appropriate for most office or business positions.

On the other hand, if you meet the physical requirements for a position and you know that employers are interested in this data then tell them. For instance, a laborer who has had a perfect attendance record, is in excellent health, and can lift 50+ pounds would benefit from listing this information on his or her resume. This is clearly personal information yet these are also strong selling points. Want-ads for construction workers request personal information such as owning tools and having reliable transportation. If you own these tools and have reliable transportation then include this information because it is a selling point. This information could cause you to be the one called for an interview. If you are willing to travel, have a security clearance or are bondable and any of these traits make you look more qualified for a particular position be sure to include them. If they don't make you look more qualified then exclude them.

Salary History

Do not list your salary history on your resume. If it is requested in an advertisement, and you feel you need to include it, put it in your cover letter. Give a range of your past salaries or a range for your current salary requirement to minimize the risk of being screened out of an interview. For example:

My salary history has ranged from $15,000 to $20,000 annually.

My current salary requirement is in the $18,000 to $22,000 range.

Be careful when stating salary requirements so that you don't oversell or undersell yourself. If you feel that including your salary will be a negative then don't include it. In Chapter 11 we'll talk more about answering salary questions during the interview process.

Reason For Leaving Employment

Don't include reasons for leaving employment on your resume. When you repeatedly explain why you've left each job it sounds like you are making up excuses and apologizing for your work history, which is not a good image to project. When completing applications consider using one of these replies to explain why you left a job:

Career Advancement   To Seek Full-Time Employment
To Continue Education   Workforce Reduction

Maintaining Your Confidentiality

If you are worried about listing the name of your current employer on your resume then consider leaving off the company's name. Instead give a description of the type of firm you work for:

Secretary, Employed with a Major Law Firm   1980 to Present.

To further ensure the confidentiality of employers contacting you, type CONFIDENTIAL RESUME above your name. In your cover letter, include a sentence like the one below if employers will need to contact you at work.

You may contact me CONFIDENTIALLY at work (206) 462-7666 between 7:00 am and 3:00 pm.

Professional Memberships

Include professional memberships if they are relevant to your objective. Decide if this information is more or less important than other data, and include or exclude it accordingly. For example, Susan wants a position as a Bookkeeper. She has a lot of secretarial experience, but very little bookkeeping experience. As a member of an accounting association she set-up its bookkeeping records and maximized this experience by placing it at the top of her resume.

Bookkeeping Experience:
- Set up bookkeeping system for the Northwest Accounting Association.
- Maintained records for 1,000 members.
- Tracked expenses to control a $20,000 budget.

You may not wish to give details regarding your professional memberships, as Susan did, yet you may want to list them. In this case your resume might read like this:

Professional Memberships:
- Northwest Accounting Association
- Greater Seattle Women's Business Association

If You Have Relocated

Several of my clients have had problems getting interviews because they had recently moved to our state. In writing their resumes they had included the city and state for each job they had held. Since these positions were out-of-state it was obvious to employers that they were not long-term residents of our state. Many employers have told me they have had problems with out-of-state employees and tend to avoid hiring them. Tony, a construction manager, had this problem with his old resume. When he came to me he had been getting about one interview for every twenty resumes he sent out. He hadn't considered his out-of-state employment as a possible cause. We certainly beefed up his resume and made it better, but the real key to his generating about seven interviews for every ten resumes he sent out was eliminating references to his out-of-state employment. In only four weeks he accepted a position he really wanted.

If you move from one state to another, it is wise to leave out all references to the cities and states where you were employed. It's also wise to provide a current address within the city or local area you seek employment in. If you don't have a permanent address, ask a friend if you can use his or her address on your resume. You might also consider getting a P.O. Box in the area where you seek employment. If you live more than forty-five minutes away from the company you are applying to, employers may be concerned that you'll have a hard time getting to work. This can be another good reason to get a P.O. Box in the area you want to work in. Be sure to cover your bases so that you appear to be an applicant who can easily get to work. Otherwise you may lose out on interviews and possibly a job.

Military Employment

If you have a military background be sure to describe it so that it sounds like the type of job you are applying for. For example, Betty, a Specialist 5, was a command clerk. Before interviewing Betty, I didn't have the slightest idea of what a Specialist 5 was or what a command clerk does. Many personnel managers or hiring officials won't know what military terms or classifications mean either. Here's what Betty's resume looked like:

U.S. Army, Specialist 5/Command Clerk 1988 - 1992

♦ Oversaw command post and provided clerical support to base.
♦ Communicated with 45 officers and enlisted men.
♦ Gave orders to clerical staff.

Instead of using the army's titles and descriptions for Betty's experience we used transferrable skills. Here's how we described her army background:

OFFICE MANAGEMENT, U.S. Army 1988 - 1992

♦ Managed all office and reception duties to support staff of 45.
♦ Prepared confidential reports and correspondence.
♦ Directed clerical projects and delegated duties to administrative staff.
♦ Maintained database, tracking over 1,500 employee accounts.

Which description do you feel presents Betty as more qualified for an Office Manager or Executive Secretarial position? As you can see, it's important to use words and phrases used in the industry you seek to describe your experience. Read ads and job descriptions to determine how employers describe the positions you want. Don't be afraid to use their wording. Be sure to highlight and draw attention to skill areas employers will be interested in.

Associations and Religious Affiliations

If your involvement with an association or church group supports your objective then consider including it, but ask yourself if an employer could have a negative reaction when reading it. If so, leave it off. Some of my clients have strong religious beliefs and feel they only want to work in a Christian environment. They feel it's important to list their church involvement. This, of course, could work for or against them depending on the job market and the religious beliefs of the employers they apply with. It's a gamble and gives control to employers. It can allow employers to screen the applicant out on paper. A better way to approach this situation is to leave religious information off the resume and generate as many interviews as possible. This allows the applicant to examine each work environment and see if it meets his or her needs. This puts applicants in control of the screening process. They are screening employers out instead of employers screening them out.

Personal and Professional References

Provide three business and three personal references on a separate sheet of paper. For business references list the person's name, title, company, address, and phone number. For personal references, list each person's name, address, and phone number. I've included a sample reference sheet below.

You may assume that when a person says, *"Sure I'll be a reference for you,"* that this person will present you favorably. However, that's not always the case. Employers will ask your references to describe your reliability, temperament, work habits, strengths and weaknesses. Such questions may cause your references to hesitate or give answers about you that are not always positive. Therefore, it's important to ask each of your references how they will describe you when answering these questions. If their answers are not positive then take them off your reference list.

AMY HAMSTEDDER
1515 16th N.E.
Normandy, Wisconsin 97803
(589) 343-3789

PROFESSIONAL REFERENCES

Mr. David Smith, President
Safeco Transmissions
2435 98th Avenue
Tacoma, Washington 98379
(375) 364-2809

Ms. Susan Berry, Billing Manager
Newfound Company
34567 116th N.E.
Forth Worth, Texas 99873
(503) 789-3456

Dr. Richard Petroskie
Newborn Clinic
3457 78th Street
Detroit, Michigan 38767
(907) 345-3765

PERSONAL REFERENCES

Christine Nims
23456 277th S.E.
Bothell, Washington 98765
(206) 376-3874

Roger Daltry
38790 30th Avenue
North Bend, Washington 98037
(206) 376-8967

Sheila Watson
1245 Fiscus Avenue
Bellevue, Washington 98006
(206) 454-9801

6

Design Gets Attention But Content Sells

To increase the number of interviews you generate it is very important that you take the time to write and design a resume that grabs and holds an employer's attention. Your resume is an advertisement that you'll want to carefully prepare. A copywriter for a major advertising campaign wouldn't expect to bang out an ad campaign in a couple of hours. He would carefully consider his product and use the primary components of a good ad - design and content. Your resume should also utilize these components. You'll want to create a great resume with design that gets attention and content that sells your qualifications. The content, or job descriptions, are the meat of your resume. It's the content of your resume that will motivate employers to interview you. That's why strong job descriptions are so important.

The advertising business is a billion dollar industry that has conducted extensive research on the effectiveness of direct mail. Advertisers have found that there is a direct correlation between the length of time a reader spends reading the mail piece and whether or not the prospective customer buys the product. As reading time increases so does the likelihood of a decision to buy. Good resume design will get an employer's attention, but it's the content of your resume that will make an employer stop and read it. The longer an employer reads your resume the more likely he will be to "buy" and call you for an interview. By using numbers and being specific in your job descriptions you will convince an employer of your qualifications and keep him reading. This doesn't mean that a long-winded resume will get an employer to spend more time reading it. In fact, just the opposite is true. To keep attention and convince an employer to interview you, your resume must be short and to the point. Convincing in as few words as possible.

Effective Design

Resume design or layout must attract attention and direct the reader's eye path to important information. Look at a typical resume sample:

<u>Advantage Temps</u>
Placed at Sega, Inc.
Consumer Service Representative:
Handled consumer service calls on multi-line phones, resolved consumer complaints, and performed data entry.

As you read the sample at the bottom of the facing page, where did your eye go first? It probably went to "Advantage Temps" which is underlined. Do you think the name of the temp agency is the most important piece of information to highlight about this person's background? Do you feel this design is effective? Now look at the sample below:

CUSTOMER SERVICE REPRESENTATIVE, Sega, Inc.

♦ Handled consumer service calls on multi-line phones, resolved consumer complaints, and performed data entry.

Did this design direct and control your eye path more effectively? Was your eye automatically directed to the title of Customer Service Representative because it is capitalized and bolded? Let's look at another set of before and after samples:

Before:

Daycare Provider, Allday Day Care: oversaw activities of children, created lesson plans, and implemented field trips.

After:

SUPERVISION, Allday Day Care

♦ Oversaw activities of children, created lesson plans, and implemented field trips.

Which sample directed and controlled your eye path most effectively? We improved the impact of the after sample in two ways. First, we selected a functional heading that fits this person's job description. The title, "Daycare Provider", doesn't present a strong image in the work world and corporate executives tend to negate the responsibility and complexity of caring for children. The functional heading of Supervision is much stronger and will attract an employer's attention much more readily than "Daycare Provider." Second, we put the functional skill heading in caps and bolded it to maximize design.

Don't Go Overboard On Design

I once saw a resume for a sportswriter that had been prepared by a graphic artist and had cost $450. The words of his resume were placed around a dynamic picture of a football player as he was running and side stepping the defensive team. He had the football nestled close to his body and fierce determination showed on his face. It was an arresting picture and certainly got my attention. However, I felt let down when I read the content of the resume. It barely focused on the person's experience as a sportswriter and it contained only three lines about the radio and TV stations he had worked for.

His resume listed information about his high school education (which was irrelevant because he had a B.A. Degree in Communications) and included unrelated personal information. I'm sure this person didn't get the results he had hoped for. At first glance, his resume looked great but there was no meat to it. It made me wonder if that was how he was in person, all show and no go. Don't feel you have to put a lot of money into preparing your resume. Just make sure that you set up sections and headings that emphasize your strongest assets.

Sheila's Before & After Resumes

Sheila, an Office Manager and Bookkeeper, came to me after being unemployed for three months. Her old resume had generated about two interviews for every 20 resumes and cover letters she mailed to open positions. These interviews were for positions ranging from $18,000 to $20,000, while her last position had ended at $24,000. Sheila was depressed and afraid she would have to take a $4,000 to $6,000 cut in pay to become re-employed.

Her new resume generated about 14 interviews for every 20 positions she applied for. Within three weeks she accepted a Bookkeeping/Office Management position starting at $26,000. She was so happy! Sheila's before and after resumes are good examples of how much impact resumes have upon the entire job search process. Her story clearly shows how ineffective design and content can cause employers to overlook your resume or to offer you lower pay. On the other hand, Sheila's after resume demonstrates how good design and content can dramatically increase interviews and salary offers. Take 10 seconds and look at Sheila's before resume on the next page. Notice where your eye goes first, second, then third.

You probably noticed the "Education" heading first.

Then the "Employment History" heading and dates of employment.

Then your eye probably searched back and forth for something that stood out.

How effective was Sheila's before resume in passing your 10 second review of it? Did you get a good idea of Sheila's experience? Do you feel this resume will stand out among hundreds of other bookkeeping and office management resumes? How long did it take to find her title as a Bookkeeper? Take a look at Sheila's after resume on page 92. What do you notice first, second, then third?

You probably noticed the "Bookkeeping" heading first.

Then the "Office Management" heading.

Then the "Public Relations" heading.

And last, the "Education" and "Employment" sections.

<u>Sheila Smith</u>
5050 S.E. 30th
Syrie, WA 98036
(206) 785-7785

<u>Education:</u>
Lynnwood Academy, Lynnwood, WA
Bookkeeping, Typing/Business Machines,
Correspondence & Office Procedures

<u>Employment History:</u>

1985 - 1993
Amsterdam Constructors
Walla Walla, WA

As a Bookkeeper maintained a full set of books
including general ledger, subsidiary journals,
accounts receivable and payable, and payroll.
Prepared financial statements and worked
with auditors. Completed monthly tax
reports. Responsible for daily billing and
collections; and credit approval.

1975 - 1985
Smith & Sons Manufacturing
Sand Castle, NY

As a Bookkeeper managed the office and
maintained a full set of books including general
ledger, subsidiary journals, accounts receivable
and payable, and payroll. Brought computer
system on-line. Entered and edited data and
trained personnel in computer usage. Answered
phones, prepared shipping invoices, maintained
personnel files, and typed correspondence.
Typing - 55 WPM. 10-Key by Touch.

<u>References:</u>
Available Upon Request

In 10 seconds did you learn more about Sheila when reading her before or after resume? Most people feel the after resume provides more information in less time. Within one to two seconds, Sheila's section headings "sell" her qualifications, drawing the eye to her job descriptions and achievements. It's obvious how much the design of Sheila's after resume directs and controls your eye path. While the content of Sheila's before resume was worth reading it didn't demand attention. As a result, it was passed over when competing with hundreds of other resumes.

Compare the before and after samples to one another. Which one would you pick up first out of a stack of resumes? Most people choose the after resume. Why? The format is attractive and uses line graphics to emphasize skills and break up sections of the resume. Important skill headings are capitalized and bolded to draw the eye to them which achieves our first advertising rule of good design. Sheila's job descriptions use detail to enhance her credibility as a Bookkeeper and Office Manager which achieves our second advertising rule of strong content. The content of Sheila's resume is what interested employers in her skills. After the design attracted an employer's attention, it was the content of Sheila's resume that generated her interviews.

Design and Typing Tips

You've probably noticed that most of the resume samples in this book have been wordprocessed. Effective resumes can also be designed and typed with a good IBM or electronic typewriter. If you type your resume avoid using an older manual typewriter. Many manual typewriters slip out of alignment causing letters in each sentence to be spaced a little above or below one another. This creates an outdated appearance compared to typing from an electronic typewriter or wordprocessor.

Remember how important appearance is. If your resume is "blah" it may not be picked up from a stack of hundreds. If it's not selected you will receive fewer interviews and it may take you longer to get a job. If you're tempted to use a manual typewriter when typing or designing your resume, ask yourself if it is worth the risk of not getting interviews. Consider this: How often have you gone into a grocery store, picked up a can with torn packaging and just because the paper was torn or wrinkled put the can back on the shelf? This happens all the time with resumes. You don't want your resume to be put back on the shelf so spend the time needed to write and design an effective resume.

Use A Wordprocessing Service

If you don't own a typewriter or a computer use a secretarial or wordprocessing service to type your resume. Make sure they have a letter quality printer. Even better, find a service that has a laser printer. That's how I printed this book. The current cost for wordprocessing ranges from $20 a page to about $35 a page.

SHEILA SMITH

BOOKKEEPER / OFFICE MANAGER

5050 S.E. 30th
Syrie, WA 98036
(206) 785-7785

BOOKKEEPING

Established complete accounting system for new plant:
- Processed A/R and A/P for 1,250 accounts and payroll for 65 employees.
- Handled complete set of books, cash disbursements, cash receipts, sales journal, general ledger postings and bank reconciliations.
- Prepared financial statements and summarizations.
- Completed and submitted all payroll and excise tax reports.
- Processed daily billing and collected on bad debts.
- Maintained personnel and insurance files, updated employee status, calculated and submitted yearly pension and W-2 forms.

OFFICE MANAGEMENT

Managed office administration for manufacturing firm to support staff of 35.
- Converted all operations to computerized system.
- Oversaw implementation of $200,000 computer system.
- Trained management and sales staff in computer procedures.
- Coordinated with exporters to compile export forms and packing slips for national and international shipments.
- Coordinated with insurance administrators to process benefit claims.
- Composed and processed correspondence, reports and proposals.
- Typing 55-60 WPM, Telex, 10-Key by Touch.

PUBLIC RELATIONS

Developed strong rapport with customers, vendors and employees.
- Elicited customer concerns and resolved problems.
- Provided speedy and accurate follow-up on billing and order verification.
- Effectively coordinated a variety of activities in a fast-paced environment.

EDUCATION

Bookkeeping & Office Administration - 2 Years, Lynnwood Academy

EMPLOYMENT HISTORY

Full-Charge Bookkeeper, Amsterdam Constructors 1985 - 1993
Full-Charge Bookkeeper, Smith & Sons Manufacturing 1975 - 1985

If you decide to have your resume wordprocessed select a resume format from this book that you like and take it with you. Be sure to point out the design elements that you want incorporated in your resume. Ask the wordprocessor if he can create a resume that looks like your sample format. If he can't, ask to see samples of other resumes that he has prepared. If they direct and control the eye path go ahead and use them. If they don't, look for another wordprocessor. Don't let someone talk you out of an important design element that may get an employer's attention. If someone's suggestions make good sense and help you create a great design, use them. Otherwise shop around until someone agrees to do what you want.

If you own a computer and are going to wordprocess your resume with it, DO NOT USE A DOT MATRIX or NEAR LETTER QUALITY PRINTER. Dot matrix print is hard to read and can't compete with electronic or wordprocessed resumes. It's not worth losing interviews. However, if you have a letter quality or laser printer you're in business. If you typewrite your resume you can produce a resume that looks at least as good as the typewritten one on page 96. Whether you type or wordprocess your resume follow the design and typing tips in the next section to maximize your resume success.

TIP #1: Typing Your Resume

If you use an electric IBM or similar typewriter with mechanical keys or a type ball clean the letters with a toothbrush. Ink that has filled up the open portions of letters will create letters that are dark in some places and light in others. This will look horrible when your resume is printed. If you clean the keys and the typing is still uneven then go to a professional wordprocessor.

Remember, it will be worth the money and time!

If you are using an electronic typewriter with a daisy printwheel, remember to check the printwheel for broken spokes or chipped letters. Clean the letters with a toothbrush if needed. On all machines check to see if you need a new ribbon. Sharp, crisp, dark lettering attracts more attention than light or faded lettering caused by old ribbons. If film ribbons are available for your typewriter purchase those rather than cloth ribbons. Film ribbons create letters that are crisper and sharper than cloth ribbons. Invest the money - it could get you a job.

If you don't have access to a typewriter consider renting one. Some typewriter companies also rent typewriters on-site by the hour at very affordable rates. You can find such companies by looking in the "Typewriter" or "Business Machines" sections of your local yellow pages book.

TIP #2: Cut & Paste

If you type your resume with a typewriter, save your sanity and time by typing small sections of it. Type a sentence across the width of your page. If it's too long, cut out a few words and re-type it. Continue to do this until all sentences fit within your margins.

Next, type the sentences in sections on separate pieces of paper. Then place the sections together on a piece of 8 1/2" x 11" paper. Move the sections around to see if a section heading or job description looks better centered or aligned to the left margin. Play with these sections until your resume looks streamlined and your eye automatically travels to the top three or four skill areas or job titles that you want to sell. When you like the arrangement use this mock-up to type your final resume. If you type your resume on a typewriter, treat your master copy like gold. Be sure to keep it in a large manilla envelope so that it won't get wrinkled or get anything spilled on it. If you spill something on your master copy use white-out to cover it. If the white-out leaves marks when your resume is photocopied then type another master.

TIP #3: Use Narrow Margins To Save Space

Use narrow margins to maximize space. Most of the resumes in this book have top, bottom, left and right margins of 6 characters or 1/2 inch. It's OK to use narrow margins as long as you allow plenty of white space between sections. Be sure that your resume doesn't look crowded. If an employer looks at it and thinks, *"Ugh!" That's too much to read,"* you may miss out on an interview.

TIP #4: Use Elite Pitch

Most typewriters have both 10 pitch (pica) and 12 pitch (elite) adjustments. Pitch means how many letters you can type within each inch of space. Use the 12 pitch setting if your machine has one. Twelve pitch will allow you to type two more letters per inch, or approximately 16 more letters per line when using left and right margins of 1/2 inch. If you use a computer to type your resume set your font size at 12 point. To emphasize your main headings or job titles set them in 14 point font size and bold them.

TIP #5: Control & Direct The Eye Path

Control the reader's eye path and emphasize headings by spreading out the letters in each heading and bolding them. Take a look at the resume on page 96. To create the headings I typed one letter, hit the spacebar one time and then typed the next letter. To create a wider space between words I hit the spacebar three times. This creates headings like the sample below:

S P R E A D   H E A D I N G S

L I K E   T H I S

For more emphasis I backspaced over each letter, striking each one a second time to make it bolder. This takes time and patience but it gives the headings more impact and pulls the eye to them. Of course, this is much easier to do with a computer.

TIP #6: Use Bullets for Emphasis

You'll notice I used periods at the beginning of each sentence in Sheila's resume. These periods are referred to as bullets and the sentences are referred to as bulleted sentences. You can also use hyphens, small o's or asterisks to bullet sentences. Which of the two examples below do you prefer to read? Which design is more effective?

Managed office administration to support staff of 35. Converted all operations to computerized system. Responsible for entry and edit, back-up/duplication and bringing multi-user 240 megabyte computer system on-line. Trained management and sales staff in computer procedures. Front office reception included handling incoming calls and interfacing with customers and vendors.

Managed office administration to support staff of 35.
- Converted all operations to computerized system.
- Responsible for entry and edit, back-up/duplication and bringing multi-user 240 megabyte computer system on-line.
- Trained management and sales staff in computer procedures.
- Front office reception included handling incoming calls and interfacing with customers and vendors.

Most people prefer the last example because the bullets break up the sentences. This attracts the eye more readily than a big block paragraph. When looking at a list of bulleted sentences it feels like you can start and stop reading wherever you want. On the other hand, a block paragraph runs all the sentences together and it feels like you have to commit to reading the whole paragraph. Because employers initially skim the resume for a few seconds they may look at a block paragraph and skip it because they feel they don't have the time to read it. Therefore, it's much better to bullet your sentences and give employers the feeling that they can start and stop reading wherever they want.

TIP #7: Quality Printing & Paper

Have your resume photocopied onto a high quality 24 pound bond paper. A light creme or off-white paper with a laid or textured finish will stand out in a stack of white photocopied resumes. Avoid anything that is too flashy such as lime green paper or stiff card stock which makes you look desperate and unprofessional. Also, avoid "parchment" paper which has light and dark mottled spots.

A Note About Professional Resume Writers

Many "professional resume writing services" print their client's resumes on parchment paper. As a result, parchment paper sets off warning signals for many employers who know that many services crank out hundreds of resumes that use the same wording.

S H E I L A   S M I T H

B O O K K E E P E R

5050 S.E. 30th
Syrie, WA 98036
(206) 785-7785

B O O K K E E P I N G

Established complete accounting system for new plant:
- Processed A/R and A/P for 1,250 accounts and payroll for 65 employees.
- Managed complete set of books, cash disbursements, cash receipts, sales journal, general ledger postings and bank reconciliations.
- Prepared financial statements and summarizations; and all payroll and excise tax reports.

O F F I C E   M A N A G E M E N T

Managed office administration to support staff of 35.
- Converted all operations to computerized system.
- Oversaw implementation of $200,000 computer system.
- Trained management and sales staff.
- Processed export documents for national and international shipments.
- Maintained personnel files and submitted yearly pension and W-2 forms.
- Coordinated with insurance administrators.
- Prepared correspondence, reports and proposals.
- Typing 55-60 WPM, Telex, 10-Key by Touch.

P U B L I C   R E L A T I O N S

Developed strong rapport with customers and vendors.
- Elicited customer concerns and resolved problems.
- Provided speedy and accurate follow-up on billing and order verification.
- Managed projects in fast-paced environments.

E D U C A T I O N

Bookkeeping - 2 Years, Lynnwood Academy

E M P L O Y M E N T   H I S T O R Y

Bookkeeper, Amsterdam Constructors   1985 - 1993
Bookkeeper, Smith & Sons Manufacturing   1975 - 1985

Many employers also feel "professional resumes" may be exaggerated and not accurately describe each client's background. This may be true because many services give their clients a one or two page form in which to write their work histories. These firms may then spend as little as 15 to 30 minutes with each client. After a client leaves someone else, whom the client may never meet, writes the resume. Whereas, I and other services like mine, sit and write the entire resume with a client. I always spend from two to three hours with each client writing the resume and asking questions. During this time the client gets to help write and approve every word that goes into his or her resume.

Often, it's not until an hour or so into this process that my clients remember something really important that needs to be in the resume. If a service spends as little as 30 minutes with a client a lot of important information may be left out. If you decide to have your resume professionally written look for someone who writes the entire resume with you. Ask if you will be allowed to have input the entire time your resume is being written. If not look for another writer! Also, ask the writer to tell you about some of the people he or she has helped. This should help ensure that you get a great professionally written resume.

TIP #8: Create A Professional Image

Purchase matching paper and envelopes for your resumes and cover letters. Submitting a resume and cover letter on matching paper presents a professional, well thought out image. Most quick-print shops carry a variety of paper, so you can select and purchase paper from them. Good quality paper can cost as little as three cents a sheet and envelopes as little as five cents apiece. Don't get carried away with paper color. Remember, a conservative color such as white, creme or very light grey works best and will generate more interviews. Splashy and fancy papers can be detrimental to the image you want to project. If you have your resume wordprocessed, but use a typewriter to type your cover letters, you may worry that the lettering doesn't match. That's OK because matching paper will pull the resume and cover letter together visually.

Content That Employers Remember

To sell, the content of your resume must be interesting and must hold an employer's attention. To do this you must create pictures or images in an employer's mind as he reads your resume. Your job descriptions must cause him to actively see you accomplishing the things you describe. Read the content of the before and after samples below and at the top of the next page:

Before:

CUSTOMER SERVICE REPRESENTATIVE, Sega, Inc.

- Handled consumer service calls on multi-line phones, resolved consumer complaints, and performed data entry.

CUSTOMER SERVICE REPRESENTATIVE, Sega, Inc.

Managed service calls dealing with up to 100 customers daily.
- Coordinated repairs with 7 departments.
- Provided technical assistance - analyzing malfunctions and recommending solutions.
- Followed up on parts orders and subscriptions.
- Input account information and verified product warranties.
- Often dealt with irate customers and diffused tense situations while promoting public relations.

Did your image of this person's abilities change and expand as you read the after example? Pretend you are an employer and need a Customer Service Representative. You can interview only one person. Which person would you call? This simple comparison demonstrates how much impact effective content has upon the success of a resume. When I use samples like these to teach my resume classes, students are always amazed at the difference between the before and after resumes. One of my classes spent 10 minutes writing the after description you just read. They used the brainstorming questions in Chapter 3 to interview this person. It was a fun process to watch. As the students realized how easy it was to create a great resume their excitement built. They became more talkative and animated, and began sharing their backgrounds with enthusiasm. Everyone's confidence level went up. I think you'll also have fun using these techniques. They can improve anyone's resume whether it's a corporate executive making a 6-figure income or an entry level worker making $10,000 a year. Let's look at another set of before and after samples:

Before:

SUPERVISION, Allday Day Care
Oversaw activities of children, created lesson plans, and managed field trips.

After:

SUPERVISION, Allday Day Care

Supervised classes of up to 30, which represented over $150,000 in annual sales.
- Prepared daily work schedules and delegated duties.
- Processed receipts, inventory and class lists.
- Trained new employees in customer service and procedural operations.

We improved the content of the after sample by answering the brainstorming questions in Chapter 3. Bobbi wanted to use her daycare experience to qualify for an office position. In her after sample we dropped all references to children and created business oriented descriptions which focused on sales, record keeping and employee training; all of which transfer directly to an office setting.

Make Your Resume Memorable

In addition to being descriptive your resume needs to be memorable. Read the following descriptions and then close your eyes and see which one you remember.

♦   Was responsible for all phases of bookkeeping.

or:

♦   Managed all phases of bookkeeping including 1,200 accounts with monthly receivables in excess of $200,000.

Of these two sentences, most people remember the last one more vividly. It's much easier to remember 1,200 accounts with receivables in excess of $200,000. The first sentence is less memorable because it is limp and wordy. It also sounds passive. By replacing *Was responsible for* with *Managed*, the impact of the sentence is immediately improved. *Managed* is action oriented whereas *was responsible for* isn't.

Use Action Verbs

By using action verbs to start your sentences you can improve the impact of each sentence and eliminate unnecessary words. We eliminated two words by using *Managed* to start the sample sentence above. By keeping your resume action oriented and short you will provide important information to employers in less time. This will make your resume stand out among hundreds. By conserving space and eliminating unnecessary words you will also have more room for important achievements and skills.

Quantifying

As the sample sentences above illustrate, using numbers to describe achievements and skills makes them memorable. A resume that is memorable will increase the number of interviews you generate. Using numbers to demonstrate how large a project was, how big the department was that you supported, or how much you increased efficiency can dramatically improve your resume. It's boring to read sentences that are full of general statements. How many novels would you read if they didn't keep your attention by describing in detail all the tidbits that make a story exciting. In essence, that is what you are doing with a resume. You want to keep the reader's attention by creating a resume that is easy and enjoyable to read.

Examples of How To Improve Your Sentences_____

On the next two pages are examples of how to improve sentences by using action verbs and quantifying. On page 101, we've improved two sentences written by a bookkeeper. Compare the original sentences in Step 1 to the final sentences in Step 5, then read Steps 2 through 4 to see how we made these changes.

On page 102, we've improved two sentences for Roger, an on-site construction laborer. Compare the original sentences in Step 1 to the final sentences in Step 5. These changes emphasize Roger's responsibility rather than his supervisor's. Roger's supervisor came by each morning and gave him a list of work to do that day. His supervisor then came back at the end of the day and checked Roger's work. As a result, Roger was left alone all day managing and completing a variety of construction tasks.

We emphasized Roger's responsibility by saying he managed and completed tasks versus working under the direction of the site supervisor. While Roger didn't manage entire construction projects valued to $2 million he certainly managed various phases of them. This is a subtle difference but you can see how much it strengthened Roger's resume. Roger also supervised crews of up to 12 subcontractors and tradesmen at any one time.

By delving into Roger's responsibilities and focusing on them we increased the impact of his sentences. Roger could label these sentences - "Supervision", "Project Completion", or "Construction Management." These functional headings sound much better than his actual job title of *"Construction Laborer."* Roger would want to choose the functional heading that most strongly supports his job objective.

Practice Using Action Verbs & Quantifying_____

Practice rewriting the sentences in the editing worksheets on pages 104 through 106. On page 103 is a list of action verbs you can use to edit the sentences. Pretend you are editing these sentences for your own resume and estimate how much you could have increased productivity or reduced costs. Be sure to quantify and use action verbs to strengthen each sentence. Cross out limp and unneeded words to create sentences that have more impact.

Words that are easily eliminated and don't add to the strength of sentences include: *I*, *the*, *was*, *a*, and *was responsible for*. When you finish editing the practice sentences turn to page 107 and compare your final sentences to mine. Even though your sentences will be different see if they have as much impact as mine do.

Bookkeeper - Sample Sentence

1. Original Sentences

Was responsible for all phases of bookkeeping for this metal goods manufacturer.

During my employment successfully increased monthly cash flow.

2. Use Action Verbs

     Controlled
~~Was responsible for~~ all phases of bookkeeping for this metal goods manufacturer.

          Increased
~~During my employment successfully~~ monthly cash flow.

3. New Sentences with Action Verbs

Controlled all phases of bookkeeping for this metal goods manufacturer.

Increased monthly cash flow.

4. Quantify & Add Numbers

        5 sets of books
Controlled ~~all phases of bookkeeping~~ for this metal goods manufacturer.

Increased monthly cash flow by <u>$12,000</u>.

5. Final Sentences

Controlled 5 sets of books for this metal goods manufacturer.

Increased monthly cash flow by $12,000.

101 ♦

Do Not Copy or Make Handouts

Construction Laborer - Sample Sentences

1. Original Sentences

Under direction of site supervisor completed construction projects independently.

Worked with subcontractors and tradesmen telling them what to do.

2. Use Action Verbs

Managed and ~~Under direction of site supervisor~~ completed ^ various phases of construction projects.

Supervised and delegated work to ~~Worked with~~ subcontractors and tradesmen ~~telling them what to do~~.

3. New Sentences with Action Verbs

Managed and completed various phases of construction projects.

Supervised and delegated work to subcontractors and tradesmen.

4. Quantify & Add Numbers

Managed and completed various phases of construction projects <u>valued to $2 million</u>.

Supervised and delegated work to crews of up to 12. ~~subcontractors and tradesmen~~.

5. Final Sentences

Managed and completed various phases of construction projects valued to $2 million.

Supervised and delegated work to crews of up to 12.

Action Verbs

Accommodated	Delivered	Increased	Provided
Achieved	Demonstrated	Informed	Publicized
Activated	Designated	Initiated	Published
Adapted	Designed	Installed	Purchased
Administered	Detected	Instituted	Realized
Advertised	Determined	Instructed	Received
Advised	Developed	Interpreted	Recommended
Altered	Devised	Interviewed	Recorded
Analyzed	Diagnosed	Introduced	Reduced
Appraised	Directed	Invented	Referred
Approved	Discovered	Inventoried	Regulated
Arbitrated	Dispatched	Invested	Removed
Arranged	Dispensed	Investigated	Reorganized
Assembled	Displayed	Lectured	Rendered
Assisted	Disproved	Led	Repaired
Attached	Distributed	Logged	Replaced
Attained	Drew Up	Maintained	Reported
Audited	Economized	Managed	Represented
Augmented	Edited	Measured	Researched
Authorized	Educated	Merged	Restored
Balanced	Eliminated	Modernized	Reviewed
Calculated	Encouraged	Modified	Routed
Charted	Estimated	Motivated	Selected
Collected	Evaluated	Navigated	Served
Combined	Examined	Negotiated	Simplified
Communicated	Expanded	Observed	Sold
Completed	Expedited	Obtained	Solved
Compounded	Extended	Operated	Sponsored
Conceived	Familiarized	Ordered	Stabilized
Condensed	Formulated	Organized	Streamlined
Conducted	Founded	Originated	Strengthened
Conserved	Governed	Oversaw	Studied
Consolidated	Grouped	Performed	Supervised
Constructed	Guaranteed	Planned	Supplied
Consulted	Guided	Prepared	Surpassed
Controlled	Handled	Prescribed	Taught
Converted	Helped	Presented	Terminated
Coordinated	Hired	Processed	Tested
Corresponded	Identified	Procured	Trained
Counseled	Illustrated	Produced	Translated
Created	Implemented	Promoted	Updated
Dealt	Improved	Protected	Utilized

Bookkeeping Sentence

	1. Original Sentence

During my employment I was able to eliminate several steps in the bookkeeping process which increased productivity.

	2. Use Action Verbs

	3. New Sentence Using Action Verbs

	4. Quantify & Add Numbers

	5. Final Sentence

Office Management Sentence

1. Original Sentence

As an Executive Secretary to the Vice President had responsibility for office management and supervision of clerical personnel.

2. Use Action Verbs

3. New Sentence Using Action Verbs

4. Quantify & Add Numbers

5. Final Sentence

Inside Sales Sentence

1. Original Sentence

Being a Secretary required extensive contact with customers, ability to quote and sell technical equipment, troubleshoot and expedite shipments.

2. Use Action Verbs

3. New Sentence Using Action Verbs

4. Quantify & Add Numbers

5. Final Sentence

Compare Your Sentences

Bookkeeping Sentence:

♦ Increased productivity 35% by streamlining bookkeeping procedures.

Office Management Sentence:

♦ Managed a national sales office, supervising 10 clerical personnel to support a staff of 60.

Inside Sales Sentence:

♦ Quoted prices and marketed technical equipment for this distributor with revenues of $2 million annually.

Your Writing & Editing Worksheet

To help you edit your rough draft sentences I've included an editing worksheet on the facing page. Copy it several times so you'll have enough copies for all the sentences you'll edit. Reword each sentence until it's strong and review the brainstorming questions in Chapter 3 if needed.

Prioritize and Use Umbrella Statements

It's important that the first sentence in each of your job descriptions, or skill groups, be the strongest. I call these sentences "umbrella statements." Umbrella is defined as "covering or embracing a broad range of elements or factors." Umbrella statements put sentences below them in context and can significantly increase the positive image a reader develops about your skills. Read the examples below:

Before:

♦ Selected and delegated responsibility to lead personnel.
♦ Coordinated subcontractors and supervised projects to completion.
♦ Managed commercial projects valued to $1.5 million.

After:

Managed commercial projects valued to $1.5 million.
♦ Selected and delegated responsibility to lead personnel.
♦ Coordinated subcontractors and supervised projects to completion.

Which of these examples is the strongest? Most people choose the after example because it starts with an umbrella statement. *Managed residential and commercial projects valued to $1.5 million* is a very strong statement and has an impact on the sentences below it. The first example doesn't have as much impact because it doesn't give you a frame of reference as to how complex this person's responsibility is until the end of the description.

Editing Worksheet_____

1. Original Sentence

2. Use Action Verbs

3. New Sentence Using Action Verbs

4. Quantify & Add Numbers

5. Final Sentence

Two More Examples

Before:

♦ Prepared projects using MS Word, Lotus 1-2-3 and PageMaker.
♦ Handled 15 incoming lines utilizing a computerized system.
♦ Managed front office administration to support President and staff of 20.

After:

Managed front office administration to support President and staff of 20.
♦ Prepared projects using MS Word, Lotus 1-2-3 and PageMaker.
♦ Handled 15 incoming lines utilizing a computerized system.

Which of these examples do you prefer? In the after example, the sentence *Managed front office administration to support a staff of 20, including the President* frames the two sentences underneath it. As an employer reads the second example he would probably think, *"This person had a lot of responsibility in supporting a staff of 20. He can probably handle a fast paced environment and can deal with executives. It looks like this person must also be good on the phone and he has strong computer skills. Look's like a person I want to interview."*

Prioritizing

It's also important that you prioritize your sentences within each job description or skill group. Place related sentences together, with the most impressive sentences first. Prioritize the rest of your sentences in order of importance, with the least important or least impressive sentence last. When you prioritize your sentences keep your objective in mind. What will the employer be most interested in? What sounds the most impressive? For example, Rosemary's objective is to obtain a Bookkeeping position. Read the following sentences and choose an umbrella statement. Mark it as number 1, then prioritize and number the rest of the sentences.

____ Handled large amounts of cash with responsibility for balancing 5 tills each day.

____ Completed cash adjustments, returns and invoices.

____ Controlled a $200,000 inventory.

____ Compiled and analyzed statistical data to develop monthly reports.

____ Assisted Manager in developing expense budgets and forecasting annual sales projections.

____ Managed accounts receivable and payable, and processed monthly billings for 2,000 accounts.

See if you selected the same umbrella statement and prioritized the sentences like I did below. I chose the last sentence from above to be the umbrella statement because it creates a "big picture" of Rosemary's responsibilities. I then chose *Controlled a $200,000 inventory* because it also presents a "big picture." Both sentences present Rosemary as someone who can handle a lot of responsibility. I selected and prioritized the next two sentences, 3 and 4 together, because analyzing budgets and statistical data are higher level responsibilities than counting money or balancing tills. Then I grouped sentences 5 and 6 together because they relate to the handling of cash. I put sentence 6 last because it is the weakest of all the sentences.

Managed accounts receivable, payables and monthly billings for 2,000 accounts.

_2_ Controlled a $200,000 inventory.

_3_ Assisted Manager in developing expense budgets and forecasting annual sales projections.

_4_ Compiled and analyzed statistical data to develop monthly reports.

_5_ Handled large amounts of cash with responsibility for balancing 5 tills each day.

_6_ Completed cash adjustments, returns and invoices.

Writing With Impact Checklist

Once you've finished your rough draft, check off each item below to make sure that you completed it. You're then ready to read the next chapter and select a resume format.

Yes___ No___ Did you begin your sentences with action verbs?

Yes___ No___ Did you avoid repeating words?

Yes___ No___ Did you keep your verbs in the same tense, using present tense for your current job and past tense for previous jobs?

Yes___ No___ Did you describe and quantify your background when impressive?

Yes___ No___ Did you use umbrella statements to begin each job description or skill group?

Yes___ No___ Did you prioritize statements within each job description or skill group for the greatest impact?

Yes___ No___ Did you write in telegraphic style and drop narrative words such as *I, a, the, of,* or *was responsible for*?

Yes___ No___ Did you avoid repetition in describing skills?

Yes___ No___ Did you keep each sentence brief and to the point?

7

Which Format Is Best For You?

You're now ready to select the most effective format to highlight your skills and experience. The format you select will have a major impact on how you present your work history and skills. As you select a format keep in mind that each format can be suitable for different employment situations and job objectives. The three basic formats used throughout this book are:

> **Chronological**
> **Functional**
> **Combination**

On the following pages, we'll discuss the advantages and disadvantages of each format. You'll also find sample resumes that illustrate each format.

The Chronological Format

A chronological format starts with your current position and goes backward listing each position you have held. This format is most widely used for three reasons:

1.   Employers are more familiar with it than any other style.

2.   It provides dates of employment which many employers like to see.

3.   It is the easiest to prepare since it requires less creativity than a functional format.

Advantages

The chronological format includes dates of employment which can emphasize and reflect well on a strong and stable work history. It can also emphasize many years of employment in a desired field. Because dates of employment are prominently displayed it can draw positive attention to advancement from one position to the next. By stacking job titles that are supportive of the job objective, it can present a strong image of one's experience. In addition, many employers prefer this format because it is easy for them to understand where you have worked and for how long. Take a look at the chronological resume on page 116. You'll see that it highlights job titles which support the objective. The dates of employment show no gaps between jobs and the job titles show consistent advancement. This format is an excellent choice for this person's work history.

Disadvantages

The chronological resume has several disadvantages for someone with an erratic, short or unrelated work history. Because dates are prominently displayed employers can see gaps in employment within seconds of looking at the resume. An employer may spot these gaps before he's even glanced at the skills or experience sections. As a result, the resume may be passed over and an interview could be lost.

This format can also be redundant if you have held similar positions. Take a look at Sheila's "before" resume on page 90. Her duties for both jobs were very similar, which made her old resume repetitive and boring. In her case, we chose the combination format on page 92 to sell her skills more effectively.

The chronological format can also result in a weak resume if your job titles are not impressive and do not support your objective. In this case, you can strengthen a chronological resume by using functional skill headings to replace job titles. Another disadvantage to the chronological format is that it doesn't work well if you want to focus on older experience. Because dates are included it draws attention to the fact that you have not worked in that field or position for several years. There can also be several more drawbacks to using a chronological format. For example, if your most recent experience is not related to your objective this format immediately draws attention to that weakness. If you have more than three jobs to list the chronological format can use up a lot of space. If several of your jobs are unrelated to your objective and you wish to omit them, the chronological format may also be a poor choice because it may show gaps between employment.

The Functional Format

The functional format is based on skill groups and can provide a list of employers but omits dates of employment. It also eliminates the need for a job by job listing as required in the chronological format. Take a look at the functional resume on page 118. This format is very effective in de-emphasizing erratic or unrelated work history as well as re-entry into the job market after a long absence. When using this format you must present your skills in a way that overcomes any concerns an employer may have about you because you have eliminated your employment history. The content of your resume must convince an employer that your skills make you worth interviewing.

Advantages

Because this format eliminates dates of employment it can de-emphasize erratic or older work experience. It can also be an excellent choice if you have no work experience. Skills gained from hobbies and household management can be capitalized upon to sell your abilities.

Disadvantages

This format is not as well received by employers, as the chronological or combination format, because dates of employment are left off.

The Combination Format

This format combines the best of the chronological and the functional formats. Because it highlights a person's best skills and includes an employment history it can have more impact than a straight chronological resume. Take a look at the combination resume on page 120. By compressing the work history at the bottom of the resume this format can de-emphasize a career change as well as an erratic, unrelated, or short work history. Minor weaknesses in your work history can be offset and minimized by first selling an employer on your skills. When making a career change this format draws attention to transferrable skills and de-emphasizes the lack of experience in a particular field.

Advantages

This format is excellent if your transferrable skills are more impressive than job titles or industry experience. It can also highlight older work experience while de-emphasizing dates of employment. If you've gained significant skills from a position that lasted a short period of time this format is a good choice. It lets you devote a large portion of your resume to these skills while de-emphasizing length of employment.

Disadvantages

There are no disadvantages to a combination format because it focuses on skills and provides dates of employment. This keeps employers from feeling that you are hiding something in your work history, yet sells and emphasizes skill areas that are most supportive of your objective. I use either this or the chronological format for most of my clients.

Choosing Your Format

Now that we've reviewed the three types of formats you're ready to select one. On the next six pages are forms and sample resumes to help you select the best format for your work history and job situation. Read each form and put check marks next to those sentences that apply to you. When you're finished, count how many check marks you have in each box. The format with the most check marks is the best format for you.

Facing each form is a sample resume that shows how you can prepare each format. Review the comments about each resume to see how your work history and job situation compares. If you do this and you're still not sure which resume format is best for you then read the beginning of this chapter again. You might also want to review the resume samples in Chapter 8 to see if one of them strikes your fancy. If so, analyze how dates of employment have been provided and how the skill areas or job titles are highlighted. Ask yourself if this layout will sell your experience and dates of employment effectively. If so, then that's your best resume format.

If you feel overwhelmed, put this book aside for a few hours and then come back to it. This really is an easy process. It's just that resume writing can stir up many feelings we have about ourselves. This can make the task seem more complex than it actually is.

Remind yourself that you've learned a tremendous amount of information about creating a dynamite resume. You know far more than 95% of the population knows about good resume design and content. If you relax and believe in what you know - you'll be fine and you'll be able to create a job winning resume. Once you've selected the best format and prepared your resume review the Resume Check List below. Congratulate yourself for all the hard work you have done. Hooray! You now have a great resume.

Resume Check List

Yes___   No___   Did you use the Brainstorming Tools in Chapter 3 to expand your job or skill descriptions?

Yes___   No___   Did you include accomplishments that prove your qualifications?

Yes___   No___   Have you asked several people to read your final draft worksheet and see what type of assumptions they make about your skills? Do these assumptions match the image you want to present?

Yes___   No___   Does your resume have impact by:

Using Action Words?
Quantifying?
Using Umbrella Statements?
Prioritizing Sentences?

Yes___   No___   Have you omitted unnecessary words or descriptions?

Yes___   No___   Have you omitted any data that could count against you?

Yes___   No___   Have you calculated your age using the method in Chapter 5 if you included dates of employment or education?

Yes___   No___   If your job titles are weak have you selected functional skill headings that support your objective?

Yes___   No___   Have you used focused experience headings for more impact? For example, look at the resume on page 118. Notice that we used "Industrial Sales Experience" versus "Employment History" as the heading above the job descriptions.

Yes___   No___   Have you used "year to year" dates instead of "month to month" dates to conceal gaps in employment?

Yes___   No___   If you have held several positions with one employer did you use a format similar to the samples on pages 76 and 77 to save space?

CHRONOLOGICAL FORMAT

Job Titles and Dates Stand Out & Get Attention

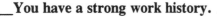_____You have a strong work history.

You have worked for each employer 2 years or more with gaps of only a few months between each position.

_____You have several years of employment in the field or type of position you seek.

_____Listing your job titles or the companies you have worked for creates an image that presents you as qualified for your objective.

_____The positions you have held show growth in your desired field.

---

① On the facing page, you'll notice that we used **"Sales & Marketing Experience"** rather than **"Employment History"** to label Debra's work history section. As you can see, "Sales & Marketing Experience" presents a much stronger image than "Employment History."

② This chronological format was a good choice for Debra because she has a strong and stable work history, spending an average of 3 1/2 years in each position. This format also highlights and draws attention to Debra's job titles which are very supportive of her goal to obtain an Outside Sales position.

③ Looking at this resume, an employer's eye is directed to the information between the double lines. These lines frame the heading **"Sales & Marketing Experience"** as well as Debra's job titles. As a result, an employer's eye will travel to and read these headings first. Within seconds an employer will know that Debra has been a sales representative which will motivate him to further read her resume.

Debra Bettinger
1515 S.E. 36th Street
Bellevue, WA 98006
(206) 238-7890

OBJECTIVE

Outside Sales position utilizing my ability to manage major accounts and identify and market new applications.

SALES & MARKETING EXPERIENCE

ACCOUNT EXECUTIVE, ABC Electronics 1989 - Present
- Cover the Northwest territory generating $1 million in annual sales.
- Hold Top Sales record competing with 25 sales representatives - 1992.
- Hold highest rating in the "Million Dollar Club" three years in a row.
- Manage major accounts such as Honeywell, Microsoft, and U.S. Bank.
- Analyze and design systems to meet client needs.
- Coordinate installation of hardware and software.
- Interface between engineering, software and operations departments to expedite orders, upgrade systems, and follow-up.

SYSTEM ADMINISTRATION, AK Construction 1986 - 1989
- Managed multi-million dollar projects on Alaska's North Slope.
- Analyzed and prepared cost accounting statements and client billings.

ACCOUNT REPRESENTATIVE, N.W. Dental 1983 - 1986
- Covered Washington & Idaho territory, marketing capital equipment and consumable products to institutional accounts.
- Major accounts included: University of Washington, Providence Hospital, Harborview, V.A. Hospital, and U.S. Navy.
- Oversaw initial clinic set-ups for graduating dentists entering private practice. Developed and presented Practice Planning seminars.

EDUCATION

B.A. Degree - Arts & Sciences, University of Washington 1980
Dean's List

FUNCTIONAL FORMAT

Skill Headings Stand Out & Get Attention
No Dates Are Listed

_____**You have very old experience.**

You are re-entering the job market after an absence of five or more years.

_____**You have little or no work experience.**

You must focus your resume on your skills and training without including dates.

_____**You have no "paid" experience.**

You must highlight skill areas gained from volunteer activities, home-management, or self-taught skills.

_____**You have a very erratic work history.**

You cannot list every position because you have too many of them, or listing dates of employment will reveal significant gaps between the jobs you have held.

---

(1) On the facing page, you'll notice that we combined Charles' **"Objective & Qualifications"** together. Within seconds of reading his achievements an employer will be convinced of Charles' qualifications. We chose to present this section as strongly as possible to overcome the weaknesses in Charles' background as discussed below.

(2) You'll notice that we didn't include any dates of employment.

(3) Charles had been with Westinghouse for over 15 years but his work history after leaving Westinghouse had become erratic. He had spent 2 years with M.H. Stollers, 1 year with Smith & Brothers, Inc. and only 6 months with Standard Products.

Listing the years of employment on his old resume had caused Charles to be screened out of interviews. He began employment with Westinghouse in 1960. Using this date it was easy for employers to calculate his age at approximately 55 years old, which had resulted in Charles being screened out of interviews.

CHARLES SMITH
PO Box 9090
Seattle, WA 98013
(206) 967-4567

OBJECTIVE & QUALIFICATIONS

Seek an Outside Sales position utilizing my ability to pioneer new accounts and maintain a strong and growing customer base.

Achievements include:

▶ Managing territories with sales from $1 million to $6 million.

▶ Increasing sales 30% and negotiating $1/2 million contracts.

▶ Calling on corporate and chain accounts; municipalities; the military; architects, engineers, builders, and management groups.

INDUSTRIAL SALES EXPERIENCE

INDUSTRIAL SALES EXPANSION, Standard Products, Inc.
Marketing industrial construction products in King County.
▶ Call on architects, contractors, builders, development and investment companies.

ACCOUNT PENETRATION, Smith & Brothers, Inc.
Generated $1/2 million in new business within 6 months of hire.
▶ Covered Western Washington and King County North territories.
▶ Major accounts included: Ernst, Pay'N Save, Associated Grocers, Western Farmers, and Cenex Corporation.

TERRITORY EXPANSION, M.H. Stollers
Took sales from $200,000 to $1.3 million, managing King County territory to the Canadian border.
▶ Consistently achieved an annual increase in sales of 30%.
▶ Called on military; municipalities; golf courses; ground and aerial applicators; and retail chains.

KEY ACCOUNT MANAGEMENT, Westinghouse (Lamp Division)
Generated annual sales of up to $6 million covering Washington, Oregon, Idaho, and Northern California.
▶ Called on wholesale houses as well as retail accounts.

COMBINATION FORMAT

Skill Headings Highlighted - Dates De-emphasized

_____**You have an erratic work history.**

_____**You have gaps in employment.**

_____**You are making a career change.**

Your job titles don't support your objective. Skill groups will be more impressive.

_____**You have used the same skills in many positions.**

A chronological resume would be redundant. Skill groups will be more interesting.

_____**You have a short work history.**

Focusing on skills and de-emphasizing dates of employment will maximize your background.

_____**Your past work history isn't related to your job objective.**

Emphasizing "transferrable" skills from a variety of positions will make you look more qualified for your objective.

_____**Older experience qualifies you for your job objective.**

You have not worked for several years and need to de-emphasize your dates of employment.

_____**Most recent experience doesn't support your objective.**

You want to focus on older experience and de-emphasize jobs that are more current because they aren't relevant to your objective.

---

(1) On the facing page, you'll notice that Linda's objective was to obtain an office position.

(2) Because Linda had never worked in an office we used "functional skill headings" to market her transferrable skills.

(3) We de-emphasized the fact that Linda's only employment had been "selling ice-cream" at Howard's Malt Shop by placing her work history at the bottom of her resume. Notice that we also labeled this experience "Management/Customer Service."

LINDA PHILLIPS
238 Boardwalk
Redmond, WA 98053
(206) 883-7821

OBJECTIVE

To obtain a general office position utilizing my office, computer and customer service skills.

COMPUTER / OFFICE SKILLS

- Processed projects utilizing MS Word and Lotus 1-2-3.
- Wordprocessing applications have included: mail merge, desktop publishing, and list maintenance.
- Data entry has included database development and accounts receivable processing.
- Handled multi-line phones with up to 10 extensions.
- Typing at 60+ wpm. 10-Key at 345 spm.

CUSTOMER SERVICE / MANAGEMENT

- Dealt with up to 200 customers, handling over $20,000 monthly.
- Coordinated with 10 stores to process $125,000 in annual orders.
- Supervised disbursement of orders with store managers.
- Assisted owner in design of media and print advertisements.
- Processed payroll taxes using 10-key by touch.
- Handled phone orders and took messages for owner and employees.

SUPERVISION / TRAINING

- Supervised and trained 9 employees in hostessing and cashiering.
- Trained 5 store managers in bookkeeping, payroll, purchasing, inventory maintenance, product pricing, and cashiering.
- Scheduled 5 shifts per day and coordinated all work hours.
- Advised owner of employee performance.

EDUCATION

Word Processing Certificate, Smith's Business College

WORK HISTORY

Management/Customer Service, Howard's Malt Shop 1984 - 1990

8

Proven Resumes
and Creative Designs

My goal in providing the following resume samples is to show you how good design makes resumes more attractive and eye-catching. I also want to encourage you to read the content of a few of the samples to see how much detail can be provided in a limited amount of space. Whenever possible I have quantified each person's achievements and responsibilities. Section headings were carefully selected to support each person's objective. If a client's work history was strong, but his or her job titles were weak we used functional headings to label experience and replace job titles. Review the "before" and "after" resume samples because they provide valuable lessons on how each client's resume was improved. These changes often made a dramatic difference in the number of interviews and job offers each person received.

Because there are thousands of different jobs, with as many different job duties, I haven't tried to provide a large number of resume samples. Having worked with over 1500 job seekers I have rarely seen someone find a resume that matches his or her background except for a few sentences. A real concern of mine is that you may find a resume that seems to match your background and then you may decide to copy it word for word. That is an easy way out and it will lead you to create a weak resume because you have not explored your unique accomplishments. It can also lead to weak interviews because you won't be thoroughly familiar with your background.

I recommend that you use these samples for inspiration in designing your resume rather than trying to write it from them. Over 20 designs have been included and each one is from a client who has been complimented on his or her resume. To protect each client's confidentiality, the name, address and place of employment on each resume has been changed to fictitious information. If you know of a particular city and the zip code or phone numbers don't match that is why.

As you work on your resume you will probably find that you have to cut back and edit what you have written. Prioritize the information you've written by numbering each sentence as we did on page 110. Then eliminate your weakest sentences in each job description or skill section. See if what you have left fits the space you have available. If it doesn't then drop a few more of your weakest sentences. Prioritizing and then eliminating your weakest sentences will reassure you that the information you eliminate is OK to omit from your resume. Remember, you will also have space in your cover letter to describe specific skills and qualifications for each job. Have fun creating a dynamic and eye-catching resume!

√ RESUME FOCUSED ON EDUCATION / TRAINING

Norma had worked several temporary positions, been a postal worker and a receptionist. Since she had worked for 3 summer quarters as a Research Assistant she chose to focus her resume on that experience combined with describing in detail the coursework she had completed to obtain her master's degree.

Norma Lindstrom
25380 30th Avenue
Portland, OR 98023
(206) 738-8902

OBJECTIVE

Position as an Applied Statistician in experimental design and analysis.

EDUCATION

- M.S. - Applied Statistics, Washington State University GPA 3.82 1993
- B.A. - Zoology, University of California at Santa Barbara 1988

MASTERS - APPLIED STATISTICS

Applied Statistics:

General Statistical Methods
Regression
Experimental Design
Advanced Experimental Design
Sampling Methods
Intro to Modeling & Simulation
Inference Survival Data Analysis
Applied Multivariate Analysis
Intro to Operations Research
Special Topics in Quality Control

Statistical Theory

Computer Programming
  Fortran

Mathematics:
  Advanced Calculus
  Linear Algebra

Biology:
  Community Structure & Analysis

STATISTICAL CONSULTING / RESEARCH PROJECTS

HORTICULTURE:	Advised graduate student in analysis of incomplete factorial experiments on factors affecting the forcing of flower bulbs.
FOREST ENGINEERING:	Assisted graduate student in the utilization and interpretation of regression equations for the prediction of stream flow.
CROP SCIENCE:	Designed experiment, appropriate test and sample size for comparing methods of moisture content determination in seeds.
RESEARCH:	Performed directed laboratory research on chitosan production methods and by-product - Sayto.
	Analyzed traffic flow and environmental data to predict pollution from proposed highways - H&R Research Labs, Inc.
LABORATORY INSTRUCTOR:	Taught Applied Regression classes for up to 40 students each quarter.

EMPLOYMENT - WHILE COMPLETING DEGREE

Lab Instructor/Tutor, Washington State University 1989-93
Research Assistant, H&R Research Labs, Inc. 1982-84
Research Assistant, Sayto 1981-82

√ **OLD STYLE RESUME WITH DATES**

Daniel had been paid $40,000 annually as an Automatic Machine Expert. Using this resume over a 3 month period he received few interviews. His last straw was when he received an offer for $5.00 an hour. The dates on this resume as well as it's poor design and content had caused Daniel to be screened out of many interviews.

Before Resume

DANIEL C. SMITH
1515 95th Street
Bellevue, WA 98006
(206) 747-4891

OBJECTIVE

I would like to take the 26 years of experience that I have gained and apply it to a more challenging and lucrative position.

COMPANY	JOB TITLE	JOB DESCRIPTION
Smith & Sons Long Beach, CA 1968 - 1993	Automatic Mech. Oper. (AME)	Developed projects and saw them through completion. Worked with engineers to change and install equipment. Did all phases of preventative maintenance. Designed and built parts of machines to make more efficient and run faster. Trained and qualified new mechanics. Troubleshoot electrical and air power systems. Took money saving ideas to management and worked with them hand in hand to completion of project. Was responsible for numerous production lines.
Resigned to take maximum advantage of 26 years profit sharing		
Standard Packaging Downey, CA 1966-1968	Electrical Trainee All around utility person	

EDUCATION

Wilson High School	Graduated 1966	Industrial Arts
Long Beach State College	1966 - 1968	Electronics Major
National Trade School	1976	Mechanical Training
Krones Labeling Machine	1992	Was taught how to tear down and reassemble and make all adjustments. Also preventative maintenance procedures in-depth.
American Can Company	1992	Was taught how to tear down and reassemble can seamer and make all adjustments.

PERSONAL

Born in Long Beach, CA Excellent Health Honorable Discharge	02-25-48. Married 21 years with two sons, age 19 & 15. U.S. Navy	

√ RESUME FOCUSED ON SKILLS & ACHIEVEMENTS

Within 2 weeks of mailing this resume to California, Daniel was flown with all expenses paid to interview in that state. He was offered and accepted a position that paid $6,000 more than his old position. His new employer also paid his family's relocation expenses, and a few weeks later he and his wife sent me a very nice card and flowers.

After Resume

Daniel C. Smith
1515 95th Street
Bellevue, WA 98006
(206) 747-4891

SUPERVISION / TRAINING

Supervised up to 20 employees on 4 high speed, heavy volume production lines - each approximately a block long.

- Controlled and adjusted all supplies, forming, filling, sealing, and packing components.
- Delegated duties and monitored production efficiency to meet schedules.
- Consulted management regarding production, employee performance and budgeting.
- Utilized computer to enter and compile production reports.
- Developed strong employee rapport being recognized for motivational skills.
- Consistently led the department in meeting all production quotas.

PRODUCTION DESIGN / COST SAVINGS

Increased efficiency and reduced labor requirements - saving over $60,000 annually.

- Continually analyzed methods to increase efficiency by re-designing antiquated equipment.
- Designed, built, and installed automatic lubrication systems, conveyors, premium feeding machines, and glue tanks; making timing adjustments as necessary.
- Dealt with vendors and manufacturers in research and selection of hydraulic lift platform and mechanical components.
- Developed and implemented preventative maintenance system.
- Received *"Corporate Commendation"* for increased efficiency and innovation.

MECHANICAL KNOWLEDGE / TRAINING

Welding	Sheet Metal	Pipe Fitting
Lathe	Basic Electrical	All Hand & Power Tools
Forklifts	Air Compressors	Hydraulics
Air Powered Systems	Pumps	Blueprints & Schematics

- Cross-Training, Production & Management Certificate, Smith & Sons
- Electronics Major, Long Beach College
- Mechanical Training, National Trade School
- Krones Labeling & Preventative Maintenance Program, Krones Manufacturing
- Seamer & Preventative Maintenance Program, American Can

EMPLOYMENT HISTORY

- Automatic Machine Expert, Smith & Sons 1980 - 1994

√ RESUME LOOKS CLUTTERED - DOESN'T SELL SKILLS

Barbara was discouraged when I met with her. She had recently completed a wordprocessing program and wanted to obtain a position using those skills. As you can see this resume is very busy and doesn't sell her wordprocessing, administrative or customer service skills.

Before Resume

RESUME OF
Barbara Symthe
3901 90th Avenue S.E.
Tukwila, WA 98201
(206) 392-7890

OBJECTIVE: To use and expand my training as a wordprocessor, to grow with the company as it grows and to keep pace with the technology in the wordprocessing field.

EDUCATION: Wordprocessing - Lake Washington Technical College, Summer Session 1992
Office Skills Refresher - Lake Washington Technical College, Fall Quarter 1992
Principles of Real Estate - Bellevue Community College, Fall Quarter 1991
Real Estate Pre-License Class - John Mykut Real Estate School, September 1987
General Studies, Washington State University 1964-66
Bellevue High School - Graduated 1964

WORK EXPERIENCE:

Saratoga College 1818 S.E. 50th Bellevue, Washington	Office Manager	12-90 to 6-91
ABC Company 5656 70th Seattle, Washington	Receptionist/ Secretary	5-89 to 7-90
Real Estate Sales 1515 80th Bellevue, Washington	Sales Agent	8-87 to 9-88
B.C. Company 6910 3rd Avenue Seattle, Washington	Clerk Typist	1-70 to 6-71

SPECIAL SKILLS: Trained in operation and understanding of 4 different wordprocessing machines. Typing speed 75-80 wpm, dictaphone, spirit-master duplicator, mimeograph, scanner, filing, telephone and all related general office skills.

REFERENCES:

James Smith, Chairman Saratoga College (526) 398-5789	Ron Piking K. Church (206) 819-7980
Betty Hill Lake Washington Voc Tech (206) 878-3756	Cynthia Billings Real Estate Sales (206) 234-7645

√ RESUME FOCUSED ON WORDPROCESSING SKILLS

Within 6 weeks of submitting this resume Barbara was hired as a Wordprocessor with the City of Kirkland. She received a $400 increase in her monthly income and achieved her goal of using her newly acquired computer skills.

Barbara Symthe
3901 90th Avenue S.E.
Tukwila, WA 98201
(206) 392-7890

WORDPROCESSING & BUSINESS MACHINES

Office Manager
- Utilized MS Word and WordPerfect on IBM Computers.
- Familiar with Excel, FoxPro, Lotus 1-2-3.
- Applications include text entry and edit, back-up and duplication, formatting, and proper storage of diskettes.

- Typing 65-70 wpm, statistical typing and transcription.
- 10-Key by Touch, mimeograph and copy machines.
- 6-line phone system with 14 extensions.

Training
- Trained on IBM Memory Writer, Lexitron, Olivetti Electronic, and Mag Card wordprocessors.

ADMINISTRATIVE SKILLS

Office Manager
- Converted manual operations to Xerox 820 computerized system for staff of 9 accountants.
- Delegated work responsibilities and monitored daily work flow of clerical personnel.
- Scheduled and confirmed staff appointments.
- Prioritized projects to ensure timely completion and meeting of deadlines.
- Maintained inventory - ordering up to $800 per month in office and accounting supplies.

Receptionist/
Secretary
- Typed daily correspondence and designed weekly newsletter.
- Coordinated volunteers for various projects.
- Organized use of church facilities by community groups.

CUSTOMER SERVICE

Office Manager
- Responsible for front office and telephone reception.
- Dealt with up to 30 clients per day scheduling appointments and verifying work in progress.
- Acted as Liaison between staff and clients to resolve public relations problems and expedite work orders.
- Increased rapport with clients by showing sincere interest in their concerns.

EMPLOYMENT

Office Manager, Saratoga College 1990 - 1991
Receptionist/Secretary, ABC Company 1989 - 1990
Sales Agent, Real Estate Sales, Inc. 1987 - 1988
Clerk Typist, B.C. Company 1970 - 1971

√ RESUME DOESN'T MAXIMIZE SALES BACKGROUND

Sandra wanted to use her inside sales experience from several years ago to go into outside sales. This resume caused her to be screened out of sales interviews because it didn't describe her sales achievements nor did it use headings to draw attention to her sales background.

RESUME OF QUALIFICATIONS

Before Resume

SANDRA WASHINGTON
4336 600TH S.E.
Issaquah, WA 98027
(206) 392-4387

CAREER OBJECTIVE: A responsible and challenging sales position which provides an opportunity for continued professional growth and advancement.

AREAS OF EXPERIENCE:

Public Relations   Supervision
Customer Service   Personnel Training
Sales   Displays
Product Promotions   Cash Accountability
Merchandising   Inventory Control
Vendor Contact   Marketing Analysis & Trends

SPECIAL ACCOMPLISHMENTS:

** Awarded for precise cash accountability
** Outstanding abilities in public relations
** Excelled in academic pursuit:
   Honor Graduate - High School
   Honor Society - Community College
** Medical Assistant Training

EMPLOYMENT HISTORY:

Trained and directed employees in sales techniques, extensive customer relations and assistance, displays, merchandising, vendor relations, product promotions, cash accountability, responsible for high value merchandise.
   U.S. Army, San Diego, California 1980 - 1990.

Promote the sale of gift items at a major airport involving extensive public relations, program implementation, monitor market trends, cash accountability, inventory control, and serve on Loss Prevention Committee.
   Airlines Hotel, San Diego, California 1990 - 1992

Help to keep in continuance a cheerful office atmosphere for chiropractic physician, receptionist, and therapist; accountable for daily bookkeeping, billing and bank deposits.
   Medical Services, Seattle, Washington 1992 - 1993

√ SALES & MARKETING HEADINGS SELL WITHIN SECONDS

Sandra accepted an Outside Sales Trainee position within 5 weeks of using this resume. In a year's time she will have an opportunity to become a Territory Sales Representative and increase her income by 25%.

After Resume

SANDRA WASHINGTON
4336 600th S.E.
Issaquah, WA 98027
(206) 392-4387

OBJECTIVE

Outside Sales Representative position utilizing my ability to generate and close sales, and promote public relations.

SUMMARY OF MARKETING SKILLS:

Sales	Supervision
Customer Service	Personnel Training
Public Relations	Vendor Contact
Product Promotions	Inventory Control
Merchandising	Cash Accountability
Market Analysis & Trends	Displays

SALES EXPERIENCE:

Technical Sales

- Generated sales in excess of $1/2 million annually in high-tech and electronic merchandise.
- Managed an in-house inventory of up to $100,000.
- Dealt with vendors selecting products.
- Utilized catalogs and manufacturer's literature in sales presentations.
- Trained staff in sales, customer service, merchandising and cash control.

- Achieved high closing ratio by gauging customer response and adjusting presentations to resolve customer concerns.
- Dealt with a diverse range of clientele in fast-paced and demanding situations.

Sales Representative

- Dealt with high volume of customers promoting the sale of catering services at a major hotel.
- Consistently met sales projections.
- Received an award for achieving highest monthly sales in 1992.
- Ordered up to $375,000 in annual catering products.
- Monitored market and sales trends to maximize sales.
- Served on "Excellence in Customer Service Committee."
- Trained new employees in sales and customer service procedures.

EDUCATION

Marketing Program, Honor Roll, Shoreline Community College
Medical Administration Coursework, Bellevue Community College
Medical Assistant Program, Health Careers Center

WORK HISTORY

Inside Sales, U.S. Army Exchange 1980 - 1990
Sales Representative, Airlines Hotel 1990 - 1992
Administrative Assistant, Medical Services 1992 - 1993

Nancy had been teaching full-time while working part-time evenings and weekends in sales. She wanted to get a full-time sales position. I've included her teaching resume on this page. On the facing page is her sales resume. It's easy to see that these resumes are completely different.

Nancy Diebold
459 Hewlett Street
North Bend, WA 98203
(206) 902-8392

SUMMARY OF QUALIFICATIONS

- 10 years Certificated Teaching experience - pre-school to eighth grade, specializing in Reading and Gifted Instruction.

- Developed teaching & testing aids correlated to School Board objectives.

- Wrote Grants for Host Program and Winetka Reading Support System.

- Presentations - International Reading Association, New Orleans to group of 120. L.A. West Coast Regional Computer Conference, to group of 100.

AREAS OF EXPERIENCE

TEACHING 1ST TO 8TH GRADE:
Reading
Language Arts
Mathematics
Social Sciences
Science (Biology)

PRESCHOOL
Activities Coordinator-Montessori Method

LEARNING DISABLED:
Slingerland Method of Instruction
Neurolinguistic Impress Method

GIFTED:
Developed Activity Centers using Bloom's Taxonomy

MICROCOMPUTERS:
Apple IIe
BASIC LOGO
BASIC Programming
Turtle Graphics
Curriculum Reading Programs

SPECIALIZED READING ACTIVITIES:
Pre-Reading Activities
Poetry to Teach Reading Skills
Alternatives to Directed Reading
Lesson Monologues Developed for
 Comprehension & Word Attack Strands
Extended Comprehension Strand of
 Adopted Basal Series
Mapping in Content Areas - 4th Grade
 Social Studies
Wrote a Dolch Sight Program
Developed Little Books using Primer,
 Pre-Primer, and Basal Words for
 K & 1st Grade
Implemented the use of Left & Right
 Hemispherical Activity in Reading

Prescriptive Diagnostic Reading Programs
Informal Reading Inventories
 (Computerized)
Remedial Math - Linear Approach
Right Hemispherical Math Activities
 for Motivation

EDUCATION

- B.A. Degree - Elementary Education, Northwestern University
- Special Education Courses for Master's Degree, Northeastern Wisconsin University

EMPLOYMENT

- Gifted Program Teacher, Winetka School District 1987 - 1992
- Teacher - 2nd, 7th & 8th Grades, North Chicago School District 1982 - 1987

√ SALES RESUME GETS $50,000 OFFER FROM MICROSOFT

Nancy's friends, who were teachers, told her to change this resume and describe her teaching skills. I know employers want to see sales achievements so I convinced her to try it. In three weeks she received a 95% response ratio and received a $50,000 offer from Microsoft.

Nancy Diebold
459 Hewlett Street
North Bend, WA 98203
(206) 902-8392

———— SALES EXPERIENCE 1980 - 1992 ————

Consistently achieved $30,000 in annual income from commission sales.

All positions were part-time while employed as a full-time teacher.

Currently seek a full-time sales position with high income potential.

- Achieved commission of $10,000 first 2 months employed with Standard Products selling residential climate control products.

- Averaged an annual income of $30,000 maintaining a 50% closing ratio. Supervised and trained canvas crew in all aspects of prospecting.

- Developed business plan and supervised marketing of an Oregon firm offering fitness equipment. Negotiated $300,000 in start-up capital.

- Achieved a 75% closing ratio as a Sales Rep for a leading fitness center.

- Marketed pharmaceuticals throughout the Northwest Territory for Squibb Medical.

- Developed a cash-out program for XYZ Corporation generating $2 million annually.

- Specialized in real estate listings for Century 21 Real Estate, listing an average of 8 homes each month - working weekends only.

- Increased monthly sales 200% for Smith's Manufacturing by implementing an innovative sales program.

- Increased annual sales from $200,000 to $440,000 within 4 years as a Telemarketing Supervisor for Midwest Memorial.

EDUCATION

- B.A. Degree - Northwestern University
- Graduate Studies - Western Washington University

√ TITLES SELL NURSING EXPERIENCE

Darlis found that her old resume wasn't generating a very strong response. When she did land interviews she kept getting passed over for other R.N.'s with "more experience." However, within 7 weeks she accepted a position as a Head Nurse with an opportunity to conduct training seminars.

Darlis McGovern, R.N.
459 Hewlett Street
North Bend, WA 98203
(206) 902-8392

SUMMARY OF NURSING EXPERIENCE

TRAVELING NURSE   *1991 - Present*
Professional Nursing Agency, Kirkland, Washington

- *Extensive experience in working with both adults and children utilizing home ventilator units (LP3, LP4).*
- *Supervised intensive care patients at home. Monitored use of Hickman catheter, IV's, IV pumps, and hyperalimentation therapy.*
- *Coordinated in-home care for dying patients.*
- *Evaluated home health needs and physical assessment.*
- *Coordinated health care between patient's needs, doctors and agencies.*
- *Promoted agency's public image, developing rapport with families in crisis situations.*
- *Instructed patients and families in use of equipment and counseled families dealing with anger and grief management issues.*

TRAUMA UNIT NURSE   *1990*
Harborview Medical Center, Seattle, Washington

- *Cared for surgical trauma patients.*
- *Utilized Swan Ganz Monitors, ventilators (Servo, Bears, KAI's), Clinitron and Roto beds, orthopedic traction devices, and IV's.*
- *Coordinated administration of drugs.*

NURSING STAFF   **1987 - 1990**
Valley Medical Center, Renton, Washington

- *Demonstrated an ability to move from department to department upon a moment's notice.*
- *Worked in intensive care unit, med/surg, OB-GYN, and orthopedic rehab.*

REHABILITATION RN   *1984 - 1987*
County Hospital, Abilene, Texas

- *Provided primary care including chemotherapy drug administration and use of Hickman catheters.*
- *Worked with long term rehabilitation patients - head injury, CVA, strokes, paraplegics and quadriplegics.*
- *Physical therapy included training patients in use of electric wheelchairs, walkers, slings, canes, prostheses and orthopedic equipment.*
- *Evaluated patients' needs to teach and redevelop skills for daily living routines, and to promote functioning in society with disability.*

---

131 ♦

√ PROFESSIONAL FOOTBALL PLAYER to OUTSIDE SALES

Ken was really defeated when I met with him. He had been a football player for the Rams and Seahawks. Off-seasons he had worked part-time and was managing a newspaper route. His new resume landed him an Outside Sales position with a major distributor at $40,000.

KEN HILL
238 Lake Quinalt Road
Bothell, WA 98021
(206) 783-9921

EDUCATION & TRAINING

- B.S., University of Nebraska, Minor - Social Sciences 1981
- Certificate in Advanced Counseling, Management Training, Inc. 1981

MANAGEMENT & MOTIVATION

- Supervised 10 agents in distribution of World News. Responsible for on-time delivery, coordination of substitutes and motivation of employees to deal with bad weather conditions and maintaining other full time jobs.
- Managed 30 high school students on a rotating basis. Dealt with problems of absenteeism, food preparation for low and peak periods, and motivated students by being consistently positive about their abilities.

BUSINESS & PROBLEM SOLVING

- Reduced vandalism on city buses by 25% by contacting junior and high school principals to set up assemblies, show films and implement motivational programs.
- Prepared cash registers, kept daily accounting records of cash flow, made deposits and assisted in purchasing.

LEADERSHIP & MOTIVATION

- Played professional football for Rams & Seahawks. Exemplified leadership on and off the field with a winning attitude, especially in pressure situations.
- Instructed a series of football clinics to train teenagers in techniques of football, sportsmanship, organization and leadership.

MARKETING & NETWORKING

- Contacted executives of 200 corporations to obtain job listings. Kept records of all placements by Employment Security to identify success of program.
- Provided managerial, financial, and marketing assistance to businesses by networking and referral to community resources.

AWARDS & AFFILIATIONS

- Red Rose Award, for service to others, Los Angeles, California
- Boys Town Alumni Association
- University of Nebraska Alumni Association
- National Football League Player Association

WORK HISTORY

- District Manager, World News, Bellevue, Washington 1993
- Career Counselor, Job Rehab, Seattle, Washington 1989 - 1992
- Assistant Manager, Rax Restaurants, Seattle, Washington 1988
- Professional Football, Seahawks & Rams, 1981 - 1988
- National Alliance of Businessmen, Los Angeles, California 1973

√ FUNCTIONAL RESUME - NO DATES

Abby had several gaps in her employment and hadn't worked for over 6 years. As you can see her skills are excellent and this resume generated her a very high response rate. Employers were so impressed with Abby's background that they weren't concerned she was re-entering the workforce.

ABBY KINNICK
13278 290th N.E., Bellevue, WA 98008   (206) 677-9800

OBJECTIVE & QUALIFICATIONS

Seek a challenging position as a Full-Charge Bookkeeper utilizing:

• Over 9 years experience in office management, bookkeeping and customer service.

• Self-motivated with ability to work under pressure, prioritize and meet schedules.

• Ability to develop new procedures with excellent attention to detail & follow-through.

AREAS OF EXPERIENCE

BOOKKEEPING	**OFFICE MANAGEMENT**	**COMPUTER**
A/R, A/P, G/L, Payroll	Supervision & Training	Conversions/Testing
Sales Journals, Billing	of Clerical Personnel	Work with Programmers
Bank Reconciliations	Workflow Scheduling	**PROGRAMMING**
Financial Statements	**CUSTOMER SERVICE**	BASIC, COBOL, RPG,
Credit Verification	Problem Solving	FORTRAN, Assembler

SUMMARY OF ACHIEVEMENTS

OFFICE MANAGEMENT — Managed general office, reception, and bookkeeping functions to support staff of 55.

• Supervised and trained clerical staff and delegated workflow. Maintained personnel files and insurance claims.
• Dealt with insurance administrators resolving claims problems.
• Developed OSHA & WISHA reports. Prepared union contracts.
• Purchased and inventoried office supplies.

BOOKKEEPING — Maintained A/R, A/P, and billing for over 1,500 accounts and payroll for up to 55 employees.

• Developed a variety of summary reports - A/R, payroll, manpower utilization, sales and cost reports.
• Researched and verified customer credit applications.
• Prepared quarterly reports and excise tax returns.
• Posted entries to sales journals and general ledger.
• Handled banking transactions and reconciled statements.
• Assisted with preparation of financial statements.
• Processed employee credit applications.

COMPUTER CONVERSION — Oversaw and implemented conversion of manual system to a Digital Mainframe Computer with PIC operating program.

• Worked with programmers in design/testing of software.
• Developed a variety of computerized spreadsheet reports.
• Completed a Computer Programming/Accounting Program with ITT, which included programming in BASIC, COBOL, RPG, FORTRAN, and Assembler languages.

Craig used this resume to apply for and win a position in California. He said his new employer was really impressed with his comments about customer service. Craig's employment had been erratic. Notice how we summarized and de-emphasized his work history.

CRAIG YOUNG
JOURNEYMAN CARPENTER
4337 89th Street
Issaquah, WA 98027
(206) 392-7890

OBJECTIVE

Journeyman level position with emphasis in finish work for remodeling/alteration projects.

REMODELING

- 75% of new remodels from strong customer referrals.
- General remodeling of $400,000 homes.
- Remodels in $20,000 - $50,000 range include additions, kitchen and bath remodels, saunas, skylights, and decks.
- Experience with commercial tenant improvements.
- Ability to roof, apply and finish drywall, make repairs and alterations of plumbing and electrical, pour and finish concrete.
- Ability to solve function, design and aesthetic problems in home improvements.
- Give special care in protecting and clean-up of homes and accessories with customers being very pleased by my project management skills.

CABINETRY / FINISH WORK

- On 99% of all jobs was given responsibility for final phase of finish work throughout my 10 year career.
- Ability to design, build and install cabinets.
- Fit and install finish trim in all applications.
- Able to work with formica.
- Can hang and fit doors.
- Attention to detail with ability to follow-through and please demanding customers is commented on and desired by contractors.

CARPENTRY

- 6 years full-time experience in $400,000+ homes, light and heavy commercial jobs to $1 million.
- Extensive call-back by general contractors requesting my services.
- Hands-on work in all phases of foundations, floors, walls, roofs, stairs, etc.
- Working knowledge of blueprints.
- Can perform basic layout and design.

EDUCATION

A.A. Degree, San Paublo College
Land Surveying Certificate, San Diego Junior College

WORK HISTORY

Remodeling	1990 - 1993
Carpentry - Commercial (Limited Residential)	1983 - 1989
Cabinetmaker	1980 - 1982
Carpentry	1978 - 1980

√ MINIMUM OUTSIDE SALES EXPERIENCE

Stephen worked as a counter person for an automotive parts distributor. Even though he spent only 10% of his time calling on accounts we focused on and expanded this experience. Stephen was very excited when he was hired as an Outside Sales Representative for a major competitor.

STEPHEN COOPER
200 N.E. Northup Way
Bellevue, WA 98004
(206) 746-9821

AREAS OF EXPERIENCE

Outside/Inside Sales	Vendor Contact	Personnel Supervision
Customer Service	Purchasing	Hiring & Training
Public Relations	DEC Computer Usage	Workflow Scheduling
Accounts Receivable	Inventory Control	Order Tracking
Deposits/Cash Accountability	Invoicing	Parts Control

SALES BACKGROUND

OUTSIDE/INSIDE SALES 1991 - Present
Wholesale Brake & Supply, a wholesale after market parts supplier and brake caliper rebuilder.

- **OUTSIDE SALES** - Call on automotive and retail centers, soliciting new business. Service existing accounts throughout Greater Seattle area.
- Products include brake calipers, drums and rotors, master cylinders, hardware, brake shoes and pads, etc.
- Recently obtained firm's largest retail account with 10 Northwest outlets.

- **INSIDE SALES** - Provide sales/price quoting to all commercial accounts.
- Deal extensively with customers over the phone researching parts, expediting shipments, and troubleshooting brake systems.

- **DISPATCH SUPERVISOR** - Supervise 3 drivers, coordinating and scheduling all deliveries and pick-ups.
- Interviewed, hired, and trained drivers in all phases of order processing.

- **PURCHASING/INVENTORY CONTROL** - Purchase parts from vendor warehouse to fill and expedite orders. Utilize digital computer to process invoices and maintain inventory control. Process accounts receivable, make daily bank deposits, and maintain cash on hand.

EDUCATION

Issaquah High School - General Education 1983

Employment While Completing High School:

Dairy Queen 1990 - 1991
Opened restaurant and prepared products to serve 500 customers daily.

Guiseppe's Italian Restaurant 1989 - 1990
Set up nightly service operations and maintained equipment.

Big Red's Restaurant 1987 - 1988
Assisted in maintenance of this 300 capacity facility.

---

135 ◆

√ FROM ASSISTANT TO ACCOUNTING MANAGER

Alice's confidence really took a boost when she saw her new resume. She was making $1350 a month. I encouraged her to apply for positions $300 to $500 more per month. After two months of encouragement she accepted an Accounting Manager position at $1750 a month.

ALICE COOPER
200 N.E. Northup Way
Bellevue, WA 98004
(206) 746-9821

OBJECTIVE

Challenging Office Manager/Administrative Assistant position, using my ability to manage projects, streamline procedures, and deal extensively with customers.

AREAS OF EXPERIENCE

Dictaphone	Collections	Computers:
Correspondence	Bookkeeping	IBM & MacIntosh
Typing 65 wpm	Inventory Control	Order Entry, Word
10-Key by Touch	Shipping/Receiving	Processing, Payroll,
PBX & Multi-Line Phones	Travel Arrangements	A/R, A/P, Inventory,
Purchasing Office Supplies	Appointment Scheduling	Spreadsheets

---

OFFICE MANAGEMENT

NEW OFFICE SET-UP

Managed and reorganized distribution office including credit management/collections operations.

- Corresponded with corporate headquarters daily.
- Developed and maintained job logs, customer accounts, inventory, invoicing, accounts payables and receivables.

WORK FLOW SCHEDULING

Directed administrative functions to support staff of 25 as Assistant Office Manager.

- Managed work flow of clerical and shipping personnel.
- Responsible for inside sales, expediting and order entry.
- Trained sales and accounts payable staff.

INVENTORY CONTROL

Controlled inventory for 3 warehouses in 2 states. Compiled year-end spreadsheet reports.

- Ordered stock and maintained vendor relationships.
- Processed parts requisitions coordinating with production, Q.C., and shipping departments.

BOOKKEEPING

General ledger, payroll, A/R, A/P, sales journals, personnel records, and bank reconciliations. Managed petty cash, controlled budgets and purchased office supplies.

EDUCATION

Accounting/Office Procedures Certificate, Edison Technical School.

EMPLOYMENT

Assistant Office Manager, Seattle Awning 1990 - Present
Office Administrator, Northwest Symetrical Products 1988 - 1989
Inventory Control, Packaging Services, Inc. 1980 - 1984

√ BROCHURE - STYLE RESUME

Sandy owns a medical transcription business and wanted a resume that she could give to physicians to market her services and possibly to generate an offer as a Clinic Manager. She's been very pleased with this design and has developed many new contacts with it.

SANDY ALLISON, R.N.
2390 89th Street
Marysville, WA 98312
(206) 889-2314

MEDICAL TRANSCRIPTION SERVICES

Medical transcription services offered at your convenience:
Free Pick Up & Delivery
24-Hour Dictaphone Service
Quality at Competitive Rates
Free Quotes & Initial Set-Up

AREAS OF SPECIALTY

General Practice	Psychiatric Reporting	Case Documentation
OB-GYN	Neurology	Insurance/Benefits
Surgical/Trauma	Internal Medicine	DSHS Reporting
Oncology	ENT	Legal Briefs
Orthopedics	Head/Neck	Expert Testimony
Pediatrics	Radiology	Operations Consulting

LIST OF MEDICAL CLIENTS / REFERENCES:

Lewis Krantz, M.D. - General Practice
Norma Kinsey, M.D. - Plastic Surgeon
Stewart Smith, M.D., FACC - Cardiologist
T.M. Edwards, D.O. - Osteopath
American Obstetrical Association

PROFESSIONAL EXPERIENCE:

MEDICAL TRANSCRIPTIONIST	Possess broad knowledge of private and corporate medical practices and governmental reporting procedures.
CLINIC SET-UP	Set-up all medical and bookkeeping files for two medical practices. Hired and trained staff and managed clinic operations.
MEDICAL MANAGEMENT CONSULTANT	Analyzed and streamlined work flow for a practice seeing over 600 patients monthly. Developed an innovative marketing program which increased sales 23%.
REGISTERED NURSE	Over 10 years hospital and private care nursing has resulted in a broad range of specialties. Recognized for providing outstanding service.

√ LABORER to BOOKKEEPER

Arnold wanted to use his computer training to move into an office position. While working in "labor" positions he had gained skills in bookkeeping, purchasing, inventory and customer service. We focused this resume on these skills and he received an excellent response to his career change.

Arnold Helms   **210 30th Street**
(206) 892-8876   **Seattle, WA 98106**

OBJECTIVE

A position utilizing my bookkeeping, office administration, and public relations skills.

COMPUTER EXPERIENCE		OFFICE ADMINISTRATION
FoxPro	Excel	Accounts Receivable & Payable
Quicken	MS Word	Computerized Billing
PeachTree	WordPerfect	Payroll/Record Keeping
Database Administration	Data Entry	Multi-Line Phones

COMPUTERIZED BOOKKEEPING ———————————————

*   Maintained over 800 A/R accounts and approximately 100 A/P accounts.
    Prepared biweekly payroll for up to 8 employees.
*   Prepared all deposits and reconciliations for 3 checking accounts.
    Converted manual payroll, A/R, A/P, and checking to computerized system.
*   Set up computerized accounts and developed client database.

PURCHASING / INVENTORY CONTROL ———————————————

*   Purchased and maintained $10,000 worth of inventory for a 55 unit condominium.
    Purchased all supplies for building, office, pools, and grounds from 15 vendors.
*   Prioritized weekly & monthly responsibilities, consistently meeting deadlines.
    Kept detailed records, documented purchases, and tracked inventory.

CUSTOMER SERVICE ———————————————

*   Coordinated with state, county, and city officials.
    Provided cost estimates, project options and company policy.
*   Dealt with irate customers, resolving conflicts and negotiating payments.
    Provided quality service by assessing and fulfilling customer needs.

EMPLOYMENT HISTORY

Computerized Bookkeeping	A-1 Mechanics, Inc.	1992 - 1994
Purchasing/Inventory Control	Hotel Procurers	1991 - 1992
Inventory Control/Customer Service	Balboa Distributors	1990 - 1991
Public Relations/Purchasing	General Vehicle	1988 - 1990

EDUCATION

Computer Applications - Certificate	B.C.T.I.	1994
Pre-Law Studies	Bellevue Community College	1990
Legal Clerk Training	U.S. Army	1989

√ AN EFFECTIVE 2-PAGE RESUME

Cynthia went from a $36,000 position in Outside Sales to a $53,000
Territory Management position with this resume. All 5 of the executives
that interviewed her complimented her on her resume and said that of 125
resumes received hers was the best.

Cynthia Moyers
4312 55th Street
Seattle, WA 98411
(206) 344-8900

OBJECTIVE

Sales Management position utilizing my national marketing, direct sales and
supervisory experience, with opportunity for high income potential.

MARKETING & MANAGEMENT ACHIEVEMENTS

**Developed and managed national marketing program, generating
sales in excess of $15 million from 12 major U.S. operations.**

- On-line to meet current sales projections - establishing 2,000 new
  accounts in 1993.

- Extensive experience developing and implementing outside sales,
  telemarketing and direct mail campaigns.

- Business and operational development has included recruitment, hiring,
  and training of sales and support staff.

- Developed and managed annual budgets, controlled expenses, purchased
  capital equipment, and oversaw accounting systems.

NATIONAL MARKETING MANAGER   1992 - Present

National Transfer, a Division of Home Management, Inc.

- Created national marketing program and established 12 U.S. sales operations.
  Within 2 months generated a client base of over 300 accounts. On-line to
  meet 1993 projection of opening 2,000 accounts.

- Traveled nationally marketing services to Fortune 500 corporations, national
  property management firms, and the general public. Conceived and
  developed telemarketing program, direct mail campaigns, promotional
  advertising, sales presentations, and customer service operations.
  Negotiated program approval with Board of Directors. Hired and supervised
  subcontractors- ad & promotional designs, office systems and installations.

- Monitored communication and marketing efforts in 7 subsidiary divisions to
  ensure quality control and compliance with company policies/procedures.
  Established new offices in hub cities - Recruit, supervise, and train sales,
  telemarketing and support personnel.

- Devised and implemented computerized spreadsheet program to maintain
  national client base, sales and account data from corporate headquarters.
  Managed budgets, projected sales, controlled costs, oversaw purchasing,
  accounts payable and receivables.

√ TITLES SELL WITHIN SECONDS

With employers spending as little as 10 seconds to screen resumes, the 2nd page must maximize and sell job titles or skill groups. Cynthia's job titles get immediate attention and cause employers to be interested in reading her resume further.

Cynthia Moyers   **(206) 344-8900**

OUTSIDE SALES REPRESENTATIVE   1989 - 1992

Northwest Press & Printing, commercial business forms & printing services.

- Pioneered Puget Sound territory, marketing supplies and services to commercial accounts.
- Consistently increased each month's sales by approximately 10%.
- Successfully re-opened several major accounts.
- Consulted and assisted clients in design of forms, four color and flat printing.
- Coordinated in-house production to meet deadlines and controlled quality of finished material.

OWNER / SALES MANAGER   1979 - 1987

Sprague Graphic Design, close-tolerance forms and four color printing.

- Created and established business, marketing services to commercial and general accounts.
- Generated 30% of sales from strong referral business.
- Developed business plan, advertising and marketing program, and analyzed overhead and expenses to project profit potential.
- Selected and purchased capital equipment and supplies.
- Gained extensive expertise in sales, marketing, customer service, and troubleshooting as an entrepreneur.

ADDITIONAL MANAGEMENT EXPERIENCE

PRESIDENT   Managed "Professional Women in Sales," a non-profit organization with local membership of 10,000.

Page 2

√ FROM $1500 A MONTH TO $40,000 FIRST YEAR

Tammy applied for two positions in the paper. A week later she interviewed with a credit service firm and was hired that day. By emphasizing and quantifying her sales background and combining it with her experience approving credit to $1 million annually she landed an excellent position.

Tammy Millett
P.O. Box 1717
Seattle, WA 98125
(206) 435-8901

─── OBJECTIVE & QUALIFICATIONS ───

Seek an Account Representative position utilizing the following:

- Pioneering the Greater Seattle Territory, successfully developing key accounts.

- Increasing sales approximately 200% within 6 months.

- Approving $1.2 million in consumer credit annually.

- Bachelor of Science Degree from the University of Washington.

Outside Sales Representative, Remedy Temporary Service 1990 - Present

Develop and maintain key accounts such as Advanced Technology Labs, Washington Natural Gas, CX Corporation, and Leviton Telecom throughout the Greater Seattle area.

- Increased sales from $62,000 to $132,000 per month in first 5 months.
- Increased hourly gross margin approximately 20%.
- Maintained a quota of approximately 60 calls per week.
- Implemented 1990 marketing plan - on track to meet projected goals.
- Developed written proposals, quoted and negotiated bill and pay rates.
- Interviewed, hired and assigned employees in a variety of industries.
- Resolved personnel and service problems with clients.

Account Representative, Adams Associates 1988 - 1990

Pioneered Seattle territory- exceeding 2nd year goals. Developed major accounts such as Ernst & Whinney, Fletcher Challenge (Wright Schuchart), and National Frozen Foods.

- Received 2 "National Key Account Awards" for outstanding achievement.
- Successfully negotiated fees ranging up to $12,000.
- Negotiated placements with top executives and personnel managers.
- Developed extensive telemarketing skills with ability to set appointments and generate orders by phone.
- Conducted confidential searches. Recruited and qualified applicants. Coordinated interviews.

Credit Representative, Frederick & Nelson 1986 - 1988

Approved approximately $1.2 million in consumer credit annually. Gathered credit and salary information from customers by phone, analyzed consumer credit reports and authorized new accounts and credit extensions.

- Awarded merit raise for "Outstanding Credit Achievement."
- Served on "The Credit Action Group" and created an 80 page procedures manual.
- Resolved account discrepancies, billing disputes, overdue accounts and writing off of service charges.

---

141 ♦

√ RECEPTIONIST / CRT CLERK to CORPORATE ASSISTANT

We relabeled Sam's CRT Specialist title to Accounts Specialist, Receptionist to Front Office Administration, and Mail Clerk to Departmental Support. Using these new headings Samantha landed a position as a Corporate Assistant making $320 more per month, with her own office.

Samantha Naples
2389 S.W. 80th
Los Angeles, CA 89202
(206) 203-8922

OBJECTIVE & QUALIFICATIONS

Position as an Administrative Assistant utilizing the following experience:

Managing front office administration while providing support to President and 8 management staff.

Prepared correspondence, quotes and proposals utilizing WordPerfect, MS Word and Lotus 1-2-3.

Instrumental in managing mail operations to support 8 departments.

Certificate - Griffin Business College.

ADMINISTRATIVE EXPERIENCE

ACCOUNTS SPECIALIST, Safeco Consulting Division

* Responsible for computerized processing and verification of up to 1,000 legal documents daily.
* Coordinated customer service and claims processing through Bank Officials, Bank Customers, Insurance Agents, and interoffice employees.
* Composed and edited client correspondence using dictaphone.
* Maintained general ledger postings - Ten-Key 372 spm, Typing 100 wpm.

FRONT OFFICE ADMINISTRATION, Abrams & Williamson, Inc.

* Managed front desk, providing secretarial support to the President and 8 management staff.
* Prepared correspondence, certificates, quotes, proposals and summaries utilizing WP 5.0.
* Managed all mail processing, including express mail for staff of 16.
* Ordered and maintained office supplies, equipment and maintenance.
* Handled 8 lines with 20 extensions.

DEPARTMENTAL SUPPORT / COORDINATION, Systems Control

* Provided general secretarial support for three departments - composed and edited correspondence.
* Instrumental in managing mail operations for 8 departments and coordinating with department heads including:

Marketing	Accounting	Medical
Administration	Claims	Eligibility
Data Processing	Customer Service	

* Prepared mailing projects and maintained filing.

Cover Letters That Get Interviews

A cover letter is a letter of introduction that you include with your resume when responding to a job opening. Many employers won't accept a resume if it is not submitted with a cover letter. Just like an objective on your resume, your cover letter tells an employer why he has received your resume and why you are writing to him. Proper business etiquette requires that you include a cover letter with your resume. If you don't include one it implies that you are not familiar with the business world and can lead to your being rejected as a candidate. Just like your resume, your cover letter is also an advertisement for you and is part of your marketing package. It should also incorporate the primary components of an excellent advertisement - design and content.

Design

Just like your resume, your cover letter may be one of hundreds received. To stand out your cover letter must get attention by using special design techniques such as indented paragraphs, bolding and/or underlining. Take a look at the cover letters on pages 145 and 146. Which letter would you choose to read first? Most people choose the letter on page 146.

Your cover letter must highlight and draw an employer's eye to important information quickly and easily. The letter on page 146 was created with a wordprocessor and the program's bolding feature was used to darken the bulleted sentences. If you don't have a wordprocessor you can use a typewriter to underline and emphasize important skill areas. Take a look at the typewritten letter on page 148. While this letter is a little more plain it still stands out more than the original letter on page 145.

Save Employers Reading Time

Christine was asked by her supervisor to sort through some resumes and select several applicants to interview. Christine was excited about the project and initially thought she'd have about 20 to 30 resumes to review. She was shocked when her supervisor gave her a box of 200 cover letters and resumes to sort that night. At first, she wanted to read each cover letter and resume. After a while she realized she had spent 30 minutes reading only 10 cover letters and resumes. She then decided to pick up her pace and spend about a minute scanning each cover letter and resume. After another 30 minutes she was dismayed at how few cover letters and resumes she had sorted. She realized she was going to be up all night if she didn't develop a faster method to sort the resumes.

So she asked herself what skills were most important for the job. Since it was a sales position she decided she would look for the word "sales" in the cover letters and would look for job titles that reflected sales experience in the resumes. She then began glancing at each letter. If nothing stood out she immediately turned to the resume and ran her finger down it looking for sales experience. If the person's cover letter or resume didn't have sales listed she tossed them. At that point she was spending about 10 to 30 seconds on each cover letter and resume.

Christine said she was amazed at how long and tedious this process was. Her eyes were tired at the end of two and a half hours. It had taken her that long to sort 200 resumes and select 30 applicants. She felt she had done a good job, but said, *"I don't want to have to do that again!"* This story shows how important it is to highlight and draw an employer's eye to important skills in your cover letter. All of the 200 applicants who had applied for the position knew it was for sales, but only 30 of them had highlighted their sales background or had explained how their experience related to sales. That meant that over 90% of the applicants did not market their skills effectively in their cover letters or in their resumes. As you can see, the design of your cover letter is very important. By using techniques that draw the employer's attention to your skills you will dramatically increase the effectiveness of your cover letters.

Content

After you've gotten an employer's attention, the content of your cover letter must convince an employer to interview you. You want to build a case for yourself, explaining and proving why you are qualified for the job. Have you ever watched a show like L.A. Law? If so, you know that the defense attorneys thoroughly analyze each client's case. They look for any angle that can help them defend their client. They build a case, presenting fact after fact that proves why their client should win.

That's exactly what you want to do with each and every cover letter you write. You want to analyze each job opening you apply for and present fact after fact that proves you are qualified and should be interviewed. By building a convincing case of your qualifications you put yourself way ahead of the majority of your competitors.

I'd like you to pretend that you are an employer and need to hire a Driver/Delivery person. Here's an advertisement you placed in your local newspaper that describes the experience and skills you seek:

> **DRIVER/DELIVERY PERSON** 2 + years experience driving and delivering high value products in the Puget Sound area. Customer Service experience dealing with corporate accounts required. Resume to: Ms. Perry, Personnel, XYZ Co., 1456 Harborview Ave, Bremerton, WA, 98212

457 Avalon Street
Bremerton, WA 98121
(206) 442-7890

September 20, 1993

Ms. Diane Perry
Personnel Manager
XYZ Delivery and Shipping
1456 Harborview Avenue
Bremerton, WA 98212

Dear Ms. Perry:

Enclosed is my resume for the Driving position you recently advertised in
the Seattle Times.

I have several years driving and delivery experience. My work history is stable
and I am looking for a position that offers challenge and adequate compensation.

I have enjoyed working with customers in the right employment settings
but prefer independent work as a driver/delivery person.

My driving and customer service experience seems to qualify me for this job.
I look forward to an interview. You may contact me at (206) 442-7890. Thank
you.

Sincerely,

Ronald Taft

457 Avalon Street
Bremerton, WA 98121
(206) 442-7890

September 20, 1993

Ms. Diane Perry
Personnel Manager
XYZ Delivery and Shipping
1456 Harborview Avenue
Bremerton, WA 98212

Dear Ms. Perry:

Enclosed please find my resume for the Driving position you recently advertised in the Seattle Times. As you will note, my experience includes:

♦ **Over 5 years driving experience within the Puget Sound area.**

♦ **Being trustworthy with an excellent attendance record.**

♦ **Making deliveries of up to $250,000 in cash and high value merchandise.**

♦ **Developing strong working relationships with key accounts such as IBM, Microsoft, and US Bank.**

The combination of my driving and customer service experience makes me well qualified for this position. I look forward to an interview and may be contacted at (206) 442-7890. Thank you for your time and consideration.

Sincerely,

Ronald Taft

With the advertisement on page 144 in mind, read Ronald's cover letters on pages 145 and 146. Which letter builds the strongest case for his qualifications? Pretend these letters are from different people and you can choose only one person to interview. Which person would you select? What are the differences between the letters that made you come to that conclusion? The letter on page 145 is typical of the majority of cover letters employers receive. Most applicants never analyze a job opening or job description. They haphazardly throw unrelated information together without building a convincing case for themselves or their skills. That's one reason why many people get so few responses to the large numbers of cover letters and resumes they mail out. The job market itself is often not as bleak as people think. It's not that jobs aren't there or that people applying aren't qualified. Rather, it's because applicants don't know how to market themselves effectively or because they don't take the time to create strong cover letters and resumes. The person with the best qualifications isn't necessarily the person that's hired or called for an interview. It's the person who has presented his qualifications in the most convincing way that is interviewed and hired.

Redundancy

Many career and resume counselors advise that you avoid repeating anything in your cover letter that's in your resume. I disagree. Studies have shown that it takes up to seven times of hearing or seeing something before it makes an impression on us. When employers spend so few seconds glancing at cover letter after cover letter how can we expect them to remember much about us? By being redundant and re-emphasizing our best skills in our cover letter we can help an employer remember our skills. In this instance, being redundant becomes a good strategy.

If you don't restate your best skills in your cover letter what will you write about? Probably general things that everybody writes about. Cover letters that go on and on about the challenge a person seeks or how wonderful the company is, do little to convince me of a person's skills. When skills are omitted, cover letters are weak and don't generate interest. Generally what employers want is specific and condensed descriptions of an applicant's qualifications.

When students bring up their concerns about repeating some of the information that's in their resumes, I feel confident recommending what has worked for my clients. Having received several calls from clients each and every week about the success of their cover letters and resumes I know that these techniques work. If you want to use other cover letter ideas and formats feel free to experiment. If they work and generate interviews then use them. If they don't then follow my recommendations. It can get you a job.

Introductory Paragraph

Generally, a cover letter is comprised of three to five short paragraphs. In the first paragraph, it's good to explain why you are writing the letter, or if someone has referred you. Your first paragraph might read like either of the two paragraphs at the top of page 149.

457 Avalon Street
Bremerton, WA 98121
(206) 442-7890

September 20, 1993

Ms. Diane Perry
Personnel Manager
XYZ Delivery and Shipping
1456 Harborview Avenue
Bremerton, WA 98212

Dear Ms. Perry:

Enclosed please find my resume for the Driving position advertised in the Seattle Times. As you will note, my experience includes:

Over 5 years driving experience within the Puget Sound area.

Being trustworthy with an excellent attendance record.

Making deliveries of up to $250,000 in cash and high value merchandise.

Developing strong working relationships with key accounts such as IBM, Microsoft, and US Bank.

The combination of my driving and customer service experience makes me well qualified for this position. I look forward to an interview and may be contacted at (206) 442-7890. Thank you for your time and consideration.

Sincerely,

Ronald Taft

Enclosed please find my resume for the _____ position you recently advertised.

or

Sally Ingrams, manager of the Better Business Bureau, informed me that you have a _____ position open. She feels my qualifications match this position and encouraged me to enclose a resume for your review.

How To Build A Case For Your Qualifications

It's in the second, third and fourth paragraphs that you build a case for your qualifications. To do this you must analyze each ad or job description and break out the skills requested in it. You will want to prioritize the skills an employer is looking for and then explain how your qualifications match them, in the same priority. The skills requested in the ad below have been underlined and then prioritized.

> **CUSTOMER SERVICE REPRESENTATIVE** <u>2+ years experience dealing with clients in-person & by phone</u>. <u>Type 55 wpm w/good computer skills</u>. <u>Corporate accounts, credit approval and problem solving experience</u> preferred. Resume to: Ms. Perry, Personnel, XYZ Co., 1456 Harborview Ave, Bremerton, WA, 98212

> <u>Prioritized skills:</u>
>
> 1. 2+ years experience dealing with clients in-person and by phone
> 2. type 55 wpm with good computer skills
> 3. corporate accounts, credit approval and problem solving experience

Read the indented cover letter on the facing page. You'll notice that Rex addressed the prioritized skills listed above in the three indented paragraphs of his cover letter. Rex bolded each skill requirement and then wrote one or two sentences explaining how his experience matched each requirement. By analyzing each position you apply for and describing your skills, as Rex did, you too can build a convincing case for your qualifications. Once you've done this you are ready to write your closing paragraph.

The Closing Paragraph

Your final paragraph is a call for action. State when you will contact the employer or ask for an interview and then thank the employer for his consideration. Say you will contact the employer the following week if you know the company name and phone number. This works better than saying you will call on a certain day. If something comes up and you forget to call that particular day you won't end up looking like you have poor follow-through.

149 ◆

457 Avalon Street
Bremerton, WA 98121
(206) 442-7890

September 20, 1993

Ms. Diane Perry
Personnel Manager
XYZ Delivery and Shipping
1456 Harborview Avenue
Bremerton, WA 98212

Dear Ms. Perry:

Enclosed please find my resume for the Customer Service position you recently advertised. Below I have outlined how my experience matches your requirements:

2+ Years Customer Service Experience:
My background includes over 5 years experience dealing with customers in-person and by phone.

Good Computer and Typing Skills:
Processing accounts by computer has been required in each customer service position I have held. My typing speed is 60+ words per minute.

Corporate Accounts, Credit Approval and Problem Solving:
My experience with corporate accounts includes companies such as Microsoft and Weyerhaeuser. Setting up new accounts and approving credit of up to $1/4 million has required strong problem solving skills.

My background makes me an excellent candidate for this position. I will contact you next week to discuss interviewing with you. If you have any questions please phone me at (206) 442-7890. Thank you for your time and consideration.

Sincerely,

Rex Schmidt

In closing, your final paragraph might read:

I am very interested in this position and will contact you next week to schedule an interview. If you have any questions please contact me at (206) 455-2789. Thank you for your time and consideration.

If you can't follow-up because you don't have the company's name, then state that you would like to schedule an interview. Your final paragraph might read:

I am very interested in this position and would like to schedule an interview with you. Please contact me at (206) 455-2789. Thank you for your time and consideration.

The Importance of Follow-Up

Many of you may be thinking, "*But, I don't want to have to call them and follow-up. I just want them to call me.*" I think there's nothing more frightening to most of us than following-up on job openings. It makes our hands get sweaty and our hearts palpitate. The fear of hearing "no" or feeling embarrassed makes most of us procrastinate and never call or follow-up on letters we have sent to prospective employers. As a result, many people send off hundreds of resumes and cover letters but never know what happened to them. By following-up and calling employers we put ourselves ahead of the majority of job seekers. Because most job seekers don't phone or follow-up, those few applicants who do stand out.

This may be one of the times I warned you about. You may be feeling a little scared or out of your comfort zone at the thought of calling employers and asking if your letters have been received. Whenever I teach job search seminars I always ask people to raise their hands if contacting employers seems a little scary to them. Usually more than half of the participants raise their hands, so it's natural to feel a little scared or worried about calling employers. You need to ask yourself why you're scared and how you can feel comfortable following-up on your job contacts. Otherwise, you're in the situation I described before in which you are learning excellent job search techniques, but are too scared to use them.

I know I was scared and breathless the first time I called to follow-up on a help-wanted ad. Having closed my resume business I had decided to go into the personnel field. I answered an ad for a Personnel Coordinator for a temporary employment agency. The ad listed the street address but didn't include the company name or phone number. When a week had passed and I hadn't received a call I got out the yellow pages. Within a few minutes I found the temporary agency's name and phone number. The help-wanted ad had stated, *"No calls, please"* which made me uncomfortable and increased my anxiety. I really wanted that job so I decided I would call and say a friend told me the agency had an opening. That way I could call and it wouldn't look like I was disobeying what the ad said. My next hurdle was that the ad listed the contact's name as M. Foss. I had no idea if this was a man or a woman which also increased my anxiety. Since a lot of personnel agencies are owned and managed by women I decided I would ask for Mrs. Foss.

After getting my nerve up and writing a script of what I was going to say, I got on the phone. I asked to speak to Mrs. Foss and the line went dead silent. After what seemed an eternity the receptionist said in a condescending tone, *"There's no Mrs. Foss here. Do you mean Mike Foss?"* Embarrassed I replied, *"Oh, yes, of course. Sorry, I wasn't thinking."* I was put on hold for a few seconds and Mike Foss introduced himself. Breathless as I was, I went into my sales pitch. I said a friend had told me about the job opening and that I had mailed my resume and cover letter for the position. He put the phone down and rustled through his papers for a minute or so and then said, *"Ah, here it is. Well, I already have someone in mind for this job but I guess it won't hurt to talk to you for a few minutes."* He then asked why I thought I could do the job.

Still feeling shaky, I jumped in and told him I had owned my own resume business and was familiar with the job requirements for hundreds of jobs. I told him I had also owned a word processing business and was familiar with computers. I thought that my knowledge of different industries combined with my secretarial and computer skills gave me unique experience to interview and place temporary employees. He seemed quite interested and said, *"Well, I do have someone in mind and I believe we'll hire her, but why don't you come in tomorrow."* Wow! Was I happy when I got off the phone. To make the rest of this story short I spent three hours at his office the next day, then had a second lunch interview that took two hours, and a final interview that took an hour and a half. I got the job because I took my fear by the horns, found the temp agency's phone number, and followed-up. I don't want to imply that everytime you follow-up on one of your applications you'll get a job, but it will put you ahead of your competitors. It landed me a job and put me into a field I really wanted to work in. Don't underestimate the power of a phone call. Follow-up! It will be worth it. If you're still feeling shaky then prepare a SUCCESS IMAGERY script, as outlined in Chapter 12, and listen to it. You can reprogram your fear into confidence by visualizing how you want to be and what you want to achieve.

Fax Your Cover Letter

Pamela found a help-wanted ad for a construction secretary. The ad included the company name, address, phone and fax numbers. That night she faxed her resume and cover letter, and called the next morning to follow-up. She was set up for an interview two days later. As she was being interviewed, the employer took out a stack of resumes and cover letters about six inches high. The employer said, *"I've received over 100 resumes and cover letters. I just don't have the time to read them. I've decided I'm only going to interview people who fax their resumes to me. I've received seven faxed resumes and yours was one of them. I'm impressed that you followed-up so quickly."*

If an ad includes phone and fax numbers as well as the mailing address - take the lead. Fax your resume as soon as possible and then follow-up just like Pamela did. If a fax number is provided, your last choice should be to mail your resume. Who knows, by the time it's received by mail the position may be filled or the employer may have received enough faxed resumes that he's not opening the mailed ones. Do whatever it takes to reach an employer as quickly as possible.

Apply Even If You Don't Have Every Skill

You may not have all the skills requested for each job you're interested in, but don't let this deter you from applying. Each time an employer advertises a position the hiring pool varies. At certain times of the year an employer may receive cover letters and resumes from many highly qualified applicants. At other times, he may feel lucky to get one or two good candidates. As a result, you can never predict how good your skills will look to an employer. Even if you are lacking in one or two skill areas, still apply for the job if it's one you are interested in. By selling the skills you possess and slanting them to the position you are applying for you can often market yourself as a top candidate.

If You Think You're Not Qualified

When I first entered the personnel field I was shocked when Ann, our permanent placement specialist, said one of my temporary employees would be a perfect match for her client. I read a page of job requirements the employer was requesting. It was pretty overwhelming. A few of the skills included typing of 80+ wpm; legal secretarial background; and experience using WordPerfect and Lotus 1-2-3. I quickly went back and reviewed my employee's application and resume. She typed 60 wpm and had worked in a legal office as a receptionist but not as a legal secretary. While she had WordPerfect experience she didn't have Lotus experience. When I told Ann this, she said, *"Oh yeah, I know. But you can see how bright and bubbly she is. My client is going to love her personality. I know she'll fit right in with the staff he already has. Once she's typing all the time her speed will go up. She's had secretarial training which included legal terminology. She can learn to be a legal secretary. I'm sure he'll hire her!"* I wasn't sure at all and felt that Ann was going to pull the wool over her client's eyes. I thought there was no way he would be interested in my employee, especially since Ann was sending him another candidate with all the hard skills he had requested.

Surprisingly, he hired my candidate. He liked her personality and felt she was very trainable. He and several other staff members interviewed both of the applicants. The person with all of the hard skills just didn't seem like a good fit to them. Her personality was dry and they felt she would want to have things done her way rather than the firm's way. On the other hand, they felt my employee had an excellent personality because she was outgoing and eager to learn. I had been in personnel for only a month when this happened and it opened my eyes as to what employers really look for when interviewing candidates. When reviewing ads or job descriptions it seems employers will only consider those candidates with all the hard skills they list. However, it's most often a person's soft skills, personality and willingness to learn that actually motivates employers to hire someone.

I recommend that you apply for any position that you are interested in and have some qualifications for. You may not always get your foot in the door, but many times you will. You'll then have a chance to sell yourself and your personality. If you skip over jobs you think you're not qualified for you will eliminate a huge segment of the job market. If you're interested - apply!

Answering Blind Ads

If you answer a blind ad, an ad that only lists a PO Box with no company name, you won't know what company you are applying to. Be careful, as you could answer an ad for the company you are currently working for. To learn what company placed the help-wanted ad, call the post office that handles the zip code listed in the ad's address. Ask the post office to give you the name of the company that holds the box number listed in the ad. This can be time consuming and makes many people feel uncomfortable, so very few people call to find out what company placed the ad. As a result, employers who place these ads receive very few follow-up phone calls from applicants. The fewer the phone calls the less competition you have. This puts you in a strategic position if you can get enough information to identify an employer and track down a phone number. By calling you can put yourself way ahead of your competitors.

Several of my clients have gotten interviews by following-up on blind ads. If calling the post office and asking for the company's name makes you feel uncomfortable then ask yourself how uncomfortable you're going to feel if you don't get an interview. This may help you to motivate yourself and to overcome your fear. Remember, by taking action and following-up you gain more control of the interview process which is much better than passively waiting for a phone call. Taking action like this is a trade off between how much you want a particular job and how much you are willing to face your fears.

Answer Ads As Soon As Possible

Apply for each position as soon as possible. If you find an ad in a Sunday paper then answer it that night or the next day. If you wait too long you may lose out. When I was employed as a secretary I helped the office manager open and review the resumes for our front office help. Generally, we'd receive from 80 to 120 resumes for a general clerk or secretarial position. From a weekend help-wanted ad we would receive about 20 responses on Monday. Tuesday we'd receive as many as 60 more. Then we'd continue to receive 10 to 20 more responses each day for about two weeks.

We often received so many responses that by Tuesday we had enough applicants to start interviewing. If this pool of applicants was good enough then the office manager kept the rest of the letters that came in but didn't open them. It was just too time consuming. If someone was hired from the first batch then the rest were thrown away. This happens all the time and is a contributing factor to the problems many job seekers experience. To increase your response ratio be sure to mail your cover letters and resumes within one day, or two days at the latest to advertised positions.

Clients are often surprised at the quick response they get when they mail a cover letter and resume on a Sunday night for a weekend advertisement. Many clients have called me on a Thursday or Friday to say they've just scheduled interviews for positions they applied to over the previous weekend. I was shocked to read one consultant's advise to executives. He recommends waiting a few days after seeing an ad before responding to it.

After thinking a few days about the opening he then suggests writing a cover letter. He even goes so far as to say it's good to wait a week or two before applying. Because his book is directed to executives he evidently thinks the executive hiring process is always long and drawn out. He seems unaware of the fact that a company may have already been looking for someone for weeks or months and could be on the verge of a hiring decision. This advice could keep someone from getting a job. My advise is to get those letters out there, and the sooner the better. Then be sure to follow-up!

Your Salary History

Many help-wanted ads request an applicant's salary history in order to screen out applicants whose salary requirements are too far above or too far below the salary being offered. For example, consider an employer who wants to pay $1,800 a month for a Customer Service Representative. He receives a letter from someone whose past salary has been $2,400 a month. The employer may decide this person will not be happy nor interested in the position at the $1,800 salary level. Therefore, it's likely the employer will choose not to interview this individual. The applicant may or may not be happy with a starting salary of $1,800 a month but loses his chance to make that decision as well as an opportunity to learn more about the position.

Just because salary information is requested doesn't mean that you have to supply it. If your resume and cover letter build a strong case for your qualifications an employer will risk calling you even if you don't supply salary information. If it's a real sticking point, the employer will ask about your salary on the phone. When the employer calls, you've achieved your goal. The employer is on the phone and you have gained greater control of your job search. You can then assess the position and decide whether or not you want an interview.

To be on the safe side, I recommend not giving salary information in your cover letter. If you feel you must include salary information then give a range. For example, if you will take $1,800 a month, but prefer a starting salary of $2,000, you might write a sentence that reads:

My current salary requirement is in the range of $1,800 to $2,000 per month.

If you are an executive and want to increase your income from $55,000 to $60,000+ annually you might write a sentence that reads:

My current salary requirement is in the low-sixties. If you would like further salary details please contact me at (206) 455-7890.

Address Your Letter to a Specific Person

It's very important that you get the name of the correct person to send your cover letter to. Not having the name of a specific person to contact makes it difficult to follow-up on your cover letter and application. Getting the names of decision makers can be difficult because receptionists are trained to screen calls and not give out information. Pointers on getting to decision makers and obtaining contact names are discussed in the next chapter.

Cover Letter Worksheet

Take a look at the cover letter worksheet on page 157. If you like this format you can easily "fill-in the blanks" by writing bulleted sentences for each skill listed in the ad or job posting you are responding to. This is a fast and simple method for cover letter writing. Analyze each job description and prioritize your skills to match what each employer is looking for, then type a customized letter for each position. I know you may be tempted to print off or copy the same letter for every ad. You may feel you just don't have the time to write each letter individually. However it's important to ask yourself if you will find the time to watch a soap opera or the Sunday night movie. If so, that time could be spent writing letters.

The Importance Of Customizing Your Letters

I just completed a job search in which I generated a very high interview rate competing with over 600 applicants for only four positions. Out of these four positions, I received three interviews and accepted a position as the *Job Placement Specialist* for the University of Washington, Bothell campus. I spent approximately 16 hours writing customized resumes and cover letters because each of the four positions was very different. The Job Placement Specialist position required experience writing resumes and teaching career seminars. The second position was for a Personnel Assistant with the City of Kirkland which required personnel and payroll experience. The third position was for a Personnel Assistant with the City of Redmond which required strong secretarial and bookkeeping skills. The last position was for a Career Assessment Specialist which required giving and grading GED exams. If I had used one resume for all these positions I would not have generated such a high response rate. This proves that the more time you put into customizing your resumes and cover letters the higher your rewards will be.

Generic Letters - A Last Resort

Stanley had no time to write customized cover letters because he worked full-time days and part-time nights. He was in sales and wanted an outside sales position. Since all of the positions Stanley wanted to apply for were in sales we created a generic resume and cover letter. In them we targeted areas of experience that were requested in many of the ads he was responding to. Using a generic resume and cover letter saved Stanley a lot of time because all he had to do was copy them, slip them into an envelope and mail them. Using the generic letter on page 158, Stanley received a little less than a 50% request for interviews. If you have absolutely no time to create customized cover letters you may also choose to write and use a generic letter. However, if it doesn't generate a high response then be prepared to write customized letters.

Cover Letter Worksheet

Your street address
City, State Zip Code
(your area code) your phone number

date

Name of Person You Are Contacting
Person's Title
Company Name
Address
City, State Zip Code

Dear Mr. or Ms. _____:

Enclosed please find my resume for the _____
position you recently advertised. As you will note, my experience
includes:

♦ _____

♦ _____

♦ _____

♦ _____

♦ _____

The combination of my _____, _____, and
_____ skills makes me well qualified for this position. I
will contact you next week to discuss interviewing with you. If you have
any questions please contact me at (your area code) your phone number.
Thank you for your time and consideration.

Sincerely,

Your Name

1467 38th Avenue S.W.
Seattle, WA 98071
(206) 783-9940

Attn: Recruitment

Please accept this letter and resume as application for the Sales position you recently advertised. Briefly, I have outlined my sales background:

Record Of Success:
- Currently generate approximately $1 million in annual sales.
- Proven experience developing and managing major commercial accounts.

Willingness to Travel:
- Past employment has required extensive travel in a marketing capacity.

Education:
- B.A. Degree in Business Administration with experience setting up, managing and marketing a high-profile business.

Communication, Interpersonal and Organizational skills:
- Over 10 years experience marketing and managing a business has required excellent skills in these areas.

Dedication to Quality and Customer Service:
- My desire is to excel and achieve my best for myself, my customers and the corporation that I work for. Excellent references can verify my dedication and loyalty to service.

The combination of my skills and experience match the qualifications you seek for this position. I am eager to meet with you to discuss employment opportunities. Please leave a message for me at 783-9940 and I will return your call that day.

Sincerely,

Stanley Roughten

Become
A "Cherry Picker"———————————————

Imagine picking cherries off a tree to make a prize desert. As you reach for the cherries you examine each one and select those that are perfect. If they are ripe you pick them. If they are green you leave them on the tree. You'll want to be just as selective in your job search and pick those employers who are best for you. To make your job search successful and enjoyable it's important to develop a "cherry picker" attitude. As a "cherry picker" you will listen for the *yes's* and pass over the *no's* you hear from employers.

Top sales people also develop a "cherry picker" attitude. The "old school method" of prospecting teaches sales people to push every prospect into agreement, overcome objections, and then close the sale. This method promotes the fear of lost sales. With this attitude a sales person feels compelled to close every sale and is disappointed if he doesn't. On the other hand, the "new school method" of sales teaches you to become a "cherry picker." With this method, your goal is to cultivate as many contacts as possible, then pick the *yes's* from them. You are not concerned with the *no's*. You make your offer and if the recipient says *"no,"* you politely say, *"Thank you very much,"* and go on to your next sales call. Your goal is to have no expectation of a sale when making each individual call. Rather, your goal is to "pick" a few *yes's* from several contacts. In this way, you become the rejector not the rejectee.

Change Your Emotional Response to *No's*—————————

Adopting a cherry picker attitude dramatically changes your emotional response to the *no's* you receive. If you have no expectation that you will get an interview when contacting an employer then you will not be disappointed if you don't get one. However, if you do get an interview you'll be pleased and excited. This is not to say that you can carelessly call employers and inquire about jobs. You want to put 100% preparation and motivation into every call. You want to develop a mind set that says, *"I know there are numerous employers out there that will benefit from my skills and experience. I just need to find them. When I do and it's a good fit then I'll be a cherry picker."* To make this system work it's important to develop a significant list of employers to contact. By using effective job search methods you'll find a bounty of employers to contact. You'll then prepare a script, or sales presentation, which markets your strongest qualifications. Once you've practiced this script, which we'll discuss later, you'll be ready to undertake your job search campaign. If you have been selective in compiling your list of employers - employers with positions that fit your qualifications - you can feel confident that out of every 100 employers you contact you will generate up to ten interviews, or more.

That means that you may hear as many as 90 *no's*, but if you've adopted the cherry picker attitude you won't care. All you will care about is getting an employer on the phone and hearing if he is interested in your skills and abilities. If he's not then you're ready to move on until you hear a *yes*. Each individual call is a small investment and can take as little as one minute to make. Unless you live in a very small town there are enough employers in your area who will be interested in your skills and abilities to make it worthwhile for you to go out and find them. Ignore the rest.

Be A Relaxed and Worry Free Cherry Picker

Consider how a cherry picker attitude will affect your personality on the phone. When you call an employer you will feel free to be spontaneous and relaxed because you won't feel like your life and job is hinging on that one phone call. This will give you an air of confidence and enthusiasm employers are attracted to. No one feels especially attracted to people who sound desperate or pushy.

If you get through 25% of your contacts and have not received a *yes* you need to re-evaluate the quality of your list. You may also need to re-evaluate your phone presentation. Ask yourself if you have identified the most appropriate position and industry to match your qualifications. If not, reassess your skills and abilities and develop a new list of appropriate contacts. Ask yourself if your phone script is working and if you are presenting your strongest qualifications, quickly and concisely. If not, rewrite your script and practice it until you come across smoothly and confidently on the phone. Don't stumble along using an ineffective list of employers. Change strategies until you begin to get positive responses to your phone and cover letter contacts. I read a story about a sales trainer who worked with a group of stockbrokers. He began calling several homes from a list they gave him. After four calls he wasn't getting a good response and asked what the salary level of the people on the list was. He was told that it was about $20,000 a year. The trainer then asked for another list. After several more unsuccessful calls, he asked if the brokers knew what type of homes he was calling. He was told they were small homes. He then requested a list of people making at least $40,000. After only two calls he hit a "cherry" and made a sale! You can see how the sales trainer applied a financial requirement to the client list he used. When he obtained a list of people making enough money to be interested in stocks he hit a cherry and heard a *yes*. You want to do the same thing. You want to find employers who have positions that match your qualifications; who can provide the salary you require; who are the size of company you want to work for; and who can provide further growth opportunities if you desire them. By selecting employers who meet these requirements you will be able to develop a successful list and become a happy cherry picker.

Where Else Can You Pick Cherries?

As you gather information on employers ask yourself where you can find more cherries. Once you've identified a good prospect or gotten an interview with an employer ask yourself what other companies are similar.

I used this technique to increase the sales of my temporary agency. We made a sale to a kitchen cabinet manufacturer and provided that company with temporary employees who sanded wood products. To gather more cherries, I asked myself what other companies or industries would use production people to do wood sanding. As it turned out there were many companies that did some type of woodworking in my sales territory. I ended up making contacts with several different companies that made modular office furniture, veneer products, grocery store salad bars, video display racks, and unfinished furniture. I increased my prospecting pool from one contact to over 60 companies, thereby picking several more cherries.

To increase your pool of employers you'll also want to ask yourself where you can pick more cherries. What other companies can you apply to that are like the ones you're already interested in? Is there a related industry or off-shoot of it that your skills can be used in? Be creative and brainstorm. Once you start this process it can blossom. It can be fun and exciting to discover all the opportunities awaiting you.

The Winning Job Search

Even though what you've just read is motivating, you may still feel a little anxious about your job search. As you read the rest of this chapter you may feel even more anxious. I know I did when I first used and applied the information you're going to learn. I want to let you know that your feelings are OK. Almost everyone experiences some degree of discomfort when contacting employers and following-up on jobs. I want to encourage you to pay attention to your feelings. Let them be. Don't hide from them - find a way to work through them. Ask yourself what frightens or concerns you and then use the appropriate tools you learn in this and the next chapter to increase your job search skills. As your job search knowledge grows so will your confidence.

Rob came bounding into my office, a big guy who was all smiles. As we talked, I asked what areas of his job search were difficult for him. It was amazing. His whole demeanor changed. His shoulders became hunched, his voice dropped, and he appeared overwhelmed as he said, *"I dread interviewing."* In an instant the sparkle had gone out of his eyes and he said: *"Everytime I think about calling an employer or sitting in an interview I feel terrible. My hands get sweaty and I imagine how miserably I'm going to do. I just don't want to interview. When I'm this nervous I feel like I can't breathe. That makes me feel wimpy, and I hate that feeling. I know I have to interview but it really scares me. That's why I've put off looking for a new job for over a year."* I then said to Rob, *"It's obvious you would like to do just about anything but interview for a job. But you know you've got to. So we need to find some tools to help you feel confident and capable of interviewing. Can you remember a time when you gave a presentation or talked to someone about something important and felt you did a good job?"*

Rob replied, *"Well, yeah, 2 months ago I recommended buying a new machine for our shop. We make surf boards and I knew this machine could increase our productivity. I did some research and ran some of our materials on it. It was so much faster.*

I talked with the sales rep about how much the machine cost and how long it would take to pay it off. I realized the extra work we could produce would pay for the machine in 6 months. So I went to our department manager and told him what I had discovered. He was really excited and bought the machine."

Getting The Sparkle Back

Within a few seconds Rob had become animated again. The sparkle was back in his eyes and he was feeling confident. I then said, *"Rob, it looks like you're really proud of what you accomplished. Do you realize how many skills you used to get that machine placed in your shop?"* Rob looked funny, shook his head and said, *"No. It doesn't seem like I used any. It was just fun."* I then asked, *"Don't you think you used your analytical as well as sales skills?"* Rob replied, *"Well, yeah, I guess so."* I then said, *"You came up with an idea, researched it and proved it, then sold your employer on it. Do you realize these are the same skills you'll use to interview well?"*

Rob looked confused for a second, then smiled and said, *"Yeah, I guess it is the same."* I then said, *"You need to research a job you want, prove how you are qualified for it, then convince an employer to hire you. If you take the excitement you feel right now and use it to market yourself you'll be amazed at how well you'll do. Now let's practice some interviewing questions. As we do, I'd like you to focus on the confidence you feel right now. Imagine that I am no different than your boss and sell me on your qualifications just like you sold your boss on that machine."*

After about 20 minutes of role playing Rob felt entirely different and had associated new, positive feelings to interviewing. As he left that day he said, *"I can't wait to start researching employers and getting interviews. I know I'll be a little scared, but when I remember researching that machine and selling my ideas I feel confident. Practicing for an interview while I'm feeling this way really motivates me. Thanks, this is great stuff!"*

By associating and linking positive thoughts to the interview process, Rob became excited and motivated. He used his past memories as a foundation of confidence while he role-played. Now when Rob feels a little scared he can remember, step by step, how he researched and sold that machine to his employer. He can bring those feelings into the present and use them to market himself in an interview.

No matter how much or how little anxiety you feel about looking for a job I recommend you go through the same process. Ask yourself what you have accomplished in the past that makes you feel confident and happy when you remember it. Use those feelings of confidence to deal with any part of your job search that makes you uncomfortable. By facing your fears, or negative associations, and turning them into positive associations you can reprogram your feelings.

F E A R

Zig Ziglar, a leading motivational speaker, discusses the acronym FEAR in one of his video programs. He describes FEAR as False Evidence Appearing Real. There's no better situation to apply this acronym to than looking for a job. When Rob came to me he was experiencing FEAR. He imagined how terrible he would do in an interview and felt he had no skills or abilities to help him succeed. However, Rob quickly realized his fears were unfounded.

Ask yourself if your fear is False Evidence Appearing Real. Our imagination can often run amuck, getting us all juiced up, believing we can't succeed and that we'll fail. If this happens to you, ask yourself, *"What strengths and skills do I already possess that will help me with my job search?"* You may get negative answers at first, but keep asking yourself this question and your subconscious mind will supply the answer. If you feel really negative about yourself it may take several times before you begin to acknowledge the skills and abilities you possess. As you remember good things about yourself keep focusing on them. Use them as a foundation to conduct your job search. Believe me it works. Only by constantly reinforcing my own strengths in this way have I been able to write this book. You can learn all about effective job search techniques, but if you can't get yourself motivated to use them the information is useless. I want to motivate you to stretch and grow. Achieve your dreams. If I can, you can.

Proven Job Search Methods

I'm sure you've heard the job search process referred to as a numbers game, and it is. The more employers you contact the more interviews you are likely to generate. The more interviews you generate the more job offers you will receive. To maximize your success it's important that you know which job search methods are most effective. The U.S. Department of Census published a survey of 10 million job seekers that reveals the effectiveness of various job search methods. Before I give you the statistics I'd like you to take the quiz below and rate each method on a scale of 1 to 6. Put a 1 next to the method you think generates the most jobs. Put a 6 next to the method you think generates the least jobs. When you're done compare your ratings to the completed list at the top of the facing page.

Rate Each Method According to Effectiveness

____ Answering newspaper want ads.

____ Networking with friends and relatives.

____ Using unemployment offices for job leads.

____ Working with employment agencies.

____ Running your own "work wanted" ad.

____ Applying to an employer even if there's no job opening.

Job Search Effectiveness Rating	
_3_	Answering newspaper want ads.
_2_	Networking with friends and relatives.
_5_	Using unemployment offices for job leads.
_4_	Working with employment agencies.
_6_	Running your own "work wanted" ad.
_1_	Applying to an employer even if there's no job opening.

Did you correctly rate each of the methods listed above? If not, you may be surprised at the information you're about to learn and the impact it can have on your job search. Below I've listed the statistics for each job search method. As you can see, the top three methods of obtaining a job are applying directly to employers, networking, and answering want ads.

Of 10 million job seekers surveyed, approximately:

1. 6.6 million **applied directly to employers** with 3.1 million obtaining jobs.
2. 8 million **networked with friends or relatives** with 2.4 million obtaining jobs.
3. 4.5 million **answered local want ads** with 1.1 million obtaining jobs.
4. 2.1 million **used employment agencies** with a little over .5 million obtaining jobs.
5. 3.3 million **used their unemployment office** with a little less than .5 million obtaining jobs.
6. 160,000 **ran a work wanted advertisement** with 21,000 obtaining jobs.

Applying Directly to Employers

Although clients come to a job search class to learn effective job search techniques their eyes often glaze over as we discuss these statistics. Even though the census survey shows that applying directly to employers is the most effective job search method, many people don't feel comfortable doing it. Many people feel just like I did when I read, *"Go Hire Yourself an Employer."* Many people think, *"Who am I to market myself to an employer?"* The idea of contacting an employer puts a lot of people way out of their comfort zones. As a result, many people avoid using this method.

Networking

In the census survey of 10 million job seekers, networking ranks second in the top job search methods. However, smaller independent surveys by executive recruitment and outplacement firms have shown that 39% to 67% of job seekers obtain jobs through networking. Either way, networking is clearly one of the top two job search methods. Yet, many people feel uncomfortable asking other people about jobs. Some clients have told me that they feel like they are groveling or begging. As a result many people avoid networking.

Answering Want Ads

Answering want ads is the third most effective job search method. Yet, many people use this as their only, or primary, job search method. In my classes I always ask why people use this method rather than applying directly to employers or networking. Everyone quickly points out that mailing a cover letter and resume to an ad is non-threatening. It doesn't require people contact and won't result in being rejected over the phone, which many job seekers want to avoid.

Working With Employment Agencies

Working with employment agencies is the fourth most effective job search method. Some people also use this as their sole job search method because applying directly to employers or networking causes them too much discomfort. They find it easier and less threatening to sit back and let an agency send them on interviews. However, there is often a price to pay since agencies usually charge a fee for their services. There is also a price to pay if you avoid using either of the top two job search methods. If you avoid applying directly to employers or networking you can't tap into what's known as *"the hidden job market."* As a result, you may end up looking for a job for a longer period of time or miss out on some of the best jobs available. It's estimated that up to 93% of all jobs that are available each year are never advertised. To tap this hidden job market you must contact employers directly or network to learn about them. I obtained my second position in the personnel field by using the yellow pages to contact temporary employment agencies. I'd call, ask to speak to the owner or manager and within two sentences summarize my experience. At least five out of ten times, I was asked to come in for an interview. Within two weeks I interviewed with six agencies and received four job offers. None of these positions had been advertised and yet each of these employers either had a current job opening or were considering a change in personnel.

Working With State Employment Agencies

Working with your state employment agency is the fifth most effective job search method. However, many people avoid working with these agencies because they believe it is too time consuming and that job listings are out of date. The Employment Security system in Washington state has been revamped and streamlined. These offices now provide new strategies in workforce training and placement. Check with your state employment agency to review its services before you rule it out.

Running A Work Wanted Ad

Running a work wanted ad is the least effective of the top six job search methods. Few people use this method, subsequently very few employers are in the mode of looking for work wanted ads. As a result, they generate little response from employers. Therefore, I recommend you concentrate your efforts on the top five job search methods.

Maximize Your Time & Marketing Efforts

It's important that you estimate the amount of time you will devote to your job search each week. Then set goals for how much time you will spend pursuing and using each job search method. For example, it makes sense to spend:

1) The greatest amount of time applying directly to employers.

2) The second greatest amount of time networking.

3) A smaller amount of time answering newspaper ads.

4) The least amount of time waiting for agencies to send you on interviews.

If you are unemployed and want to obtain a job as soon as possible, work on your job search 40 hours a week. Spend 15 hours each week researching employers and contacting them; spend 15 hours networking with business contacts, friends and relatives. Then spend 10 hours answering want ads and working with private and state employment agencies. By setting goals and completing scheduled activities you will gain control of your job search. You won't be passively waiting for the right job to come along. You'll get out there and find it. By using all the job search methods we've discussed you can cultivate a broad range of contacts and leads. If you use only one job search method your contacts and leads will be limited.

Your Comfort Zone

Before we go on, I'd like you to rate your comfort level in using the job search methods listed below. Let ten represent a lot of anxiety and zero represent no feeling of anxiety in using each method.

Applying Directly to Employers
0 1 2 3 4 5 6 7 8 9 10

Networking with Business Contacts, Friends and Relatives
0 1 2 3 4 5 6 7 8 9 10

Answering Want Ads
0 1 2 3 4 5 6 7 8 9 10

Working with Private Employment Agencies
0 1 2 3 4 5 6 7 8 9 10

Working with your Unemployment Office
0 1 2 3 4 5 6 7 8 9 10

If you rated any of the job search methods four or above you may have a tendency to avoid using that method. You'll need to be aware of this tendency and work to overcome it. Learn all you can about that particular job search method, which should lessen your anxiety, and then practice the skills needed to use that method. Read Chapter 12 to create a SUCCESS IMAGERY script that boosts your confidence and listen to it. By doing these things you will increase your comfort and success.

Applying Directly to Employers

As we've discussed, you should spend the greatest amount of time applying directly to employers. You can do this in two ways either by phone or letter. Calling by phone is quick and can yield results in the shortest amount of time. If this puts you too far out of your comfort zone then mail a letter explaining your skills and abilities.

Many people feel they are being pushy or presumptuous to get on the phone and call employers. However, I recommend you do just that. Within an hour's time you can make ten to fifteen calls, or more. On the other hand, you may be able to write only two letters in this amount of time. Then you have to wait several days for each letter to be received before you can call and follow-up. After each letter is received, you still have to muster the courage to get on the phone and follow-up. Otherwise, sending your letter was a waste of time. So you might as well get motivated and call in the first place.

Before you begin your phone calling campaign you'll want to develop a targeted list of employers. Shortly, we'll discuss how to use the library to develop a good list. You'll also learn how to generate the maximum number of interviews in the shortest amount of time by calling and speaking with decision makers.

Narrow Your Focus

To be effective in researching job leads you must have a good idea of the type of position you want and the type of industry you want to work in. Otherwise, you have no way of narrowing your focus among thousands of employers. It's important to identify those positions and industries your skills and abilities will be the most valuable to. After I gained experience in the temporary industry and began looking for a new job in that industry my phone calls generated a high response. This happened because employees who have experience in this industry are rare, which made me more valuable to employers in that field.

Later, when I left the personnel field I knew I wanted to teach. Knowing my skills and education were a good match for vocational schools I called a friend who worked for one. As timing would have it, her company had an opening for an instructor. I interviewed the next day and was hired three days later. Neither of my job searches would have been as effective if I had not identified the position and industry I was interested in. By targeting specific industries I was able to selectively market skills that made me an excellent candidate for each one.

Spend time thinking about the position you want and the industry you want to work in. You may decide to stay in the same industry or to make a career change. Either way, determine the skills and abilities you have that make you an excellent candidate for a particular position or industry. John had been a building contractor until he hurt his back and could no longer do that type of work. As a contractor he had marketed his services and had an extensive knowledge of construction procedures and materials. In mulling over his work experience, he realized he really liked the construction industry and enjoyed dealing with customers. Based on these insights he decided he would like to become an Inside Sales Representative marketing construction materials. He developed a list of 25 prospective employers and presented his best qualifications to them over the phone. Within two weeks he had five interviews and was offered two positions. He was amazed at how quickly his job search progressed once he became focused.

In the first column on the next page I'd like you to list the skills you would like to use in a job. In the second column list the types of positions that use these skills. In the third column list the type of industries that employ people in these positions. For easy reference, I've included a space to list each industry's standard industrial code (you'll learn about this code in the next section). If you're still not sure what type of position you want to work in, review your local want ads. You'll probably find it easy to determine which jobs you're not interested in. This reverse process of elimination can help you find those positions that you think sound OK. Hopefully you'll find several you are excited about pursuing. To be a successful cherry picker you need to focus on and contact companies with positions that most closely match your skills and abilities. When making a career change you must be ready to show how your transferrable skills fit the new career you are seeking. By presenting your strongest qualifications for each position or industry you will dramatically increase your chance for an interview.

Lead Development & Library Research

Once you've identified the type of position you want and the industry you'd like to work in then you can begin doing library research. If you've never been to the library to do job research you may feel a little anxious about it. However, using library materials is easy and the librarians are there to help you. In this section we're going to discuss the types of materials you can use to learn more about employers. Knowing this information will increase your confidence and allow you to ask the librarian for help.

Business Directories

Many companies that sell mailing lists lease them to libraries. Locally, *Inside Prospects* and *Contacts Influential* lease business listings for over 10,000 employers. All employers are broken into these 4 categories:

1. Alphabetical
2. Zip Code
3. SIC Code
4. Key Individual

Skills	Positions	Industries	SIC
_____ →	_____ →	_____ →	_____
_____ →	_____ →	_____ →	_____
_____ →	_____ →	_____ →	_____
_____ →	_____ →	_____ →	_____
_____ →	_____ →	_____ →	_____
_____ →	_____ →	_____ →	_____
_____ →	_____ →	_____ →	_____
_____ →	_____ →	_____ →	_____

Alphabetical Section: Each company has been sorted alphabetically. If you know the name of a company you are interested in, turn to the alphabetical section and locate it. You will find the address and phone number as well as other data we'll discuss below.

Zip Code Section: Each company has also been sorted by zip code. This is very handy if you prefer to work in a specific geographic area. Make a list of the zip codes for the areas you wish to work in, then turn to each zip code section. Within each section you'll find an alphabetical list of businesses located within that zip code area.

SIC Section: Each company has also been sorted by its SIC, or Standard Industrial Code. This a governmental code given to each industry. Look in the front of each directory and find the industry you want to work in. Next to the industry you will find a 4 digit standard industrial code. Then go to the volume that contains the SIC's and look up your 4 digit code. This section will contain an alphabetical listing of all employers classified within your industry.

Key Individual Section: The key individual section can come in handy if you've heard someone's name and would like to contact that person but you don't know the company he works for. Locate his name in the key individual section and you'll also find the name of the company he works for.

Keys to Each Listing: At the bottom of each page is a small list of keys that provide information about each company. Here's a sample of the keys below:

Type of Office:

H = Headquarters Office
B = Branch Office
S = Subsidiary Headquarters

Number of Employees

A = 1-4	D = 20-49	G = 250-499	J = 5000-9999
B = 5-9	E = 50-99	H = 500-990	K = 10000+
C = 10-19	F = 100-249	I = 1000-4999	

You can see how easy it is to classify employers and break down job leads using these directories. Let's say you want to work as an Office Manager for a doctor's office or clinic. You prefer working in Bellevue or Mercer Island. Bellevue has 5 zip codes - 98004, 98005, 98006, 98007, and 98008. Mercer Island is 98040. The SIC code for physicians and clinics is 8060. With this information you can turn to the 8060 SIC section and look for physicians and clinics within your 7 zip code areas. Or, you can turn to the zip code section and look for the 8060 SIC codes. If you start your search by zip code you can concentrate on those zip code areas closest to you first. Then gradually make more and more employer contacts farther away from your home. As you look at each listing, you can select or eliminate employers based on annual sales, how long they've been in business, and how many employees they have. To help you gather employer information I've included an employer worksheet on page 173. Be sure to copy it several times before you write on it.

Other Directories & Reference Materials

There are numerous reference materials available in larger, metropolitan libraries. Below we'll discuss several and give you an idea of how you can use each of them in your job search.

Computerized Periodical & Newspaper Indexes: These indexes provide a wealth of information about companies and current happenings within them. You'll use the computer to do a search of magazine and newspaper articles for subjects or companies you are interested in. The computer's database will give you a short synopsis of what each magazine or newspaper article is about. Many of the magazine and newspaper articles are available on tape which you can put into a viewing machine. If it's an article you are interested in the machine has the ability to photocopy it for you.

This is a fun, easy and fast way to get information about major employers and news on industries. Before interviewing with Dunhill Temporary Systems I used this process to get information on the temporary industry. I copied over 40 articles and learned a lot of valuable information. I was surprised to learn that this was a $12 billion dollar industry. I took all the copies of the articles into my interview and used them as a selling tool to show how interested I was in that position. I casually pulled them out of my attache case, spread them out about six inches and said, *"I've really enjoyed doing library research on the temporary industry. I learned that Dunhill Temporary Systems has 148 offices throughout the U.S. and Canada. One of the articles rated Dunhill 4th in sales among 28 temporary agencies."* Wow, was the person interviewing me surprised and impressed. Evidently no one else had gone to that much work before an interview. I was really glad I had taken the time to do the research, even though I had been anxious and out of my comfort zone while doing it. In addition to learning industry information you may also uncover names of companies and employers you can contact that you had previously been unaware of. It really is fun to see all the information that's out there at your fingertips.

Newspaper Clipping Files: Ask if your library keeps newspaper clippings on major employers in your area. If so, you have another source of information to use.

Manufacturer's Directories: There are numerous directories of manufacturing companies published by state and private publishing firms. These directories describe the goods and services produced by each manufacturer. They also provide information on the size of each company, the SIC code, and how long it has been in existence. My local library carries the *Washington State Manufacturer's Guide* and *Advanced Technology in Washington State Directory*. The latter provides information on high tech companies involved in computer based products and services.

Dun & Bradstreet Directories: These directories provide financial information on companies with sales of two million dollars and up. If you are interested in a larger firm, these directories can be one more source of information.

Standard & Poor's: This directory lists over 30,000 corporations and provides financial data as well as biographical data for over 75,000 key officers.

Annual Reports: Ask if your library keeps a file of annual reports and publicity packets for major employers in your area. These reports offer a wealth of financial information and describe the goods or services each company provides. You can learn excellent information for your interviews from these packets.

Companies with New Business Licenses: Many libraries receive lists of companies that have been granted business licenses within the last month or quarter. If you can verify that a start-up company will be stable then getting in on the ground floor can be a growth opportunity. These lists are generally updated on a regular basis so it's wise to ask if there is a recent addendum.

Networking Sources & Leads

Chamber of Commerce: Many chamber of commerce offices are interested in helping their citizens find employment. These offices can provide detailed information on companies that are members. Call and ask to speak to the chamber's manager. Tell him or her what type of work you are looking for. Ask for referrals to local employers that can provide the type of job you want. You may luck out and get several referrals. Many chamber of commerce offices sell lists of their business members. If this information is critical to your job search consider buying it.

Kiwanis and Other Organizations: Local civic and charity organizations can be a good source of information and networking leads. Get your courage up and talk to people. Send anyone who's interested in helping you, and that you feel comfortable with, a copy of your resume and ask them to pass it on. You could get a job doing this alone.

Associations: Look for associations in your yellow pages book that might be able to help you in your job search. There are hundreds of professional sales, secretarial, bookkeeping, teaching, public speaking and business groups that meet on a regular basis to network. If one association isn't quite right for you then ask them if they know of any other associations that might be helpful.

171 ♦

Church Employment Offices: One of my clients said she had used an employment referral office set up by the Church of Latter Day Saints. According to her it was open for use by anyone, not just church members. She received several good job leads with employers in her local area. Check with local churches in your area to generate referrals and to network.

Networking

Networking with friends, relatives and business contacts can yield a bounty of job referrals. Be creative. No matter where you are strike up conversations with people. Subtly mention that you are looking for a job. Many people will respond by asking what type of job you want. Then ask if they know of anyone you should talk to. When someone refers you be sure to get his or her name and spell it correctly. Be sure you also get the correct name and spelling of the employer you are being referred to. When calling the prospective employer be sure to mention the name of the person who referred you. This generally gets the employer's attention, especially if that person knows the employer well. Be sure to send the person who helped you a thank-you note to show your appreciation. The goodwill you generate by thanking people will come back to you.

My brother-in-law's networking happened in a roundabout way. Fresh out of the Navy with experience in communications and electronics, he had problems being considered for jobs because he didn't have a four year degree. My mother-in-law went into action knowing he wanted to work for Boeing. She networked with one of her neighbors who was a retired Boeing executive. She asked him if he would contact his associates at Boeing and set up interviews for my brother-in-law. After several referrals and contacts he got an interview and was hired. He's been with Boeing for several years now. This is an excellent example of how networking works. When faced with some difficulty, such as the lack of an educational requirement, getting a referral can often diminish that problem and result in a job.

In my networking classes, clients have cultivated good job leads in the most unexpected situations. Rita struck up a conversation with a person at her bus stop. He gave her a referral and she had an interview within three days. Many of my students network with one another. When Rachel received a new job she told Felicia about her old job and set Felicia up for an interview. In two weeks Felicia was hired. After closing our temporary business my husband used networking to get his current job. He called several of his friends and asked them about employment opportunities that matched his background. Over the next couple of weeks his friends called to tell him about possibilities. Within two and a half weeks of beginning to network he was offered and accepted a new position.

Complete a Networking List

I've included a networking list for you to complete on page 184. Make at least 10 copies of it and compile the names of 50, or more, people you can network with. As you complete it be creative. Include your doctor, dentist, attorney, mechanic, grocer, dry cleaner, and anyone else you can think of.

Employer Worksheet - For a Happy Cherry Picker_____

Person to Contact: _____   Phone #: _____
Company: _____   SIC #: _____
Address: _____   # of Employees: _____
Zip Code: _____

Notes: _____
_____
_____

Person to Contact: _____   Phone #: _____
Company: _____   SIC #: _____
Address: _____   # of Employees: _____
Zip Code: _____

Notes: _____
_____
_____

Person to Contact: _____   Phone #: _____
Company: _____   SIC #: _____
Address: _____   # of Employees: _____
Zip Code: _____

Notes: _____
_____
_____

Person to Contact: _____   Phone #: _____
Company: _____   SIC #: _____
Address: _____   # of Employees: _____
Zip Code: _____

Notes: _____
_____
_____

Person to Contact: _____   Phone #: _____
Company: _____   SIC #: _____
Address: _____   # of Employees: _____
Zip Code: _____

Notes: _____
_____
_____

If contacting these people makes you uncomfortable then prepare a script before talking with them. You might say something like this, *"Dr. Willis, I'm looking for a _____ position. Do you know of anyone it might be helpful for me to contact regarding employment possibilities?"* Even if you're told *no*, but you believe this person can help you, send him a thank you note after your conversation. Include your resume and ask him to pass it along if he happens to hear of anything. Mention that you hope to get your name out to as many people as possible and would appreciate his help. In a few days he may hear of a good contact and pass your resume along to a prospective employer.

Diamonds in Your Back Yard

In *The New Success*, Pamela Murray provides an excellent chapter on business networking. Here's an excerpt from her book:

> You probably have a diamond mine in your contacts right now. Open up your current network and mine the diamonds hiding there. Persist with those folks you want to add to your network. Don't give up after the first one or two calls. Persist gently, but consistently. One client, a Realtor, after attending a seminar and learning about the Law of Seven, in which you build a plan to contact someone seven times over the course of eighteen months, told me the following story:
>
> *"I wanted to meet and get to know this gentleman, mostly because he was so well-known in a field of my interest not related to real estate. I decided to try your Law of Seven. I went to two of his public lectures and afterward spoke with him, asking him questions like you suggested. For my third contact, I sent him a note, telling him how much I had enjoyed hearing from him. Finally I got up enough courage to call him and ask him to lunch. He was quite defensive and wasn't sure he wanted to go, but I convinced him that I really wanted nothing more than to chat with him about our mutual interest. After he consented to go, I was nervous that maybe I shouldn't have done this. At lunch we had a grand time. As it was drawing to a close, he finally asked me a little about myself. I told him I was a commercial Realtor. He said, "You know, I'm looking to buy a couple of buildings for investment, probably in the two million dollar range....I'd like you to represent me."*
>
> Pamela's client had been nervous about calling the other fellow and even wondered if it had been a good idea. However, his persistence paid off and in the long run was worth it. Pamela's advice as a professional success coach is: *"The diamonds are in your back yard. Mine them."*

Sell Yourself With Integrity

As Pamela's story illustrates, networking pays off. One reason her client experienced so much success was because he was sincerely interested in this person. He wasn't out to "get" something. We've all had people talk to us when their only goal was to get us to do or buy something.

When approached in this way, most of us don't react positively. Therefore, it makes sense to make networking a routine habit of talking to people and getting to know them versus asking what they can do for us. I used these tactics in my resume consulting business. I ran yellow page ads and, of course, people calling were also shopping other services. However, I marketed my services much differently than my competitors. When prospective clients called, I didn't go into a high pressure sales pitch, withhold the cost of what I charged, or push people to make an appointment before hanging up. My strongest selling tool didn't seem like a selling tool at all. By asking callers about their backgrounds I was able to get them actively involved in our conversation. I'd ask what type of job they were looking for and what their work histories were like. Then I'd tell them stories about other people with similar backgrounds whom I had helped. I might say a few sentences of how we could describe their work experience. Then I'd wait. I never asked for appointments or tried to "make a sale." Often, there would be a pause while callers waited for just this type of approach. When it didn't happen they'd sound a little surprised and ask if they could make an appointment.

Using this technique, I demonstrated an interest in clients which quickly established my integrity and honesty. At least 80% of the people who called me from an ad either made an appointment then or called back to make one. That's a very good closing ratio and I wasn't even closing! I let my customers close themselves. That's what happened with Pamela's client. He let his networking contact sell and close himself, and it looks like he got the opportunity to represent a two million dollar deal.

Even though these examples are from business transactions they are applicable to your job search. By showing an interest in others as you network you will be amazed at the rewards you receive. Remember, networking is the second most effective job search method. If it makes you uncomfortable then spend some time thinking about how you can talk to people without feeling pushy or coming across as needy. It's worked for me and hundreds of my clients, and it can work for you!

Job Lines & Governmental Openings

Another resource to help broaden your job search contacts is job lines. Almost every employer with one hundred or more employees provides a job line. All you need to do is locate the proper telephone number and call it. You'll hear a tape recorded message that describes each position, the closing date (the last day you can apply for the position), the salary, education and experience requirements. If you are asked to complete an application then do so. Many large corporations and governmental offices require that every applicant follow a standard hiring and application process. You will waste your time if you send a cover letter and resume without including an application.

If you are interested in a city, state or federal position ask your librarian to direct you to current job postings. Notices for these positions are often mailed to libraries on a regular basis. There are also several good books that tell you how to apply for governmental work. Ask the librarian to help you find them. Then read them and follow their recommendations.

A good tip to remember when applying for a governmental position is to use wording in the job posting to prepare your resume and application. Select key words that have been emphasized and use them as skill group headings or in your job descriptions. This makes it easy for personnel reviewing your application to see that your experience matches the position you are applying for.

Use Old Help-Wanted Ads To Find Employers

As you review each week's want ads, keep an eye out for companies you would be interested in working for. Even if they advertise a position that you're not interested in they may still have unadvertised positions that you qualify for. Be sure to cut these ads out and keep them with your list of employers to contact.

Another excellent strategy is to go back over help-wanted ads for the last three months up to a year's time. Using this method you can compile a larger list of employers who have advertised for the types of positions you want. To speed this process select three or four job categories to look for. This way you won't have to read the entire help-wanted section. For example, I could look in the C column for Career Counselors, I column for Instructors, T column for Trainers, or V column for Vocational Counselors. If it's been some time since the last ad was placed there's a good likelihood that one or more of these employers are in need of filling that or a similar position.

Working with Permanent Placement Agencies

Since I've worked in the personnel industry and owned a permanent and temporary placement agency I'd like to share some of my experience with you. As you enter an agency, be aware that you will be scrutinized from the moment you step in the door until you leave. Qualified applicants are always in short supply and everyone in the agency will be watching to see if you can fill one of their orders. Be polite and courteous to the receptionist. She can have a lot of power. The owner of an agency I worked for was at the front desk one day. An applicant came in for an interview and assumed the owner was "only the receptionist." She was quite rude when told her counselor would be 10 minutes late. That applicant ruined her chance of being sent out on an interview because she was rude to the "receptionist." When the applicant left the owner pulled her application and said there was no way she wanted someone with that kind of attitude sent on jobs from her agency.

I always asked our receptionist her opinion of each person's skills and attitude since she spent more time testing and completing paperwork with each applicant than I did. If her opinion wasn't favorable I didn't send that person out. Any time you are applying for a job watch your P's & Q's - be friendly and courteous to the receptionist, don't chew gum, smoke or ask to use the phone. Take a resume and have all the reference information you need with you. Complete your application thoroughly and when asked to take tests don't complain. Act confident and sure of yourself.

Be aware that you will be checked out by each job counselor as you fill out applications and take tests. Agency consultants are always on the look-out for people to fill positions. Each consultant may have several job orders to fill. As a result, anytime a new applicant comes in that looks and sounds good the consultants will swoop through the front office and check him or her out. If the applicant tests well the consultants may soon be competing to see who gets the applicant. In permanent and temporary placement, demand is always higher than the supply of qualified applicants.

That's one reason why working with an agency can result in good jobs. Many times an agency may have only two or three qualified applicants for each job. If you are selected and sent on an interview then the pool of people you are competing against is very small. Having so few competitors can put you way ahead of the game. Whereas, you may be competing with hundreds of applicants when you answer a want-ad or posted job opening.

Agency Fees

If you find a permanent position advertised by an agency check to see if it is Employer Fee Paid. That means the entire placement fee is paid by the employer. If the ad says it's a Split Fee then the employer is willing to pay some part of it and you'll have to pay the balance. If it's Applicant Fee Paid, that means you have to pay the entire fee. You'll need to decide if a job is worth the fee. Nowadays fees can run up to 24% of your first year's salary. Read the fine print before signing a contract or accepting a job through an agency. Samantha accepted an applicant fee paid position and was happy she did. She was able to move from being a CRT Specialist to being a Regional Assistant. I still remember when she came to class and said, *"I can't believe it. I have my own office with a door and a view. I'm a Regional Assistant and I'm making $320 more a month."*

Keep in Touch

If you have applied with an agency but aren't sent on interviews call them once a week and keep in touch. Remember, agency counselors interview several hundred applicants each month. Just because you haven't heard from them doesn't mean you're not a good candidate. It may be that your counselor is so busy interviewing applicants that he or she doesn't remember you and has already filed your application.

If your agency advertises a position you're interested in, contact your counselor and ask to be sent out on an interview for it. When you call don't assume your counselor will remember you. State your name and quickly summarize your strongest qualifications to get your counselor's interest. While working with an agency may result in a good job offer, don't depend on an agency to generate all your job contacts for you. Even if they "sell" you on their service and it sounds like they're going to find you a lot of interviews - don't believe it until it happens. The nature of this business is to get as many candidates in the door as possible. Even though an agency may have only a few positions available they may make it sound like they have many. If this happens you may wait weeks or months before being sent out on an interview.

If you decide to work with agencies be sure to register with four or more. Remember to spread your eggs around - don't put them all in one basket. Agencies always want to know if you've signed up with other agencies. Just because they ask doesn't mean you have to tell them. It's usually best if they think you are working exclusively with them.

Working with Temporary Placement Agencies

If you need money or have a hard time competing for permanent positions consider working as a temporary. You can often get very good permanent positions this way. Many employers like to hire on a "temp to perm" basis and see how the person works for a week to several months. If an employer wants to hire the temp they then "buy out" the temp from the agency. With a temp agency there should never be a fee to you. If someone tries to charge you for a temp or "temp to perm" position call your local Department of Labor and Industries to see if this is legal.

Because temp agencies have small pools of qualified applicants you may be sent on interviews for jobs you could never get on your own. This happened to my daughter, Melissa. She left a job she wasn't happy with before finding another one. Just like most of us, she hoped she'd have a job within a week or two. However, that didn't happen. She went on several interviews but lost out to applicants with more experience. This went on for several weeks. I couldn't stand seeing her discouragement so we made up a resume for her. Knowing that she would be considered a good candidate in the temporary industry I recommended she register with several. *"Who knows"* I told her, *"you may get sent out tomorrow."* To her surprise she did. She worked for one agency for two weeks and then had a few days with no work. I recommended she contact another agency.

She went in that day and was set up for an interview for a "temp to perm" receptionist position the next day. After her interview, we wrote a thank you letter, dropped it off, and two hours later she was hired. She feels her new job is the best one she's had and she's making a dollar more per hour. Melissa found out that only three people had been sent on interviews for her job. If she had competed with a large pool of applicants her chances of being hired would have decreased. If you have a hard time competing when applying for advertised positions then consider temping. Call several agencies and ask them if they specialize in "temp to perm" openings. Apply with those that do. It may get you a job!

Before Contacting Employers Determine Your Objective

Before calling or mailing letters to employers determine what your goal in contacting each employer is. Your objective should be one, or all three, of the following:

♦ To ask for an "informational interview"
♦ To determine if the company has a current or future need for the position you seek
♦ Or, to ask for referrals.

Informational Interviews

The first time I read about informational interviews I thought it was farfetched to believe that employers would grant such interviews. It is true, however. Many employers will take the time to chat with you about themselves and their career goals as well as about opportunities within their companies. I hadn't used this strategy until recently when I wanted to work for a technical college. I obtained the name of the evening program director and called her. I decided before getting on the phone that I wanted a face to face meeting. I knew such a meeting would give me valuable information in case I was granted a "real interview." Even though I felt nervous and pushy, I called. Our conversation went something like this:

Me: *Hi, my name is Regina Pontow. I am interested in teaching courses for your evening program and have experience as a computer and career development instructor for a local business college. I have also owned a personnel agency and would like to see if my experience fits any of your current programs.*

Lori: *It sounds like it does. We offer computer training in MS Word, Lotus, and Excel. Do you have experience with those programs?*

Me: *Yes, I am currently teaching MS Word and training in Excel.*

Lori: *We also have a supervisory program. Do you have supervisory experience?*

Me: *Yes, managing my personnel agency required interviewing, hiring and supervising all of the employees we placed.*

Lori: *Can you send me a resume and cover letter?*

Me: *Yes, however, I would like to meet with you for 10 to 15 minutes to gather a little more information before putting together a packet to send you. Is there a possibility we could meet late this week or next week?*

Lori: *Well...I guess so. But, this wouldn't be an interview. I select applications but give them to a committee that does the interviewing. This would only be to tell you an overall idea of what the college offers.*

Me: *That would be great! It would help me target my resume and highlight more specifically how my background fits your programs.*

Lori: *Let me get my calendar. Would next Tuesday be good for you?*

As a result of this conversation I met with Lori and two weeks later was called to interview for the "Stepping Up To Supervision" program. Before meeting with Lori, I could tell she was much more interested in my computer rather than my supervisory experience, but I was more interested in the supervisory program. I knew I would really have to sell myself for her to consider me for that program. To prepare, I thought about what the dynamics of teaching such a course would be. Then I developed a list of ideas and selling points I could talk about. It worked and I landed an interview. I don't think Lori would have considered me for this position if I hadn't met with her.

Prioritize Your Employer Lists

You may have a large list of employers to contact and don't have the time to schedule informational interviews with all of them. If this is an issue you can control your time by prioritizing your list of employers. Try to schedule informational interviews with those companies that most strongly fit your career goals. Call those that are not as high on your list and ask if they have any current or future openings.

If your skills are highly specialized you may not have a large pool of employers to contact. If this is your situation make sure you prepare thoroughly before contacting an employer. In this instance your goal should be to generate as many face to face informational interviews as possible. Because your pool of employers is small, you will have to maximize your success in making each and every contact. For example, Doreen was a R.N. over 10 years ago and is completing her Bachelor of Science in Nursing degree. Her goal is to work for one of three community agencies. When she contacted the first agency she said, *"I am currently completing my B.S.N. degree"* and before she could finish the person answering the phone cut her off and said, *"We only hire people with experience."* This left Doreen not knowing what to say and feeling she had blown her opportunity with that company. In talking with Doreen, it came out that she had met the director of this agency at an association meeting. Even though she felt a little intimidated we brainstormed on how she could re-introduce herself to the director and say, *"My name is Doreen Smith. We met at the nursing convention and I enjoyed chatting with you. My background includes over 10 years acute nursing experience and I am completing my BSN degree next month. I would like to meet with you for a few minutes next week to explore possibilities in the field of community nursing."* You can see that contacting the decision maker and presenting Doreen's skills in a strong fashion will greatly increase her success.

On the other hand, Roxanne had a large list of real estate employers she was willing to work for. The script we prepared for her was worded a little differently than Doreen's because her goal was to contact a large number of employers and quickly determine if they had an opening. Roxanne's script appears on page 181. You'll notice that she used her executive secretarial experience combined with her real estate bookkeeping experience to sell herself as a Project Manager in that industry.

A Script To Determine If There's An Opening

I've developed a short phone script worksheet on page 182 that you can use to determine if an employer has an opening. On a separate piece of paper make a list of questions you anticipate employers will ask you and prepare strong answers. Transfer your questions and answers to the phone script worksheet. This form is merely a guideline. If you need more space improvise and create your own form. You may want to refer to Chapter 11 and review the interviewing tips before you complete it. Stand in front of a mirror and rehearse your script before each call. Remember to smile. It's amazing how much a smile can change the inflection and tone of your voice. Before you make any calls get yourself into a friendly, happy, motivated state. If you do, you will transmit these qualities by phone.

Sample Phone Dialogue_____

Receptionist:	*XYZ Real Estate, how may I help you?*
Roxanne:	***May I speak with Tom Galley?***
Receptionist:	*Yes, may I tell him who's calling?*
Roxanne:	***Yes, my name is Roxanne Woodry.***
Receptionist:	*May I ask what this is regarding?*
Roxanne:	***Yes, I have over five years real estate experience and would like to talk with him about employment opportunities.***
Receptionist:	*Can you hold, please?*
Roxanne:	***Certainly.***
Tom:	*This is Tom Galley, what can I do for you?*
Roxanne:	***Mr. Galley my name is Roxanne Woodry. I have over five years experience in real estate office administration and bookkeeping. I'm looking for a comparable position and want to inquire if you have or anticipate a similar opening.***
Tom:	*Well, I'm not sure. Just exactly what type of position did you have in mind?*
Roxanne:	***I am interested in an Office Management position which will allow me to coordinate and manage projects. I managed the administrative details for real estate transactions valued in excess of $1 million.***
Tom:	*Well, I'm not considering hiring an Office Manager, but I am considering hiring a Project Manager to assist my sales agents. That position would involve a lot of coordination with escrow companies. You would be out of the office quite a lot overseeing projects and completing details. Does that sound like something you'd be interested in?*
Roxanne:	***It sounds perfect!***
Tom:	*Are you familiar with escrow operations?*
Roxanne:	***Yes, while I was with Ammes Real Estate I coordinated with numerous escrow companies to track monies being held. In this capacity, I gained a broad knowledge of escrow operations.***
Tom:	*Well, how about coming in Thursday at 3:00 pm to discuss possibilities?*
Roxanne:	***That's great! Thank you for your time. I will see you at 3:00 pm Thursday.***

Phone Script Worksheet_____

Receptionist: *XYZ Company, how may I help you?*

You: **May I speak with** _____**?**

Receptionist: *Yes, may I tell* _____ *who's calling?*

You: **Yes, my name is** _____**.**

Receptionist: *May I ask what this is regarding?*

You: **Yes,** _____
_____
_____

Receptionist: *Can you hold, please?*

You: **Certainly.**

Employer: *This is* _____, *how may I help you?*

You: **My name is** _____**.**

I have over ___ years experience in_____**.**

I am looking for a comparable position and wanted to inquire if you have or anticipate a similar opening.

Employer: *Well, I'm not sure. Do you have* _____
_____*experience?*

You: **Yes, I have** _____
_____
_____

Employer: *Well, I'm not sure what I've got coming open but it wouldn't hurt to talk with you. Can you come in at* _____*?*

You: **Yes, and thanks for your time. I'll see you at** _____
_____**.**

Don't Ask, *"Are You Hiring?"*

When calling, don't ask the receptionist or employer, *"Are you hiring?"* or *"Can you tell me if you are accepting applications?"* When a receptionist or an employer is busy and harried it's too easy for them to say *no* and get you off the phone. Quickly state your top selling points before the receptionist or employer can interrupt you. In this way, you give the listener enough information to interest him and motivate him to begin a conversation with you.

Remember to Ask for Referrals

If you are unable to schedule an informational interview, or you find out that the company is not hiring, be sure to ask for referrals. Many people will be willing to refer you to other agencies or employers that may have openings. If you approach people in a polite and friendly way you'll be surprised at their willingness to help you. Asking for referrals works. This strategy helped me build my personnel business. Anytime I got a *"No"* from a prospective client I asked if they knew of anyone else who might use our temporaries. Very often, they would then talk with me for another five minutes or so. I sometimes eased the way by asking about the current economic situation in their business community. This helped me find out about their competitors or other happenings I might not have otherwise known about. As you conduct your job search be creative and try to uncover as much information as you can.

Dealing with *"No"*

If you receive a negative response from an employer you really want to work for, send a cover letter anyway. The name of the game is sales. I used this tactic to get a major account for my personnel agency. I called a client who was very obnoxious over the phone. She said she didn't want me calling her and not to bother her again. Even though she was rude, I really wanted that account. I knew she ordered over $250,000 a year in temps. Still stinging from her rebuff I wrote her a very nice letter and outlined some great hourly temp rates. Was I surprised when she called me a week later and apologized for how rude she had been. She told me that no one else had ever sent her a letter and we received our first order that month. Just because someone says *no* doesn't always mean they will continue to say *no*. In fact, sales people are trained to expect at least five *no's* from a prospective client before hearing a *yes*. If you persevere in your job search, as a salesperson must, you will generate more responses than you expect and you will become a happy cherry picker.

Get Organized and Prepared

The better prepared you are the better response you will get from employers over the phone. Gather all the information you will need in front of you and then make sure you can call employers in a quiet and uninterrupted environment. It sounds very unprofessional when dogs are barking, the kids are crying, or your spouse wants to know what's for dinner.

Networking List - For a Happy Cherry Picker

Who You Networked With: → Who You Were Referred To:

Name _____ Referred to _____
Phone _____ Phone _____
Company _____ Company _____
Address _____ Address _____
City _____ State _____ Zip _____

Notes:_____
_____

Name _____ Referred to _____
Phone _____ Phone _____
Company _____ Company _____
Address _____ Address _____
City _____ State _____ Zip _____

Notes:_____
_____

Name _____ Referred to _____
Phone _____ Phone _____
Company _____ Company _____
Address _____ Address _____
City _____ State _____ Zip _____

Notes:_____
_____

Name _____ Referred to _____
Phone _____ Phone _____
Company _____ Company _____
Address _____ Address _____
City _____ State _____ Zip _____

Notes:_____
_____

Name _____ Referred to _____
Phone _____ Phone _____
Company _____ Company _____
Address _____ Address _____
City _____ State _____ Zip _____

Notes:_____
_____

Gather together your notepad, resume, reference sheet, phone script, ad or job description, and your appointment calendar. Have several pens ready to take down notes. Know ahead of time when you are available for interviews so that you don't waste an employer's time. Write down all the questions you want to ask an employer before getting on the phone. Refer to your phone script as you need to and use it to build your confidence. Having practiced it confidently several times, just looking at it will give you a positive association while you're on the phone.

Be sure to breathe normally. Speak calmly and pronounce your words fully. Use the tone of your voice to show that you are interested in the job and that you are listening to the employer. Put your best voice forward and use it to develop rapport with both receptionists and employers. Don't mumble your words or fumble with your paperwork. Be prepared and present a confident professional image.

If You Feel Like Giving Up

My resume business tended to drop off during the summer and one July I was feeling rather desperate for sales. Knowing I needed to cultivate more referrals I decided to call employment agencies. I felt it would be good business to provide referrals back and forth. I could send agencies people who were looking for work and they could send me people who needed resumes. I had never done sales other than my resume business and soon found out why. I called twenty agencies. The receptionists acted like I was a sleazeball salesperson. I could almost feel them cringe and see them push the phone away thinking, *"Ugh, this person is trying to sell me something."* I didn't use the phone marketing skills we've talked about and many receptionists wouldn't even put me through to their bosses.

Even though I was feeling more and more deflated with every receptionist or manager that rejected my proposal I kept trying. Finally, three agency managers wanted to talk with me and I scheduled appointments with them. When I got off the phone I cried. I felt like such a failure. Even though three people were very interested in what I had to propose, dealing with 17 rejections had demoralized me. I felt like giving up. However, I kept those appointments and you'll never guess what happened. Two of the agencies consistently referred clients to me which increased my sales up to 50%. Was I ever glad I had made those phone calls. But that day when I was so depressed I would have never believed I could get so much good from so few *yes's*.

I'm sure you can guess the morale of this story. Hang in there. The *no's* may get you down, but remember that you only need a few *yes's* to make your career dreams come true. If I had known about being a cherry picker before contacting those employment agencies I would have dealt with their *no's* much better. I would have said to myself, *"I know referring back and forth with agencies is a good idea. I just have to find the right ones to work with. I need to find the agencies who see the value in what I have to offer. Those that aren't interested - I'm not interested in either. But when I do find an agency to work with, it will be well worth my calls. And, it will be exciting too!"*

Keep plugging away - persistence pays off!

Ten Strategies
For Interview Success

Thinking back over the hundreds of interviews I've conducted and pinpointing what's most important to interview success, one thing comes to mind - preparation. It seems that everyone would automatically prepare before an interview, but many people don't. People often say they must have a particular job at a certain salary level, yet many don't ensure their success by practicing and preparing for interviews. I'm always curious why such people don't put more effort into interview preparation. My guess is that they tell themselves it's not important or that they don't need it. I think it also puts many people out of their comfort zones. Rather than face their fears or anxieties it's easier to pretend that those feelings don't exist. It's like the ostrich who thinks if he hides his head in the sand he'll be safe.

I remember my first career class. One young man was cocky, slouched during class and acted bored a lot. Yawning and stretching was his favorite pass-time. When it came time to practice interviewing he still acted bored although he wanted a job starting at $10 an hour. As it turned out, he slurred his words, got embarrassed, and wanted to redo his practice interview. He didn't do much better the second time around. When I asked him to describe his skills he didn't know what to say even though I had coached him before our mock interview. I guess he had been too busy acting bored to pay attention. He evidently thought interviewing was going to be a breeze, but he came across weak and unsure of himself. To my surprise he said he realized how poorly he had done and that he had better begin to practice. His poor performance forced him to realize how much work he really needed to do. Better for him to have realized it during a practice session than after a real interview. This is an extreme example, but I believe this example applies to many of us to one degree or another. Maybe we say, *"I just don't have the time to practice answering questions."* Or, *"It's embarrassing to role play and I don't want to do it."* Or, *"I've always done well in the past so I don't really need to practice."*

You Control Your Success

You hold the success of your interviews in your own hands and you determine that success by how much effort you put into practicing and preparing for an interview. Therefore, you cannot put the responsibility on anyone else for how you perform during an interview.

Even if you are saddled with a lot of additional duties during a day's time you can still take time while driving or showering to review and rehearse your interviews. By sincerely applying yourself you will dramatically increase your interview success. This is much more important than trying to learn slick interview maneuvers. When you admit how much you really want to succeed and are willing to risk going for it 100%, you will succeed. Dedication to your own success is what will keep you going even though you may be scared or anxious.

How Committed Are You?

As you read this chapter, ask yourself how much effort you are willing to put into your success. Is it 50%, 75% or 100%? How much effort do you think it will take to get the job you really want? How far are you willing to go? I hope your answer is 100%. I hope you will do all that you can to succeed. Some of you may be thinking, *"But, I'm an executive and this stuff is really beneath my level. I already know all this."* No matter what level you're at - ask yourself if there aren't some areas you can improve in. Unless you're dead, there's always room for improvement. Improving even 1% may be just enough to put you ahead of your competition and cause you to be the one who is hired.

Resumes Don't Get Job Offers - You Do

A resume may land you an interview, but it's not going to get you a job. You have to do that. You have to convince employers with your verbal presentation skills that you are the best applicant. If you can't do that, you won't get the job you want no matter how many interviews you have. As you read this chapter I challenge you to complete each exercise. Only by thinking through and completing each exercise will you improve your responses during an interview. Only by thinking through and completing each exercise will you commit to your success 100%.

As you begin this process be sure to give yourself credit for all the hard work you've done with your resume and in researching employers. Looking for a job is a job, and it is sometimes the hardest job of all. Be nice to yourself. Give yourself a treat when you learn something important in this chapter. The happier you are with yourself the happier you will be with others, and this comes across in interviews.

A Strategic Approach To Interviewing

In writing over 1,500 resumes I came up with a workable system that I have used over and over again. Otherwise, writing each resume would have been re-inventing the wheel. In teaching people how to interview effectively I've also developed a system that works.

This system incorporates 10 steps or "power strategies." We'll go step by step through these power strategies and then we'll look at the most common interview questions employers ask. By that time, you will have already created many custom answers which can be used for these questions.

Step #1 - Identifying the Skills Required

Your first step to interview success is to identify the top five job requirements for the position(s) you want. Unless your objective has changed you've already listed these requirements and shown how your skills match them on page 39. Turn to that page and copy the information you have listed there to the worksheet below. If you didn't complete that worksheet then complete the one below.

In the left hand column list the top five skills required for the position(s) you want. In the right hand column write sentences that sell these skills. Practice saying and re-writing these sentences until they feel comfortable to you. When you can present each skill smoothly and confidently you're ready to go to the next section. Don't worry about memorizing these practice sentences word for word. As you practice them over and over, you'll become more comfortable in paraphrasing them. You'll be amazed and pleased when you hear yourself repeating your practice sentences in an interview.

#1 Job Requirement: How Your Skill(s) Match:

_____   _____

                                _____

                                _____

#2 Job Requirement:

_____   _____

                                _____

                                _____

#3 Job Requirement:

_____   _____

                                _____

                                _____

#4 Job Requirement:

_____

_____

_____

#5 Job Requirement:

_____

_____

_____

_____

Step #2 - De-emphasize Your Weaknesses

To increase your success in interviews it's important to identify your weaknesses and turn them into strengths. If you can't turn a weakness into a strength then you must deflect an employer's attention away from it. Sherry wanted to become an accounting clerk but didn't have experience. She had completed a bookkeeping program and wanted to capitalize on her training. When employers asked what her accounting experience was she said, *"I recently completed a course in bookkeeping and received a 95% average. Using this training I want to move into the accounting field."* Employers replied, *"Well that's nice, but we really need someone with experience. Send in your resume and we'll keep it on file."* Sherry was disillusioned and worried, however, while writing her resume I learned that she had very strong skills. As a Sales Associate she had handled over $60,000 each month for a major retail store and had tracked all sales receipts for her department. Since this part of her job was accounting oriented I knew we could use this as a selling point. We then role-played how Sherry could sell her skills when an employer said, *"Tell me about your accounting background."*

Here's what she practiced saying, *"While at Frederick & Nelson I processed over $60,000 each month, tracking and reporting all sales receipts for my department. In addition, I have a Certificate in Bookkeeping and Office Procedures."* It took Sherry at least ten times practicing these sentences before she stopped giggling and being embarrassed. After about 30 minutes she felt comfortable with this new image of her skills. Sherry found an accounting clerk position and called to apply the next morning. Afterwards she breezed into class, happy and confident. Sure enough, the first thing the employer had said was, *"Tell me about your accounting experience."* Sherry gave her practiced answer and said her mouth dropped open when the employer replied, *"Great, it sounds like you have just the experience we're looking for. Can you come in this afternoon?"* Sherry was offered the position after her second interview, but turned it down to accept an even better one.

189 ♦

As you can see, Sherry identified her weakness of not having accounting experience but drew upon a related skill to offset it. This focused the employer's attention on her strength not the weakness. As you list the skills required for each position ask yourself how your background relates. Even if there is only a small thread in your experience that relates, take that thread and expand upon it. Focus your sentences on that experience and minimize or eliminate what you don't have. Remember, many qualified applicants are never hired. Applicants that market themselves effectively are the ones that get hired even if they don't have all the skills an employer is looking for. Maximize what you do have. It will get you a job. List at least four of your weaknesses in the left-hand column below. Then describe your best selling point to offset each weakness in the right-hand column.

#1 Weakness: Strength That Offsets Weakness

_____   _____

                                  _____

                                  _____

#2 Weakness:

_____   _____

                                  _____

                                  _____

#3 Weakness:

_____   _____

                                  _____

                                  _____

#4 Weakness:

_____   _____

                                  _____

                                  _____

Step #3 - Answer Questions You're Afraid Of_____

It seems we all have one or two questions we worry about being asked in an interview. It might be a question about our education, experience, or work history. The question Sherry had worried about the most was, *"Can you tell me about your bookkeeping experience?"* When she thought of having to answer that question in an interview her mind went blank. She'd then imagine how terrible she'd do in an interview. This made her extremely nervous and caused her to dread interviewing. However, we came up with a terrific answer that got her the interview and two great job offers. By practicing how she was going to answer that question she slowly built her confidence. After several role-plays her whole demeanor changed and she left feeling motivated, excited and proud of herself. That's exactly what you want to do. You want to identify any questions you're afraid of being asked and then write and practice answers that boost your confidence.

By overcoming your fears you will gain control of your emotions. Rather than letting fears run wild in your mind, face your fears, deal with them and move on. If you don't face your fears and gain control of them they will control you. Studies show that public speaking is a number one fear for many people. Interviewing must rank a close second. Fear of interviewing can cause you to procrastinate in your job search or botch an interview, so it's very important to identify your fears and overcome them. I'd like you to identify at least three questions you worry about being asked in an interview. List them in the left-hand column and then write strong answers to them in the right-hand column.

#1 Question: Your Answer:

_____   _____

_____   _____

_____   _____

#2 Question: Your Answer:

_____   _____

_____   _____

_____   _____

#3 Question: Your Answer:

_____   _____

_____   _____

_____   _____

Step #4 - Demonstrate Your Knowledge

An incredibly strong selling technique in an interview is to subtly mention important facts you've learned about a company. This worked for me. I had gathered about 40 articles on the temporary industry and took them to my first interview. At an appropriate moment, I casually spread them out about six inches and said, *"I was able to copy about forty articles on the temporary industry. I was impressed to learn that Dunhill is ranked 4th in national sales."* With this simple strategy I made a strong statement about my interest and desire to work in this field. I didn't need to say, *"I really want to work in this industry."* My actions proved it far better than words could. Think of creative ways you can share the information you learn about companies as a natural part of the conversation during an interview. Below, write several sentences that describe your research:

_____

_____

_____

_____

_____

_____

_____

Step #5 - Ask Questions You Can Sell Yourself Into

Rather than let the employer direct your interview by asking all the questions make a list of your own. Select questions that you can sell yourself into. For example, Susan noticed there were 10 incoming phone lines and a staff of about 20 while waiting to be interviewed. Early in the interview she asked, *"The front office looks busy. How many phone lines will I be responsible for?"* The interviewer replied, *"We have 10 incoming lines with 22 extensions."* Susan jumped in and said, *"Great, while I was at XYZ Company I handled 15 incoming lines with 30 extensions. I love a busy office."* By asking a question and selling herself into it, Susan gained control of the interview and directed it to one of her selling points. It also presented Susan as a dynamic, curious and capable person. This approach is much more dynamic than if Susan had waited to be asked, *"How many phone lines can you handle?"* You can use this strategy to observe each office environment while waiting for an interview. As you observe each office and it's operations formulate questions which will allow you to sell your strongest skills.

After my first interview with Dunhill Temps I spent several hours thinking about the duties of a personnel coordinator. The owner mentioned he would have his sales rep attend our second interview. He had discussed how important it was for the sales rep and the placement person to work together as a team. Therefore, I tried to imagine what it was like to be the sales rep. I visualized her going out, calling on clients, getting orders, and then turning them over to me to fill. This made me think about how I feel when I develop a relationship with a sales rep and then get switched to someone else for servicing. I usually don't like being switched. Having developed a sense of trust in the sales rep I want to keep working with that person, not someone else. I figured clients probably felt the same way when switched from the sales rep to the personnel coordinator at Dunhill.

Using this thought, I brought it up in my interview with the sales rep. I asked, *"Do you ever worry about turning a new account over to the personnel coordinator for the first time? I think I probably would."* She replied, *"Yes. Clients sometimes resent that I'm no longer dealing with them as much."* I then said, *"I know when I buy something from a sales person and get switched to someone else after I've bought the product I usually don't like it. Therefore, it seems very important that I get to know your style and provide a similar sense of style in handling the accounts you've developed. By following your lead and working as a strong team I believe we can make each transition smooth and enjoyable for your clients."* Both the owner and the sales rep loved this response. I think this one point is what got me hired.

This dialogue demonstrated that I had put a lot of thought into the position, that I understood the dynamics of the position, and that I was a team player. It also showed that I understood that the sales rep took the lead with accounts and that I was willing to support her. This dialogue was much more powerful than if I had merely stated, *"I understand this position and want to be a team member. I know the sales rep will take the lead and I'm willing to support her."*

As you think about the dynamics of each position and company you will interview with, brainstorm on how you can sell yourself, your ideas, and your skills. As you can see, I had a substantial impact on how my interview went. If I had not identified this selling point and expressed my idea about it then it wouldn't have been brought up. Therefore, I created a great opportunity to sell myself.

Below I'd like you to make a list of at least three questions you can ask and sell yourself into. They don't have to be complicated. If you have a hard time thinking of questions then review your top five skills. Take each skill and ask yourself, *"What question can I ask that will allow me to tell an employer about this skill?"* Let's say you managed a warehouse with over 10,000 square feet of inventory and you estimate that the warehouse of the company you are interviewing with is about 8,000 square feet. You could ask, *"Your warehouse looks fairly large, do you know how many square feet it is?"* You're told, *"About 8,000."* You say, *"Good, that fits right in with my experience managing over 10,000 square feet of inventory."* Remember, the purpose of your questions is to direct an employer's attention to your strongest selling points.

Skill #1: _____

Question: _____

_____

Statement That Sells This Skill:

_____

_____

Skill #2: _____

Question: _____

_____

Statement That Sells Your Skill:

_____

_____

Skill #3: _____

Question: _____

_____

Statement That Sells Your Skill:

_____

_____

Step #6 - Weave Selling Points Into The Interview

In addition to the strategies we've already discussed, I'd like you to list five more of your top selling points and then write sentences about each one. Practice different ways you can present each selling point. My top five selling points to teach a secretarial and office automations program were:

- Having taught college classes for groups of up to 25.
- Over 10 years secretarial experience.
- Owning and managing my wordprocessing business.
- Experience processing quarterly taxes and reports.
- Proven ability to motivate others to achieve their potential.

I wove each of these skills into my interview. Every few minutes or so, I brought one of them up if the interviewer had not already touched upon it. The interviewer hadn't talked about the coaching skills required to be a teacher so I said, *"While teaching classes and writing resumes I have really enjoyed helping clients increase their confidence. That's probably the biggest reason I get so many referrals. Knowing your students don't have office skills I assume that many aren't very confident about changing jobs. My ability to help people identify their best skills and build on them is a plus for this position."* The interviewer responded by saying how hard it is to find teachers who enjoy motivating others. By his response I knew I had made several points with him.

However, the interviewer did seem concerned that I hadn't been a bookkeeper so I responded, *"Having managed a small business I am familiar with full-charge bookkeeping functions and I prepared all the quarterly taxes and reports for my business."* Then I stopped and didn't say anything else. This satisfied his concerns and he went on to his next question. While I was *familiar* with full-charge bookkeeping functions I had never done it so I knew I would have to review the bookkeeping portion of the course. But, I didn't want him to know that. Knowing in advance that bookkeeping was my weakness I was prepared to offset it with my strengths which were being familiar with bookkeeping functions and having prepared my own taxes. It worked and I was successful in this position. By identifying my strengths before the interview I made sure I incorporated all of them into my interview. Below and on the next page, list 5 more of your selling points and write a sentence or two describing each one.

#1 Selling Point: What To Say To Sell It:

195 ♦

#2 Selling Point: **What To Say To Sell It:**

_____   _____
                           _____
                           _____
                           _____

#3 Selling Point: **What To Say To Sell It:**

_____   _____
                           _____
                           _____
                           _____

#4 Selling Point: **What To Say To Sell It:**

_____   _____
                           _____
                           _____
                           _____

#5 Selling Point: **What To Say To Sell It:**

_____   _____
                           _____
                           _____
                           _____

Step #7 Summarize to Close Your Interview

To close your interview, it's important to summarize your strongest skills for the position. After I interviewed for the position with the temp agency I said, _"My secretarial and computer background combined with my customer service experience gives me unique skills to place your clerical personnel. Having marketed my own business I also understand the importance of handling customer accounts and generating repeat business. I'm very excited about this position and look forward to our next interview."_

Summarizing your skills at the end of your interview will present you as both dynamic and purposeful. This creates a much stronger image than letting the interview wind down and then being dismissed. A typical interviewer might end the interview with a statement like, *"I've still got several people to interview. I'll call you in a couple of days."* Then you stand up and say, *"Thank you"* and leave. Which strategy presents a stronger image? Most people choose the first one. However, that doesn't mean that they necessarily feel comfortable using this approach. Many clients have told me that selling themselves this strongly puts them out of their comfort zones. If you're not feeling confident this strategy can seem a little threatening. If so, it's important to acknowledge your feelings and work through them. Find ways to sell yourself that you feel comfortable with.

Below, practice writing a strong summary statement that you can use to conclude your interviews. You may be surprised. After you practice saying the statement several times you may find that your comfort zone expands.

Summary Statement to Close Interviews:

_____

_____

_____

_____

_____

Step #8 - Use Power Words & Quantify

While writing your resume you learned how to quantify and use action words. You'll also want to quantify and use action, or "power words", when answering interview questions. Using them can have a tremendous impact on the image that an interviewer develops of your skills and can result in a higher quantity and quality of job offers.

Rex was an outside sales rep who had interviewed for a sales position. During his interview he was asked, *"Can you tell me about your account management experience?"* Rex replied, *"Well, I set up and handled key accounts. I also increased the sales to my accounts substantially."* Compare that response to his new one, *"While managing key accounts such as Key Bank, Nordstrom, and Microsoft I increased sales by over 35%, or $170,000 annually."* Which response do you think sells Rex most effectively as a top sales person?

Tony was a truck driver who wanted to go into an office and customer service position. During his interview he was asked, *"Can you tell me about your customer service skills?"* Tony's first response was, *"While driving truck I deal: with customers when I dropped off goods and had them sign their paperwork. "* After Tony practiced using quantifying and power words his new response to this question was, *"With XYZ Company I provided customer service to a client base of over 2,000. Delivering products from $1,000 to over $10,000 per order often required strong problem solving skills. If there was a problem with an order I had to resolve it to the customer's satisfaction as quickly as possible. Because I had become so good at dealing with customers, over one-third of our client base had requested that I be assigned to service their accounts. "* I'd like you to go back and review each of the interviewing worksheets you've already completed. See if you can strengthen your statements by quantifying and using power words.

Step #9 - Show Enthusiasm and Use Props

When interviewing for each and every position be sure to show your enthusiasm for that position. Hiring officials who have conducted a lot of interviews will tell you that many applicants hardly ever smile or act genuinely interested in the position they're applying for. Even though an applicant may really want the position if he shows a lack of enthusiasm an interviewer will probably assume that the applicant can "take or leave" the job, which often results in the applicant not being hired. I interviewed one person for an office position which required a lot of recordkeeping and paperwork. While interviewing he said he didn't like bookkeeping and wouldn't really be happy dealing with paperwork all day. Even though he had read the job requirements he was still applying for this job and wanted me to hire him. When I reminded him that the position required a lot of paperwork he tried to backtrack and said, *"Well, I don't really like doing it, but I'm good at it. "* The impression he gave me was that he'd take this job and as soon as something better came along he'd be gone. Of course, I didn't hire him.

I almost didn't get my last teaching position because I hadn't determined what I wanted before the interview. Having closed my temp business I had wanted to take a couple of months off before going back to work. However, when I contacted a friend she set me up for an interview the next day. During the interview the employer kept asking when I would be available and I kept giving a vague answer because I hadn't really made up my mind about going back to work. After I left the interview I went to the library and called several vocational schools to see if I could find similar positions. During this process I discovered there were very few similar positions I would qualify for without a master's degree. After that my attitude changed. The job was suddenly exactly what I wanted, other than having to go back to work sooner than I expected. I wrote a thank-you letter knowing that I had to use it to overcome the lukewarm response I had given during my interview. In my letter I stated the following: *"This position is an excellent opportunity for me. Being able to use my secretarial and computer skills combined with my teaching and motivational skills will provide me with a tremendous amount of job satisfaction. I would like to accept this position if I am selected and will be available in two weeks. I look forward to talking with you on Monday. "*

I'm sure I wouldn't have been hired if I hadn't rescued my interview with that thank-you letter. This experience shows how important it is to cover all your bases when interviewing even if you're not sold on the job 100%. I ended up staying in that position for two years and would have been very upset with myself if I had lost that opportunity because of my lack of enthusiasm. Below, list all the reasons you are excited about the position(s) you are applying for. It could be that the job is close to your home; that it will allow you increased career growth; or that you excel in a particular skill and this position uses that skill. Each of these reasons can be turned into a selling point during your interviews and can be used to convince an employer to hire you. Be creative and show your enthusiasm:

Position: **Why You're Excited About It**

_____   _____

                         _____

                         _____

                         _____

Position: **Why You're Excited About It**

_____   _____

                         _____

                         _____

                         _____

Use Props

Another great selling tool to use in an interview is what I call a prop or visual aid. The articles I took into my interview with Dunhill Temps were a prop. Having them in hand was much more impressive and convincing than just saying I had done a lot of research. Letters of recommendation; great performance evaluations; awards; and examples of work you've done are all excellent props and visual aids. Using them allows you to be actively involved in your interview and helps to draw attention to your selling points. I also consider attache cases and nice folders as props. Using a nice case or folder helps me feel more professional and confident.

Carefully plan what props you are going to use. You'll want to make sure that they are easy to use and that you understand them thoroughly. For example, one of my clients took a report he had prepared into an interview. The employer seemed impressed until he asked my client several questions about the report which my client couldn't answer. He had been doing great up until that point, but then lost control of the interview. If he had practiced using this prop and had anticipated questions about it he would have been prepared. Afterwards, he felt that if he had taken these steps he would have been hired.

I like to use an attache case that holds my keys and all the items I normally carry in a purse. Fumbling with both a purse and a case makes me feel awkward. In a similar way I also consider clothes and shoes as props. Just like an actor or actress going into wardrobe to select clothes and props for a big scene - you'll want to select props that help you put on the best show. Below, I'd like you to take a minute and make a list of the props you can take into an interview. Select items that increase your confidence and will help sell you. If you need more room, list the rest of your props on a separate piece of paper.

Prop: How You Can Use It & What You'll Say:

_____   _____

_____   _____

_____   _____

_____   _____

_____   _____

Step #10 - Answering The Most Common Questions_____

By now you've practiced and planned for your interviews by completing the worksheets we've already discussed. If you haven't, stop and go back and complete them. Don't kid yourself into thinking it's not important. It is!

Now you're ready to answer some of the most common interview questions. As you probably know, there are several types of questions you'll be asked. Some will be very specific while some will be "open ended." Open ended questions generally get people in the most trouble. For example, *"Tell me about yourself,"* is an open ended question. Many people have no idea how to answer this question properly and as a result fall into the great interviewing pit while trying to answer it. They begin rambling. One woman told me she was getting a divorce and then proceeded to tell me about her marital problems. I felt she was going through some very difficult times and assumed it might be hard for her to concentrate on work. I also assumed she might have a hard time making it to work. As a result, I excluded her as a candidate.

Open Ended Questions

To answer open ended questions effectively it's important that you're prepared for them. Use them as an opportunity to sell your professional skills and abilities rather than talk about your hobbies or where you're from. While some interviewers may want to know about your personal history, most employers want to know about your skills and experience. Many employers interview dozens of people in a day, so it's important to keep your answers short, to the point, and related to the position you are applying for. As you answer each question your ability to communicate and think on your feet will be judged. That's another reason why it's important to have anticipated the questions you'll be asked and to have practiced your answers. You'll want to come across as smoothly and confidently as possible. Watching an award winning actor or actress we often forget how much work they've put into being so polished and convincing. As a result, we marvel at their talent. However, their talent is in large part, hard work and rehearsal.

Stress Interviews

Another problem area can be stress interviews. Angie came back from an interview feeling rather miffed. She said the person interviewing her had said, *"You seem a little too confident and qualified for this position,"* in a snotty tone of voice. Angie replied firmly but pleasantly, *"No ma'am, my qualifications match this position. It requires someone who has good problem solving skills and is confident, and these are two of my strongest skills."* When she went back to her second interview she was told she had answered that question very well. The employer was looking for someone who could think on his or her feet and handle tough situations. As a result, Angie was hired.

By completing the worksheets in this section you've already put yourself ahead of most of your competition. Just like Angie, by knowing your strengths and weaknesses, and having practiced presenting them you will be ready to deal with a stress interview or a stress inducing question.

The Most Common Questions

Now let's go through some of the most common interview questions. Below each question I've included a work area for you to answer it. I've also included an effective answer to each question. The answers I've given are meant only as a guideline. Be creative. Write answers that sell you and your unique skills. Ask yourself what kind of assumptions the employer will make about you based on each answer you give. Make sure the assumptions made about you match the image you want to present just as you did when writing your resume. If they don't then change your answers.

1. Tell me about yourself.

_____

_____

_____

Keep your answer short, to the point, and related to the position you are applying for. Spend one to two minutes answering this question.

Answer: *"I have over five years experience in office administration which includes bookkeeping and supervision of clerical personnel. I enjoy a fast-paced environment and like a challenge. Having a variety of duties to perform each day such as coordinating projects and solving problems makes a job fun for me. Your office seems busy and challenging, just the type of environment I thrive on."*

2. What are your three greatest strengths?

_____

_____

_____

In answering this question, employers will make assumptions about your personality and soft skills, as well as your values. For example, a machinist might answer, *"I like designing mechanical parts, using my hands to make things, and solving problems to make my designs work. These are three of my greatest strengths."* This answer would be fine if the machinist were continuing in his line of work, but this response wouldn't be effective if he wants to go into customer service. In this instance his answer doesn't apply. The employer will probably assume the machinist prefers working alone and with objects rather than with people. As a result, he probably wouldn't get hired for a customer service job. As you answer this type of question give answers that support the image you want to project and the position you are going after.

Answer: *"Being an outgoing person I enjoy dealing with people and customers. I'm a good listener and problem solver and have the ability to put people at ease while diffusing tense situations. All three are strengths that contribute to my skills in customer service."*

3. What is your greatest weakness?

_____

_____

_____

When answering this question be sure to select a weakness that you can talk about confidently and can turn into a selling point. Many people feel guilty if they don't pick their worst weakness. Don't fall into that trap. Pick a weakness that you're not embarrassed to talk about and then explain how you deal with it effectively. This is a good example of how to answer this question:

Answer: *"I tend to be creative and used to get sidetracked coming up with new ideas rather than sticking with systems that are already in place. I've learned to analyze current systems and determine if they need to be changed before I try to improve them. If they don't need changing I leave them alone. If they do, I go to my supervisor to discuss possible changes. This seems to work very well for everyone concerned."*

4.   Why should I hire you over other candidates?

_____

_____

_____

As you watch the person interviewing you be aware of subtle buying signals. If the person leans forward during your interview and seems more interested in a particular skill be sure to talk about that skill when answering this question. If the interviewer seems overly concerned about the habits, skills or traits he desires in an employee then be sure to give an answer that demonstrates you meet those needs.

Answer: *"It seems you need someone who is reliable and trustworthy in this position. While working at XYZ Company I demonstrated these traits. Handling up to $10,000 a day in sales and receipts I consistently balanced each till to the penny. This position also required someone with excellent attendance and reliability. Based on my proven abilities I believe I fit what you are looking for in an employee."*

5. Where would you like to be with this company in a year?

_____

_____

_____

Keep your answer tied to the position you are interviewing for. Make sure you present an image that you will be happy in this position for quite some time. Many people make the mistake of saying they want rapid growth and promotion, which conflicts with the needs of many employers.

Most employers want to count on new employees to stay in the position they are hired for, for a good length of time. It's important to let the employer know you will do your best to excel in the position you're applying for. Let him know that after a substantial period of time in that position, and after you have proven yourself, that you would like to be considered for promotion and growth.

Answer: *"I am very interested in this position and will work to be the best Account Manager I can be. My goal is to grow within this position for as long as possible. After a substantial period of proving my abilities I would then like to be considered for growth opportunities as they become available."*

6. Why are you looking for a new position?

This question causes many people to fall into the great interviewing pit. It's tempting for many people to unload how dissatisfied they are with their current employer. Avoid the temptation. Instead say that you feel the position you are interviewing for is a growth opportunity and sounds challenging. If the company you are leaving is experiencing turnover or isn't stable mention these facts, but do so without showing anger or irritation. Avoid painting a negative picture of any of your employers because most interviewers will assume you are the problem, not the employer.

Answer: *"Having been with XYZ Company for over two years I wasn't actively seeking a new position. However, a friend gave me your advertisement and your ad intrigued me. This position seems to be a perfect match for my career goals."*

7. Why are you interested in our company?

If you're asked this question and you haven't done any research then you will feel very foolish. So, it's a good idea to gather information on each company before your interview. However, if it's a small company you may not be able to find literature at the library. In this instance, ask the receptionist if you can look over the company's brochures as you wait for your interview. Pick out information that will help you sound knowledgeable. If you can't get information about the company then describe the job requirements that make you want the position you're applying for.

Answer: *"I am very interested in working for XYZ company because the accounting position will utilize and expand my best skills. In observing your office it seems to be relaxed yet very busy and your employees seem to be happy and interact well. A relaxed yet professional business environment is exactly what I'm looking for."*

8. How would you describe your last supervisor?

_____

_____

_____

Never say anything negative about your supervisor. If you had a poor relationship with your supervisor or thought he or she was incompetent be aware of your body language as you answer this question. You may say pleasant things but if your foot begins to twitch or you get an irritated look on your face the employer's intuition will kick in and a warning signal may go off in his or her mind about you. Find something positive to say about your supervisor that you actually believe. If you believe it, then you won't have a problem between what your mouth is saying and what your body is doing.

Answer: *"My last supervisor has excellent organizational skills. She plans ahead and has an innate ability to delegate projects to the right employee for each job. I learned a lot by working with her."*

9. Why were you fired?

_____

_____

_____

Don't become defensive, embarrassed or sad when answering this question. Be honest yet slant your answers so that they put you in the best light. I was fired because I wouldn't sign a non-compete agreement. My explanation was that I had already decided to leave and it didn't make sense to sign the agreement. Given this explanation companies I interviewed with didn't have a problem with my being fired. No matter why you were fired, role-play answering this question until you can answer it confidently. Be sure to give examples of how you have overcome your problem and provide documentation if possible. Present yourself with pride and that's how others will view you.

Answer: *"I was let go for poor attendance. Since leaving that company I have completed a two year college program and have three letters of recommendation with me (you pull them out) from my instructors. During this time I missed only one class. Would you like to read my recommendation letters?"*

205 ♦

Do Not Copy or Make Handouts

10. Why have you held so many jobs?

If you have had a sporadic work history be ready for this question. Be honest, yet have answers prepared that put you in the best light. It may be that you've gotten bored, been fired, or had car problems. Don't mention any of these reasons if you can avoid it. If you left one job for another one say that you were offered a position with better pay or better growth opportunities. If you worked while going to school then be sure to point this out. Role-play until you have an answer that presents you as reliable.

Answer: *"Relocating here, I accepted my first position out of financial necessity but moved to a higher position in only three months. Two of the firms I worked for went out of business so I had no control over leaving them. If you exclude them, I have left only one company by choice over the last five years."*

More Interview Questions

Here's a list of additional questions you should practice answering. Read through the list and pick out at least ten more that you feel you will be asked. Role-play answering each one until you can do so confidently and smoothly. To project a dynamic image be sure to quantify your achievements, use action words, and give examples of what you have accomplished. Keep your answers short and to the point.

In Chapter 9 we talked about building a case for yourself when writing your cover letters. Be sure to build a strong case for your qualifications as you interview. If you apply the Ten Power Strategies we've just reviewed you'll be amazed at how much more confident you will feel during your interviews. Following this list, I've included a few more interviewing tips as well as tips on follow-up and salary negotiation.

1. What will previous employers tell me about you?
2. What are your long-term career goals?
3. Describe your perfect job.
4. Why do you want to change fields?
5. Why have you been unemployed for so long?
6. How long do you plan on staying with our company?
7. Describe your organizational skills for me.
8. Describe your ability to handle stress.
9. Describe your problem solving skills.
10. What do you find most frustrating in a job?

11. What type of people do you dislike working with?
12. What do you think makes a good employee?
13. Do you feel you are a good employee? Why?
14. How can you contribute to our company?
15. How would you handle a problem with a co-worker?
16. Can I contact your references? If not, why not?
17. What has your attendance on the job been like?
18. How do you feel about working overtime?
19. Are you willing to take work home if needed?
20. When changes are needed how do you react?
21. Where did you go to school?

The Ten Hottest Skills

Studies show that the ten hottest skills employers look for are transferrable or soft skills. These soft skills are used in every industry and form the foundation for changing careers. Read the list below and check off those skills you feel you possess. Then go back and review the answers you've written in this section to see if you can further improve them. Give specific examples of how you've used each skill to solve a problem, increase efficiency or streamline procedures. Remember, employers want people who will be an asset and can contribute to the overall well-being of their company. Employers look for these abilities:

1. Problem Solving Skills
2. Ability to Work Independently
3. Strong Verbal and Written Communication Skills
4. Leadership and Motivational Skills
5. A Team-Player Attitude
6. Strong Organizational & Time Management Skills
7. The Desire to Learn and Improve
8. Being Reliable and Trustworthy
9. Being Customer Service Oriented
10. Having Supervisory and Management Skills

Let Employers Sell Themselves

Wait for the employer to bring up the issue of pay. If you do, you will be in a much better bargaining position. By letting the employer sell himself on hiring you, he will be more likely to consider a higher pay rate than if you bring up pay on the first interview. This is the same tactic car salespeople use. They usually avoid talking price until we've driven a car and become excited about buying it. Once we begin to feel we really want the car, then salespeople talk price. They know that once we begin to "own" the car we will be more likely to pay a higher price than when we first walked on the lot. You want to do the same thing with employers. You want an employer to feel that you are the best candidate and that he should do everything he can to hire you. If you talk price before the employer feels strongly about hiring you then you may lose out in salary negotiations.

The Question of Pay

When an employer asks you, *"What pay rate or salary level are you looking for?"* Answer by saying, *"I am flexible. At this time, my primary concern is obtaining a position that offers stability and career potential. Can you tell me the salary range for this position?"* Just like a salesperson you want to find out what the employer is willing to pay before you state what you are willing to accept. If you state a pay rate that is lower than what the employer was going to offer you may lose out. If you mention a pay rate that is too high the employer may worry that you won't be happy at a lower rate and may not hire you. Your goal is to get the employer to state the pay rate first, which gives you the advantage of increasing or lowering what you'll accept. This strategy makes many people uncomfortable, but I've seen it result in many clients receiving higher salaries. One person received $800 more per month than he expected.

To make this strategy work, you must confidently turn the question back on the interviewer. If you mumble, avoid eye contract or act nervous many employers will push you to tell them the salary you expect. However, if you look someone straight in the eye and in a friendly yet confident tone say, *"Pay is not my primary concern. I'm flexible. Can you tell me what range this position offers?,"* nine times out of ten the interviewer will answer your question. This works and is worth practicing because it can result in a higher pay rate. It's like getting a raise before you're hired!

What's Your Bottom Line

Before going on an interview determine what your rock bottom salary level is. Make sure that this is the least you would be willing to take, even if your dream job came along. By determining and being sure of this amount you will know where you stand on salary issues when asked. You don't want to lose a great opportunity and regret it later because you weren't ready to negotiate. Determine what you are willing to accept as your bottom line. If the position is below that level then you won't regret passing it up. When considering what your bottom line is take into account other factors such as health care and sick leave benefits, vacation allowances, bonuses, and frequency of performance reviews.

Negotiate A Better Job Title

If you are offered a rock bottom pay rate then consider negotiating a better title to offset it. I used this tactic as a receptionist. My employer couldn't afford pay increases one year so I negotiated for a better title. I was researching and solving health benefit problems for our members and negotiated a new title of Health and Welfare Coordinator. It didn't result in a pay increase that year, but the next year I received an hourly increase of over $3.00. Many of my clients have also used this strategy when their employers had to stick to a budget but were willing to be flexible regarding job titles. In the long run clients have used their new job titles to either progress within companies or to move up when leaving.

Turn On Your Listening Skills

Having thoroughly prepared for interviews you may find it hard to listen to employers because you are so busy anticipating questions and formulating answers to them. As a result, you may interrupt or cut short the interviewer's comments or questions. I know I tend to do this when I'm nervous. Be aware of this tendency and put a lock on your lips. Listen. Then respond accordingly. I remember doing a practice interview with an older client. I asked him a question, listened to his answer and then asked him a new question. Not hearing my new question he continued answering my first question. I interrupted him and told him he hadn't heard my last question. He became defensive and didn't believe I had asked him another question although other people in the class reassured him that I had. My impression was that he had a hard time staying focused and that his thoughts tended to drift. In a real interview this would have been a strike against him, but he easily overcame it with practice. In our next interview he forced himself to listen to each of my questions before responding. Surprisingly, he said this actually made him more relaxed and confident because he had to calm his mind. Listen carefully to each interview question and let the interviewer finish his thoughts before you speak. Put your nervousness aside and focus on the interviewer. This will help you stay on track and project a positive image.

Hiring Decisions Are Made In Minutes

It's estimated that employers make hiring decisions within as little as four minutes of speaking to potential employees. This means that you can't waste time trying to organize your thoughts in an interview. It also means that you don't have time to overcome a negative impression. Once an employer's impression of you is formed it is very difficult to change. Therefore, you need to put your best foot forward from the moment you step into a prospective employer's office until the moment you leave. You only get one chance at a good first impression and you must make it count. In my interviewing classes I show a picture of professional women sitting at a boardroom table. I ask clients to pretend that these women are going to interview several applicants. Then I hold up several pictures of male and female applicants. It's amazing. Within seconds everyone has assessed the applicants and determined who would get hired. When you go into an interview the same thing will happen to you. Your clothing, your demeanor, and your verbal communication skills will be assessed within minutes, even seconds, of meeting prospective employers. That's why role-playing and preparation for interviews is so important.

Your Appearance & Interview Success

Most of what we've discussed so far has related to your verbal presentation during an interview. Equally important, as shown above, is your appearance or physical presentation. This is such a common sense notion that it seems everyone would automatically dress their best for each interview and yet, that doesn't always happen.

209 ◆

I've had female applicants apply for office positions wearing low cut blouses, short skirts, too much perfume, and rings on every finger; all the while chewing gum. I've interviewed men with stains on their ties, buttons missing from their shirts, jackets that are too small, and pants that are too short. What type of assumptions do you think employers make about these individuals?

My assumptions about applicants who have dressed like this are: that they haven't worked in an office before and don't understand the importance of office attire; that they are trying to make a career change but don't know how; that they are too rough around the edges for many professional offices; that they don't care enough about being hired to put more effort into their appearance; or, that they enjoy wearing provocative clothing. If any of these assumptions are made by an employer it can result in not being hired. Ask yourself, *"Are these the type of assumptions I want employers to make about me?"*

If you are making a career change it's important to know how employees dress in the industry that you want to move into. What you wear also depends on the level or status of the position you are applying for. You'll want to dress to meet that level or standard. For example, my husband is a consulting engineer. In his field, engineers do not wear three piece suits. They wear wool jackets with color coordinated slacks. If my husband wore a three-piece suit to an interview in his industry it would be obvious to an insider that he had not worked in this field. It's always safer to dress conservatively than to overdo. If you have time before an interview, pop your head in the door of the office you'll be interviewing in and see what the employees are wearing. You can also sit outside the office at the beginning or end of the day to see what employees wear. Dressing to each office's standards will give employers the impression that you're just like everyone else in the office and that you'll fit in.

It's Hard to Change Habits

When an employer is faced with a choice of hiring an employee with all the skills needed and poor appearance, or an employee with fewer skills and excellent appearance, most employers choose the latter. The reason for this is that it is easier to train someone to learn a new skill than it is to get someone to change a habit. For most of us, our appearance and the effort we put into how we look, is based upon our habits. It's a habit to clean and press our clothes. It's a habit to polish our shoes regularly. We all know it's very difficult to change habits. We can change, but only when we want to.

Therefore, an employer takes a big risk when hiring someone who has developed poor habits regarding his appearance. The employee can be counseled regarding his appearance, but that doesn't mean the employee will change. Employers know this and this is often one of the reasons many applicants don't get hired. To ensure your success follow the tips listed on the next page. If you do, you will come out the winner when the hiring decision comes down to you or someone who has poor grooming or appearance.

Appearance Tips For Women

No perfume
Always wear nylons with no runs
Polish your shoes and press your clothes
Clothes shouldn't be tight in the bust, hips, or waist
Blouses shouldn't be low-cut or revealing
Skirts should be no more than an inch above the knee
Sit down in front of a mirror and see how your clothing fits
Wear conservative jewelry such as a string of pearls and wedding band
Wear clear or very light colored nail polish with no chips
Make sure your fingernails are clean and trimmed
Make sure your hair is fresh and in a business style
Wear antiperspirant
Don't wear heavy foundation or heavy eye make up
Wear light colored lipstick that coordinates with makeup and clothing

Appearance Tips For Men

Polish shoes and press clothing
Wear matched two or three piece suits or jackets with color coordinated slacks
Wear a conservative tie and shirt
Take off earrings, necklaces or bracelets; wear only a watch and wedding band
Sit down in front of a mirror and see how your clothing fits
Avoid pants or shirts that are too tight
Avoid jackets that bunch on your upper arms
Avoid jackets and shirts with sleeves that are too short
Don't wear ankle boots
Wear dark or color coordinated socks; do not wear white socks
Make sure your fingernails are clean and trimmed
Make sure your hair is freshly washed and neatly trimmed
Wear antiperspirant

Your Eye Contact & Handshake

As you meet a prospective employer, make eye contact and shake his or her hand, smile and radiate a friendly demeanor. Throughout your interview maintain good eye contact. If this is hard for you, find a spot on the interviewer's face that you can focus on. I tend to focus on the eyes, move to the mouth, and then scan the entire face of the person I'm listening to. If you are extremely shy or nervous have a friend practice interviewing with you. Ask your friend to tell you if your eye contact presents you as confident. If not, practice until it does. Remember, your goal is to come across as friendly and as someone employees will enjoy working with. If you can barely maintain eye contact, employers won't get that impression.

When practicing handshakes with some of my clients their palms are so sweaty that they make my hand damp. I have to admit that isn't a pleasant experience. If your palms sweat profusely consider putting an antiperspirant on them before interviewing. Be sure it is an antiperspirant (not deodorant).

You can also keep your shaking hand palm down against your skirt or pants just before shaking hands or put a tissue in your pocket and run your hand over it prior to shaking hands. In addition, many people don't realize how weak and limp their handshakes are. A weak or limp handshake creates the image of someone who is shy, insecure, or afraid. Such an image is not good to give prospective employers. Practice shaking hands with your friends and ask their opinion of your handshake. If they say your handshake is too weak practice it until you can give a firm, confident handshake, but not a bone crusher.

The Importance of Rapport

As you make your initial introductions and shake hands you are beginning to build rapport. Before working in the personnel industry I didn't think that chit chat at the beginning of an interview was important. However, I do now. I've given you examples throughout this book of employees getting hired not because they have all the skills an employer wants but because the employer liked them. Employers want to hire people who will get along with existing employees. Therefore, your goal when meeting an employer is to show him that you are an enjoyable person who will be liked by co-workers. If you are so nervous that you can hardly speak, it's hard to show people that you are likable. To show that you are friendly and outgoing make small talk for the first couple of minutes of your interview. Look around the interviewer's office and comment on awards, family pictures, or unique pieces of artwork. Or, you might compliment the interviewer on a piece of jewelry he or she is wearing. Remember to be yourself, relax and smile.

Ask If You're a Top Candidate

If toward the end of your interview the interviewer doesn't state that you are a top candidate be sure to ask, *"Do you feel my skills and experience qualify me as one of your top candidates?"* This question gives you an opportunity to hear the employer's concerns about hiring you before you leave his office. Once you've heard his concerns you can then deal with them. For example, if you are interviewing for a customer service position and the employer replies, *"I'm not sure you have enough direct customer experience."* You might ask, *"Can you tell me what you mean by direct customer service experience?"* The employer might reply, *"Yes, we generally need someone who has dealt with customers in person rather than by phone."* You reply, *"Great, while I was at XYZ Company I managed front desk operations and took orders from customers in person. I dealt with up to 40 customers per day processing individual orders valued at over $7,000. This required strong problem solving, organizational, and prioritization skills because I often had several people waiting at one time to be helped. Is this the type of experience you generally look for?"* The employer might then reply, *"Yes, this is exactly what we look for. Let me ask you a few more questions ..."*

Asking, *"Do you feel my skills and experience qualify me as one of your top candidates?"* makes many people uncomfortable. Therefore, only a small percentage of applicants inquire about their standing, which is another reason why so few people come out as top candidates at the end of an interview. Sales people use this tactic all the time. If we are hesitant to buy a product it's their job to find out why and overcome our objections. They ask us questions to see if we are concerned about price, quality, or product benefits. Once they know our concerns they can then explain how their product meets our needs. This tactic substantially increases sales. You want to do the same thing when interviewing. Practice the question above until you can ask it confidently. Then anticipate and practice overcoming any concerns an employer may have about hiring you.

Ask When Second Interviews Will be Conducted

Before leaving your interview find out when the employer will conduct second interviews or make a hiring decision. You might ask, *"Do you know when you'll be conducting second interviews?"* Once an employer is asked this question he will generally tell you when you can expect to hear from him. If he doesn't, ask, *"May I follow up with you on such and such date if I haven't heard from you?"* By following-up on a specific date you'll be able to determine where you stand and won't be left wondering what has happened to the job.

Writing a Successful Thank-You Letter

After your interview write down areas of your background that most impressed the employer you talked with. Also note any small talk that was unique and would cause the interviewer to remember you. If you both own Dalmatian dogs and had a discussion about that, put it in your notes. In your letter, thank the interviewer for meeting with you. Be sure to mention the reasons you are excited about the position and mention anything unique that you talked about. Your goal in writing a thank-you letter is to demonstrate follow-up and to remind the interviewer of your best qualifications and who you are. When an employer interviews a dozen people or more it's very hard to remember which candidate is which. This can be disastrous for you, especially if the interviewer misplaces his notes about you and can't remember your name even though he wants to hire you.

As a result, thank-you letters often come to the rescue. Make sure your letter will spark the employer's memory about you and that it summarizes your best qualifications for the job. I'd like you to read the thank-you letters on pages 215 and 216. Then ask yourself which letter would be most effective in making you remember an applicant? Which letter is so general that anyone could have written it? You'll notice the second letter includes a postscript. Direct mail advertisers know that a P.S. is often the first thing we read in a letter. If you have something important and unique to say add it with a P.S. After you've written your letter deliver or mail it so that the employer receives it at least one to two days before making the hiring decision. A thank-you letter won't do you much good if the employer receives it after he's made a decision.

213 ♦

Follow-Up After The Interview

If you have been told to contact the employer on a certain date - be sure and do so. If you know the employer will make a hiring decision on a certain date and you do not hear from the employer get your courage up and call that day. If the employer is still deciding on whom to hire, your call may put you in the forefront.

How's Your Self-Image

Ronald came to me and said he had done miserably in an interview. When I asked why, he said, *"I guess I just don't see myself as being anything more than a laborer."* When I said how bright he was and reminded him of how well he had done while completing a drafting program he said, *"Yeah, I know you think that, but I've got to think that. When the employer started asking me about my drafting skills I just fell apart. I imagined myself in my dirty blue jeans and just didn't feel confident."* I then said, *"You're right. Until you believe how much you've learned, how bright you are, and how far you can go - you won't be able to interview well."*

This principle applies to all of us no matter what salary level we are at. If you are experiencing a similar conflict I urge you to read Chapter 1 and Chapter 12. Make yourself a SUCCESS IMAGERY script and listen to it. Until you bring your beliefs about your abilities and self-worth in line with your career goals you risk sabotaging yourself. While a part of Ronald wanted to succeed, another part didn't believe he could and his self-doubt came out in the interview. We worked for about two hours identifying Ronald's motivators and de-motivators. We then made him a SUCCESS IMAGERY script. He listened to it for two weeks and then went on an interview and was hired. I know it sounds amazing that something so simple works, but it does. Do it - you will be glad you did.

Competing In Today's Job Market

In today's job market you must use any and every strategy you can to compete. Each strategy puts you a little ahead of your competition. By the time you've written a great resume and cover letter; interviewed exceptionally well; submitted a thank-you letter; and followed-up you will have substantially increased your chances of being hired. I hope that you have taken to heart each and every job search strategy offered in this book. I also hope that you are willing to feel a little uncomfortable while you stretch and grow in researching and obtaining your new career. Please refer often to this book as well as others recommended in the appendix. Knowledge is the springboard to change and to success. Absorb as much as you can. Read Chapter 12 and create a SUCCESS IMAGERY script to further increase your success and confidence.

Sherry Hill
5920 200th S.E.
Bellevue, WA 98005
(206) 745-8900

October 20, 1993

Mr. John Smith
XYZ Company
24389 2nd Avenue
Seattle, WA 98021

Dear Mr. Smith:

Thank you for taking the time to meet with me last week. Our conversation was very enjoyable.

In discussing the position of Administrative Assistant with you, I am confident that I have the skills and experience you are looking for. The position offers growth and advancement and matches my career goals at this time.

As we discussed I am available for a second interview at your convenience and may be contacted at (206) 745-8900. I look forward to hearing from you and hope that I am a prime candidate.

Sincerely,

Sherry Hill

Sherry Hill
5920 200th S.E.
Bellevue, WA 98005
(206) 745-8900

October 20, 1993

Mr. John Smith
XYZ Company
24389 2nd Avenue
Seattle, WA 98021

Dear Mr. Smith:

Thank you for interviewing with me today. I enjoyed learning about your plans for expanding the XYZ department.

My experience providing administrative support to executive and management staff makes my background an ideal match for the Executive Assistant position. Having significantly increased the efficiency of our computerized order processing department I would be pleased to assist you with the implementation of a similar project.

Your company's interest in maintaining and encouraging family values is also appealing to me. We both struck chord when discussing the need to spend quality time with our children.

I am very excited about this position and would like to be considered as a top candidate. I look forward to hearing from you and may be contacted at (206) 745-8900. Again, thank you for your time and consideration.

Sincerely,

Sherry Hill

P.S. I've enclosed the article we discussed. Hope you enjoy it.

Success Imagery

Many of us can identify our career goals but we often experience fear and self-doubt about our ability to achieve them. My career goals include finishing this book, marketing it, and writing ten more books over the next five years. While I can easily describe these goals, my confidence still fluctuates. One moment I feel like I can do it. The next moment I may ask myself, *"Who are you kidding? You can't do those things!"* Because my self-confidence is so much stronger than it used to be, I am now able to deal effectively with these doubts. I've realized that I'm not going to fix myself once and for all. I've given up the fantasy that someday I will find the magic key that opens the door to total self-confidence. I've realized that self-confidence is gradually built and improved upon. Just like a garden, my self-esteem must be nurtured and cared for. When my mental weeds begin to grow I need to pull them before they spread and SUCCESS IMAGERY is the process I use to weed my mental garden.

Throughout this chapter I'd like to talk with you about this process. You'll learn how to write SUCCESS IMAGERY suggestions that will help you increase your confidence and deal with your fears. Then you'll create a SUCCESS IMAGERY script and record it on a cassette tape. Listening to your SUCCESS IMAGERY tape on a regular basis will motivate you and help you to achieve your goals. We'll also discuss why and how SUCCESS IMAGERY works.

Your Intangible Desires

We hear a lot about goal setting yet many of us can't seem to achieve our goals. I believe this happens because most of us view goal setting in a superficial way. For example, we decide we want to buy a car because it will be dependable or safe, yet what we really want is to feel young and sporty. Without knowing why, we may search and search for a car until we find one that fills this unspoken desire. Because we can see and touch the car it's easy to think that buying the car is our only goal, while our real motivation is our desire to feel young and sporty. Because our intangible desires can't be seen or touched most of us don't realize what they are or how much they motivate us. Another issue which gets in the way of identifying our intangible desires is the feeling that we shouldn't have certain desires. For example, if we come from a poor background it may seem that we are being greedy or self-centered to want an attractive car that makes us feel young and sporty.

This same process happens with our careers. When we decide to look for a new job we come up with an obvious list of requirements such as salary, job duties, and growth opportunities. Yet what many of us really want is a job that helps us feel good about ourselves.

We may want to feel respected and honored by our co-workers. Perhaps we long for security, creativity, or challenge in our careers. When we identify the intangible desires that make us feel fulfilled and satisfied in our careers, we can then find ways to meet these needs. If we are unaware of our desires we may bounce from one job to another. At times we may perform job duties that give us satisfaction. Most of the time, however, it seems we perform job duties that give us little satisfaction. I need a job in which I can have a positive impact on other people. This is important to me because it makes me feel good about myself. I also need a job in which I can be creative and implement my ideas. In jobs that have been "just jobs" for me these intangibles have been missing. As a receptionist, I often felt that if I had to do that job for five more minutes I was going to explode. My intangible desires were not fulfilled and I dreaded going to work every day. Many of my clients have expressed similar feelings about their careers. Therefore, it makes sense to design our careers around our intangible desires. Yet, most of us learn certain skills, often without knowing whether or not they are a good fit for us, and then try to build our careers around these skills. To our disillusionment, we often find that the careers we build based on these skills provide little job satisfaction. However, once we identify our intangible desires we can find or create satisfying job environments that use many of these same skills.

As a receptionist I had developed strong secretarial skills and used those skills to start my wordprocessing business. Owning a business afforded me more job satisfaction than being a receptionist, but not enough. It wasn't until I started writing resumes that I began to tap into my intangible desires. I was still using many of the skills I had used as a receptionist, but my level of job satisfaction greatly increased. Writing resumes and counseling others satisfied my intangible desires and exploited my skills to the fullest extent. When I began writing this book I thought my goal was to make money. Yet, the real drive that has kept me going is the desire to express my ideas and have a positive impact on others. It's extremely important to be aware that superficial, tangible goals are not the most powerful, motivating forces in our lives. Intangible desires are, and in tough times they are what keep us going. For example, when I feel like giving up on this book I think of all the intangibles that motivate me to complete it. The money I will make is important; but it's not the money that actually motivates me. It's the opportunities in my life that money will help me create that motivate me. My dream is to work for myself part-time, yet make a good living. This will give me control over my life and time. I see myself writing in a warm, rustic house overlooking the ocean. I also see myself leading seminars and helping others. These desires motivate me to move forward and achieve my goals.

What Are Your Intangible Desires?

I'd like you to think about your intangible desires. Ask yourself what would make your career exciting. You may find that you need to change only a few of your job duties to make your career more fulfilling. Or, you may find that you are attracted to an entirely different career or field of interest. Either way, let yourself relax and daydream. Ask yourself what a work day would be like if you had a "perfect" job designed to your specifications.

Once you become aware of your intangible desires you can begin to integrate them into your career. This knowledge can also help you identify new job situations in which they can be fulfilled. If you are unaware of your intangible desires your chance of fulfilling them is negligible. For example, a small part of Sharon's job allowed her to analyze and improve her department's operations. As she identified her intangible desires she realized how much she enjoyed the feeling of competency she gained from this part of her job. These realizations increased Sharon's confidence and helped her face her fear of asking for more project duties. Within a few months, she was selected as the project coordinator for her department.

Below, I'd like you to describe ten of your intangible desires. Choose desires that if fulfilled would make you feel satisfied, happy and content with your career. For example, you may desire more challenge, more free time, more responsibility, or more leadership on the job. Go ahead and dream. The insights you learn can motivate you in your job search and can help you choose positions which will provide you with increased job satisfaction. If you find it hard to identify your intangible desires, you're not alone. Many of us have had our dreams squashed, often inadvertently by well-meaning parents, teachers or loved ones. We all have dreams and desires, although it's sometimes hard to uncover them. Reach inside and find the caterpillar in you that's waiting to become a butterfly. Imagine that all your money, housing, health, and other worries are gone. A magic genie has just given you ten wishes to do whatever you would like to with your career. These wishes are just for you and can't be used to help anyone else.

Describe Ten Of Your Intangible Desires

_____
_____
_____
_____
_____
_____
_____
_____
_____
_____
_____

If That Exercise Was Hard For You

It's hard for many of us to identify what our dreams are, or to admit them to ourselves. Having read hundreds of self-development books I've often felt anxious while reading them. Many have encouraged me to pursue my dreams and I've spent a lot of time thinking about why so many of us have a hard time achieving our dreams. Most of us certainly have the brain power to become whatever we want to be, yet we often don't pursue or fulfill our dreams. When I'm told to identify my dreams I experience a wide range of emotions such as feeling scared, excited, overwhelmed, or unworthy.

Underlying these feelings is the fear that if I believe in my dream, but can't attain it that I will be crushed. I tend to shy away from going too far out on a limb to succeed. If I don't get my hopes up too far, and then fail, I won't be so disappointed. When my mother and father divorced I was very attached to my dad. I dreamed of living with him and taking care of him. He fueled this fantasy by telling me stories of the apartment and life we would have together. Then he met my step-mother. I was crushed when I met her and realized I was never going to live that fantasy life with my father. I was never more disappointed in my entire life than at that moment. It hurt so much that I would rather never have had the fantasy at all. Life was disappointing before the fantasy, but it seemed desolate and bleak after I realized it would never, ever happen.

I think that many of us also fear identifying and pursuing our dreams as adults. Our dreams are so precious to us that if we strive to achieve them and fail, we fear we'll be crushed emotionally and possibly even financially. It seems better to coast along at a mediocre level, ignoring our hopes and desires, rather than face disappointment. We then travel through life feeling half-empty and unfulfilled. Ironically, we forget that our fears are often unfounded and when examined they often lose their power over us. Research and careful planning in implementing our plans also helps to offset our fears and increase our chance of success. I encourage you to identify your intangible desires, face your fears, and build your dreams on well-laid plans.

Identify Your Fears & De-Motivators

Once you've identified your intangible desires it's important that you acknowledge what frightens, immobilizes or intimidates you about pursuing your desires. For example, one of my worst de-motivators in completing this book was because I had been writing resumes. Resumes require a short and condensed writing style. Switching from this mode to the task of writing an entire book overwhelmed me. When I tried to write sections for this book my mind froze, and my neck and shoulders ached. I would write one or two sentences and then couldn't think of anything else to write. I automatically said very negative things to myself like:

"Who cares about all this stuff? And even if they do, who do you think you are to tell them? You're no expert. You can't even write a half a page, let alone all this other stuff. What a fool to think you could write a book."

To deal with my fears and de-motivators I wrote SUCCESS IMAGERY suggestions that put them into a positive context. I used words like relaxing, fun, easy, and exciting. I wanted to relax and enjoy writing and have my thoughts come to me easily. Relaxing was very important to me because feeling tense and anxious had caused me not to want to write. I also wanted writing to be a fun and exciting process so I would look forward to doing it. As a job seeker you may also experience a variety of de-motivators that cause you to procrastinate or to avoid activities that cause you discomfort. Therefore, it's important that you identify your de-motivators.

SUCCESS IMAGERY will allow you to turn your de-motivators into motivators which relax you and increase your confidence. When you've written SUCCESS IMAGERY that works you'll feel inwardly motivated to work on your job search. You'll no longer dread it nor will you have to push yourself to complete your job search activities. For example, Julie was nervous when she came to my office. She stuttered quite a bit during the first few minutes of our interview. Once she relaxed her stuttering decreased. When we finished her resume I asked Julie if she was worried about stuttering in an interview. She said,

> *"I'm terrified of it. I know that once I stutter, stuttering is all I'll be able to think about. Then my stuttering just keeps getting worse. I can't seem to stop myself. It's terrible."*

Julie felt that stuttering made her appear unintelligent and hard to communicate with. She worried that her stuttering would ruin her chance for a good interview and the opportunity to advance on the job. Julie's biggest de-motivator was stuttering. She told me that the fear of stuttering had caused her to stay in her present job for over two years, wishing she could change but being afraid to. Julie was relieved to learn about SUCCESS IMAGERY and we wrote suggestions which helped her feel intelligent, confident and relaxed while speaking. Key phrases we used to create these images were:

> *Feeling comfortable... speaking calmly and slowly... feeling intelligent... thoughts being clear... feeling calm and relaxed... words rolling off my tongue with ease and confidence... feeling happy and content at communicating so well.*

We came up with the following suggestions for Julie. Notice that stuttering is not mentioned:

> *"You see yourself being interviewed. You notice how very relaxed and confident you feel. You also feel very comfortable with the interviewer and feel the interviewer likes you and is interested in what you are saying. You're very pleased when the interviewer compliments you on both your verbal and written communication skills. You see and feel yourself speaking calmly and slowly. As you speak calmly you feel very intelligent and confident. Your thoughts are clear. It feels great to be so calm and relaxed."*

About three weeks after Julie began using her SUCCESS IMAGERY script she dropped into my office. She was bubbling over with excitement because she had just had a second interview and hadn't stuttered at all. It was heartwarming to see her so happy.

De-Motivators Cause Anxiety

While some de-motivators may seem minor to you, many are not. Our de-motivators are what cause us to experience anxiety and to procrastinate. The feelings generated by these fear inducing components are generally the reason we put aside our goals and give up on them.

Clients have told me some of their de-motivators include *fearing they will fail in a new job, feeling unworthy of promotions or jobs with better pay, worrying they won't be able to answer interview questions without being embarrassed, and being ashamed of their level of education.* Below I'd like you to make a list of the fears and de-motivators you are facing in your job search. A little later you'll learn how to turn your de-motivators into motivators by writing SUCCESS IMAGERY suggestions.

Your Fears and De-motivators:

_____
_____
_____
_____
_____
_____
_____
_____
_____

Facing Your Fears

A few days ago I watched Oprah Winfrey talk about how hard it was for her to lose weight. She read many entries from her journal that described how disgusted she had felt with herself for regaining her weight. I was reassured and comforted to know that someone as talented and wonderful as Oprah Winfrey has had many of the same thoughts and feelings that I have had. Her journal entries included phrases such as being out of control... trauma... battle... agony of it all... bordering on disaster... in dire need of help... thoroughly disgusted... good intentions then failure... lost resolve... feeling afraid... hating myself... trying to reckon with myself... feeling guilty... and feeling diminished as a person.

I was struck by how many of these same thoughts and feelings I have carried around with me on a daily basis, hidden from my friends and co-workers. It was liberating to know that other people also have private worlds where they express their utmost discouragement with themselves. We say so many negative things to ourselves on a consistent basis that we don't even realize we do it. Yet, realization can be the first step to change. I know that when I am inactive and don't pursue my intangible desires on a daily basis thoughts and feelings such as these run rampant in my mind. I feel diminished and dissatisfied with myself.

As Oprah continued her discussion about weight loss she described how important it had been for her to deal with her fears. She said she had been afraid of standing up for her ideas and disagreeing with people. She said she really wanted everyone to like her and had a hard time confronting people. She said she had realized she used food to cover up these feelings. Oprah said that as she faced her fears and overcame them, she began to win her battle with food. She recommends that we examine any area of our lives that is not working and look for the fears that are holding us back.

If you are experiencing self-sabotage in your career or life ask yourself if you are struggling with fear or a self-image issue. As you face these issues and deal with them you will win satisfaction and happiness in your life.

Pain and Discomfort Can Become Motivators

Most of us will do almost anything to avoid taking an honest, close look at our lives because we fear we will find pain, unhappiness and discontentment there. Yet, pain and discomfort can be powerful motivators. My discomfort and dissatisfaction as a receptionist was so high that the fear of starting a business seemed inconsequential to me. When my discomfort grew to what seemed to be gigantic proportions I was driven to make a change. The same process happens to alcoholics, drug addicts, and compulsive overeaters. When they hit rock bottom their disillusionment and self-contempt becomes so strong that they decide to face their fears and do whatever it takes to change. In a more healthy way we can use this same phenomenon to change our lives and motivate ourselves whenever we feel stuck in a rut.

Many years ago I attended a workshop on eliminating self-defeating behaviors. One of the exercises was to describe all the thoughts and feelings you experience as a result of maintaining a self-defeating behavior. This exercise was extremely painful, so painful in fact, that it was like hitting rock bottom without having to be there. It was amazing to see the transformations and realizations that people made about their lives. I decided to identify why I chose behaviors that made me appear stupid. As a result of doing this exercise, I learned that "acting stupid" in stressful situations was all I knew. Having been ridiculed and hit if I did things wrong as a child, I had developed the strategy of "acting stupid." If I acted like I couldn't do something then someone else in my family would have to do it. If they did it wrong they'd get hit instead of me. This was a successful strategy at the time. However, as an adult I realized that by continuing this behavior I perpetuated negative feelings about myself. When I made a list of the icky feelings I had as a result of acting stupid, I automatically began to change my behavior. When I realized there was real pain attached to this behavior and there were no longer any benefits to be gained from it, I no longer had a compulsion to continue it. I was then able to implement new behaviors that presented me as intelligent.

The Pain of Doing Nothing

Only four months ago I was struggling with feelings of self-contempt because I wasn't working on this book. Remembering how powerful the above exercise had been I decided to use it again. The chart on the next page lists the painful feelings I was experiencing as a result of not working on my goals. I put a much larger version of this chart on my bedroom wall. I realized that being a couch potato wasn't worth all these feelings. When I used SUCCESS IMAGERY and coupled it with looking at this list, my perception about writing this book changed within a few days. It no longer felt like drudgery to write. In fact, I woke up every morning with new ideas and excitement.

223 ♦

Wanting to Run Away

Regretting What I Didn't Do

Feeling Discontent

Missing Out On Life

Feeling Pessimistic About Life

Feeling Depressed

Mom and Dad Were Right

Feeling Taken Advantage of

Feeling Out of Control

Feeling Scared

Not Growing

Losing My Independence

Not Valuing my Ideas

Can't Help Daughter Financially

Stagnating

Being Old & Regretting Life

Is This all There Is?

Pain of Doing Nothing

Feeling I Won't Succeed

Feeling Dreary

Feeling Overwhelmed

Setting Poor Example For Daughter

Disappointed With Myself

Not Seeking Challenges

Feeling Discouraged

Feeling Lazy

On A Treadmill Going Nowhere

Having To Work For Someone Else

Never Having Enough Money

Doubting Myself

Feeling Wimpy

I'm Not Worthy Of Success

Disgusted With Myself

Not Stimulating My Mind

Feeling Lonely

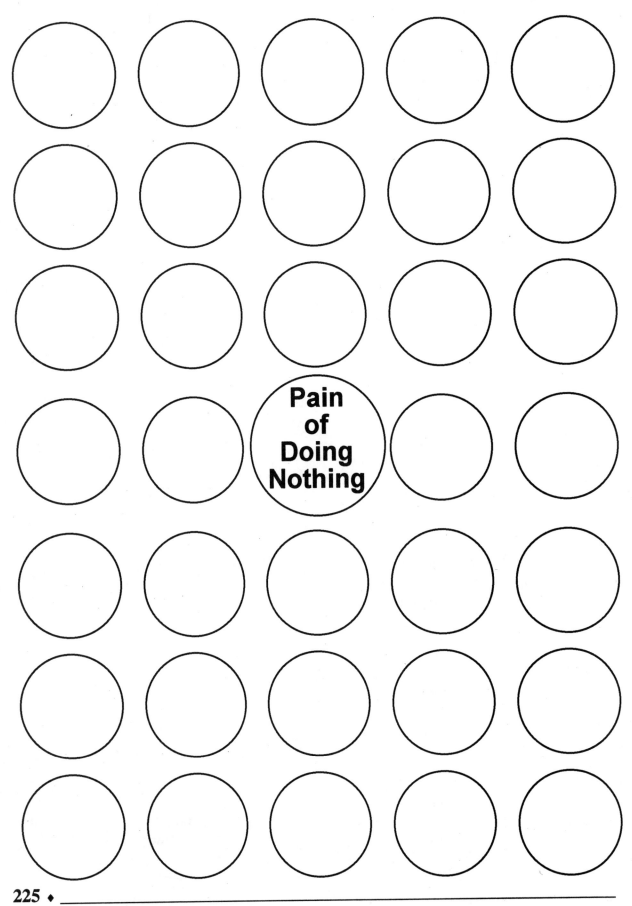

I've written this section because we often become mired in a rut and can't move ourselves to action. If you are in a rut, make a list of the negative feelings you experience as a result of your inaction. I called my chart my "pain of doing nothing" chart because that's how I feel when I do nothing and avoid working on my goals. When I admitted the pain I felt as a result of doing nothing, it just wasn't worth continuing to do nothing. If you're in a rut, list the feelings you experience as a result of "doing nothing." Use the chart on page 225 to list your deepest feelings. They can move you to action.

I questioned if the topics we've discussed in this chapter are appropriate for a career book. However, I was reassured when I read a book titled, *"Quiet Desperation."* The author surveyed a group of extremely successful men and found that over 60% of them feel they are living lives of quiet desperation. While they have been very successful financially they report having little satisfaction in their careers. If they had their careers to do over many say they would build a new career around activities that fulfill their intangible desires. Many of the men surveyed believe this would result in a better self-image with fewer negative feelings about themselves.

The Pleasure of Success

We all yearn for the "pleasure of success." and I believe we can all attain this pleasure by building our lives around the feelings we wish to experience. The hope of attaining these feelings can keep us motivated and directed in hard times. Whenever I feel discouraged about my writing I imagine how content I will feel when this book comes back from the printer. The desire to feel that contentment excites and motivates me to continue my writing.

When you identify the feelings you would like to experience there are numerous activities that can give you those feelings. For example, you might love the feeling you get from organizing a chaotic office system, but might find that you enjoy organizing an overseas convention even more. When you want to experience a certain feeling be creative. Experiment with different activities and see which ones give you the most enjoyment. Whenever you need a sense of direction in your career ask yourself what feeling or intangible desire you yearn to fulfill. Then identify the skills you can use, or the activities you need to complete, in order to fulfill this feeling or desire. You'll find that paying attention to your feelings and fulfilling your desires is a very powerful way to improve your life. To motivate myself I made a "Pleasure of Success" chart in which I listed all the good feelings I want to experience. When I read and experience these feelings I get excited and want to do something to attain them. Here are some of the feelings and desires I listed:

- Feeling satisfied and content with myself
- Being in control of my life and time
- Waking up feeling excited and happy about my future
- Loving to come up with new ideas and write about them
- Feeling life is worth living
- Getting happy goose bumps when someone's resume really comes together
- Feeling content that I have a legacy to leave my daughter

Pleasure
of
Success

On the facing page I have provided a "Pleasure of Success" chart for you to complete. List all the good feelings you would like to experience in your life, then use this chart to find activities that give you those feelings. You'll be amazed at all the opportunities which can give you pleasure and fulfill your life.

I put a larger version of my "Pleasure of Success" chart on my bedroom wall. When I wake up in the morning I read my chart and savor the good feelings it gives me. It's a great way to start my day. Consider doing this too.

Prioritizing Your Time

Another reason many of us think we can't achieve our goals or intangible desires is because we're so busy getting through each day. To finish this book I had to change how I viewed my time. It seemed I had no time for anything other than preparing for work, going to work, and worrying about work. If I drew a cartoon, I would have been a person who looked overwhelmed. Work would have been a gigantic cloud hovering over and around me. My book would have been a tiny little thing in the corner I wanted to get to, but couldn't.

While I had enjoyed my job, it felt burdensome to me because it seemed to be preventing me from fulfilling my desires. I had to keep working but realized that I needed to build my life and thoughts around my book rather than my job. Each day I needed to wake up feeling excited about writing. In recreating that cartoon I needed to see myself as a person who was in control of my life and time, and needed to see my book as a much larger part of the picture. Then I needed to see my job as important, but taking up a much smaller part of the picture.

I had also felt dragged down by work and dreaded spending my free time writing because I felt that I'd never have any time to relax. After reading my "Pain of Doing Nothing" list I realized that I wasn't enjoying or relaxing during my free time anyway. I was spending this time feeling bad about myself. To change these feelings and perceptions I created a SUCCESS IMAGERY script that read something like this:

"It's wonderful to wake up and feel so excited about writing. Even when you are doing other activities your mind returns again and again to your book. It's amazing how little time it takes to get ready for work and how little energy it takes to go to work and teach your classes. It's amazing how quickly they are over each night and how soon you can return to writing your book. You see and feel that your job is an excellent way to learn more about public speaking and improve your skills. You are also thankful that this job allows you to pursue your dream and become a best-selling author."

I know that this probably seems corny, but it works. Before I began listening to this script I felt that I should work on my book, but also thought, *"Ugh! I don't want to. It's too much work and takes too much time."* After about two weeks of listening to this script my thoughts changed. Amazingly thoughts would spring into my mind at the end of each work night such as, *"Gee, tonight went quickly and it was fun. I can't wait to get home and do some writing."* It's hard to describe how differently I view my time now. I don't feel encumbered by my job because my emphasis is on achieving my personal goals.

If you feel like I did and need to change how you feel about your time and your ability to accomplish your goals complete the worksheet below. Be honest with yourself and use this information in your SUCCESS IMAGERY script. You'll be glad you did.

How You View Your Time

_____
_____
_____
_____
_____
_____
_____
_____
_____
_____
_____

How You Want To View Your Time

_____
_____
_____
_____
_____
_____
_____
_____
_____
_____
_____

Changing Your Self-Image

Bringing your self-image in line with your goals is very important and an excellent way to do this is by using your imagination to experience positive feelings about yourself and your goals. To successfully change your self-image it's important that you understand how your mind works. Your mind can be viewed as having two parts, the conscious and the subconscious. You use your conscious mind when you focus your attention on tasks like talking to a friend, learning computer commands, or cooking. Your conscious mind is that part of your mind that you are aware of. You are using your conscious mind to read this book. While it appears that your conscious mind is the largest part of your mind, it is not. Your subconscious mind is the dominant and strongest part of your mind. You use your conscious mind only in your waking state while your subconscious mind operates 24 hours a day, in both your waking and sleeping states. It is your subconscious mind that controls involuntary functions such as breathing, circulation, and immune response. These functions must be maintained 24 hours a day or you will die. If you try to consciously regulate your breathing it requires effort although your subconscious mind performs this task so easily that you are unaware of breathing.

Your subconscious mind also has stored within it all the feelings, sights, smells, and sounds you've ever experienced. Your subconscious mind is always busy bringing these memories to your conscious mind. Each time you look at an object, experience a particular smell, hear a sound, or feel a certain way your subconscious mind acts like a super-fast computer. It sorts through your past experiences and gives you the words to identify these sights, smells, sounds, and feelings. Since your subconscious mind contains all of your feelings and memories, it is your subconscious mind that you must deal with to change your self-image. Your subconscious mind records your thoughts and feelings much like a computer does. You can experience an imaginary event and your subconscious mind records it as if it really happened. This imaginary event influences you the same way a real event or memory does. For example, your subconscious mind creates dreams that cause you to experience real feelings. Even though your dreams are not real you respond to them feeling fear, excitement, anger, and happiness, just as if they were real. We've all had nightmares and awakened feeling frightened. We tell ourselves the dream was not real but the frightening feelings still linger.

Success Imagery

By using SUCCESS IMAGERY you can reprogram your subconscious mind and improve your self-image. World class athletes have been using positive imagery for years to improve their athletic performance. Football players can sit in a locker room and increase their scores without touching a football. They increase their confidence and skill by using their imagination to vividly see, hear, and feel the crowd cheering them on as they make good moves on the field. They can imagine feeling the ball in their hands and feeling their feet hit the ground as they run with ease and confidence. Imaginary feelings such as these become a part of the football player's memories and self-image with repetition. Experiencing these imaginary feelings repeatedly increases a football player's confidence and ability to score a touchdown.

Reba McEntire accepted an award for Best Female Country Singer in 1984. She told the audience that she had rehearsed her acceptance speech back when Merle Haggard received his award for 'Okie from Muskogee'. Reba used her imagination for many years to see herself as a star. Just like Reba, successful people throughout all walks of life use positive imagery to motivate and propel themselves toward their goals. In the same way, you can use positive thoughts and feelings to replace negative ones and achieve your goals.

The Dynamics of Success Imagery

To replace negative feelings with positive ones it is important to bypass your conscious mind and deal directly with your subconscious mind. You want to avoid communicating with your conscious mind because it is very critical. If you tell yourself you can speak to a group of 200 people, but this causes you tremendous fear, your conscious mind will immediately reject the idea. You will spontaneously experience negative self-talk such as:

"Oh yeah? Remember in the 3rd grade when you had to give that book report and you were so bad that all the kids laughed? You think you can do better now? What a laugh. You'll die of fright and embarrassment."

Thoughts like these and the feelings they evoke will quickly convince you that there's no way you want to speak to a large group. More than likely, you'll abandon your goal because it causes you too much self-doubt and fear. To overcome negative thoughts you must give new instructions to your subconscious mind, where all your memories are stored. For example, if you want to speak to a large group without fear or intimidation you could imagine the following:

"Seeing the audience smiling at you and being very interested in what you are saying. Hearing the audience applaud when you make a good point. Feeling yourself become more confident because the audience is reacting so positively."

With consistent repetition of these imaginings, you develop the belief that you can speak to a large group. You believe that people are smiling at you. You believe that what you say is so good that it makes people want to applaud. In this way, positive imagery is believed and stored in your subconscious mind as a real event or memory. The next time you think about speaking to a group this memory is recalled by your subconscious mind and increases your confidence. If you think SUCCESS IMAGERY sounds corny and farfetched, or it makes you feel anxious, you're not alone. Many of my clients have related such feelings to me. I remember how I felt when I first read about positive imagery. It was exciting, yet I doubted that these techniques worked. I knew I needed some way to feel good about myself and to accomplish my goals, so I took the time to analyze my feelings and to use positive imagery. I coined the term SUCCESS IMAGERY because I've developed additional techniques which increase the power of imagery and affirmations. Integrating your intangible desires, dealing with de-motivators, and prioritizing your goals increases the power of SUCCESS IMAGERY. I can't tell you how glad I am that I spent the time to turn my thoughts around. I know that if you take the time to develop your own SUCCESS IMAGERY script you'll benefit from it tremendously.

Daydreaming

We all daydream and often daydream without realizing it. When was the last time you drove home and realized five or ten minutes had gone by with your mind on something other than driving? You were on auto-pilot. Your subconscious mind had made sure that you made all the right turns, braking and shifting as needed, yet when you think back it seems like you weren't aware of driving at all. Whatever you were thinking about was so strong and vivid that you experienced an altered state of consciousness. This altered state of consciousness is excellent for planting new memories and imaginings in your subconscious mind. Performers enter an altered state of consciousness each time they practice their acts, pretend they are playing to an audience, or imagine themselves achieving their goals.

In *Storms of Perfection*, Andy Andrews has compiled a collection of memoirs by successful people. Letters written by fifty celebrities such as Bob Hope, Norman Vincent Peale, Shirley Muldowney, Bart Starr, and Phyllis Diller describe how each of these stars has dealt with rejection and failure. As you read the letters, it's clear how much these celebrities have used their imaginations and dreams of success to keep them going in rough times. Joan Rivers recounts how she was fired from many nightclub jobs. Her mother told her that she had no talent and was throwing her life away trying to be a comedienne. Joan's letter describes how desperate she felt, yet her drive to succeed kept her going and became her most valuable asset. Joan's message is that perseverance is just as important as talent. She says to never stop believing. You can imagine how many times Joan Rivers practiced her act, pretending and daydreaming that she was in front of an audience. By sticking to her dreams and using them to step over failure she has succeeded.

Another very touching letter in *Storms of Perfection*, was written by Mel Tillis, a well-known country music star. Spending a lot of time alone as a child Mel created his own stage productions. Mel cut pictures out of the Sears and Roebuck catalog to make cardboard men and women as well as furniture for his miniature sets. He loved pretending and making up his own stories. In junior high school he decided he wanted to audition for the junior play. When he told the teacher he wanted a part she seemed uneasy. While she didn't want to hurt his feelings she felt the speaking parts would be difficult for him because he stutters. Even though he was disappointed, he wasn't about to give up. He was eager to be involved even if it meant only pulling the curtain. He told his teacher he'd be the best curtain puller she ever had. When I've had other people read this letter from *Storms of Perfection* they've gotten teary eyed. I think that's because Mel Tillis' story exposes how vulnerable many of us have felt as children in pursuing our dreams. By asking to pull that curtain, Mel let his courage and perseverance shine through.

Stories such as these relate how successful one can be by identifying a goal and then imagining how it will feel to achieve that goal. By breaking your goal into a step by step process and imagining it repeatedly, you can achieve success in any area you pursue. I recommend you purchase a copy of *Storms of Perfection*. Read it when you need inspiration. It provides wonderful stories that will help you understand how others have dealt with failure or doubt and come out winners.

Why It's Important To Identify Your Goals

Many popular self-help books discuss how important it is to turn on your reticular activating system in order to achieve your goals. By definition, reticular has to do with vision or the ability to see. As you define your goals you are able to see them. If you have purchased a car then you've already experienced a very literal example of your reticular activating system being turned on. Before you decided to buy your car you probably never noticed other ones just like it. However, once you selected the one you wanted you probably noticed cars just like it everywhere you went. It's amazing. How does this happen?

You didn't consciously say to yourself, *"I want to see every car that's just like mine."* However, your mind was filled with thoughts and excitement about your car. You were probably fantasizing about how wonderful you would feel as you got in and out of your car for the next year or so. You may have imagined what a racy or sexy feeling you would get while driving it. You knew you'd feel happy and successful each time you opened the door and smelled that new car smell. While you didn't drive around looking for cars just like yours, your thoughts were focused on your car. Your imagination was in full swing and without realizing it you were sending very powerful messages to your subconscious mind. As a result, your subconscious mind directed your attention to other cars just like yours even if they were only in your peripheral vision.

This example illustrates how we are subconsciously attracted to those things or activities that we spend a lot of time thinking about. For this reason, it's imperative that we identify and focus on the intangible desires and goals we want to have fulfilled. If we float through life without direction or aim, our reticular activating system is never turned on. Or, it is turned on to the negative things in our lives. Wonderful opportunities can be before us and we never recognize them. Once we identify our goals and focus on achieving them, our subconscious mind directs us toward opportunities that will help us achieve them. If Mel Tillis had not spent his childhood producing his miniature stage productions he might not have had the courage nor the perseverance to ask to pull the curtain. Having focused on his plays for all those years his reticular activating system kicked in and urged him to persevere and secure his dream. He had seen himself on a stage so many times that his subconscious mind propelled him to ask to pull that curtain and his reticular activating system directed him to an opportunity to achieve his dream.

This concept is also well illustrated by a study of Yale graduates. A group of 100 students graduated in 1973. Ten years later a research team interviewed all 100 graduates. The research team wanted to determine how many of the graduates had become successful in their own estimation. Sadly, only 3% were satisfied with what they had achieved over this ten year period. The common element among the 3% was that each person had written down his or her goals back in 1973. These people had developed short as well as long term plans for achieving their goals. Goal setting had turned on each person's reticular activating system and directed each one to opportunities which ensured his or her success.

By using their imaginations to see into the future and project their success, they became successful. As a result, it's critical that we pay close attention to our thoughts. If our thoughts are negative, we are much more likely to attract something negative to us, or to put ourselves into negative situations. If we feel we'll never be successful our subconscious mind is not directed to find opportunities to make us successful. On the other hand, the more we identify positive goals for ourselves and think about them, the more our reticular activating system will kick in and show us opportunities that we wouldn't have been aware of. It's also interesting that many of us think we can't succeed without an education. Obviously, an education from Yale didn't ensure the success of the graduates surveyed. Identifying and focusing on goals made the difference.

I had never paid much attention to goal setting before writing this book. I tended to set my sights on achieving something, think about the steps needed to get there, and then proceed in a haphazard fashion toward completing those steps. We've all heard sayings like, *"If you don't know where you're going, how will you ever get there?"* I had discounted this saying because I had thought I was pretty goal oriented. However, my views of goal setting have changed.

I now understand how clear and specific goals give us direction in achieving them. We need to outline the steps and time needed to achieve our goals, and until we do we are like a boat adrift without oars, sails, or motors. Life's daily currents can easily push us off course. We may have the intention of going to the library to do job research, but then a friend asks for a ride to the bus stop. Our family then needs us to get groceries for a school get-together. The kids get out of school and they want us to rent a movie. Pretty soon the day's gone and our good intentions are out the window. Not having committed to specific activities it was easy to get sidetracked and lose a day.

When I've been urged to outline my goals and commit to a schedule to achieve them I have felt anxious. I worry I can't stick to my goals, fear that I will fail or think I'm not successful enough to finish it anyway, so why bother? However, a wonderful thing happened when I faced my fears and mapped out a daily, weekly and monthly plan for completing this book. I was relieved to see that by sticking to a six month schedule I could finish a project that I had started over eight years ago. At that moment, completing my book became a reality. The saying, *"If you don't know where you're going, how will you ever get there?,"* became crystal clear to me. I finally understood that until I list each activity, accept that I need to do it, and then commit to do it, that the chance of my achieving the goal is very small. I realized this process was exactly why the 3% of Yale graduates who became successful, were successful.

I recommend that you use this process. Decide how quickly you want to have a new job. Is it a week, a month, or a year from now? Are you willing to commit to completing enough job search activities to ensure that you obtain a job within this time limit? After you've determined how quickly you want a new job complete the calendar on page 249. This calendar covers one month's time. If your time limit is longer than a month then make a copy of this calendar for each month you intend to spend looking for a job.

Allocate time on Sundays or Mondays to review newspaper help-wanted ads and to write cover letters. You might then schedule Tuesday to do library research and write more letters. Wednesday might be a day to contact employers and write more letters. Thursday might be a day to network and write thank-you letters. By Friday you might need to conduct more library research and write more letters to employers. Also schedule time to listen to your SUCCESS IMAGERY script three times a day. Interspersed between each day's activities may be interviews or networking lunches you've scheduled. If this sounds like work, it is! Schedule your time as if you are on the job. Then stick to your schedule. Imagine that each activity has to be finished on time and has to be reported to a supervisor at the end of the day.

When you write your SUCCESS IMAGERY suggestions describe the job search activities that you need to complete on a daily and weekly basis. Also describe how competent and in control of your life you will feel by following your schedule. Describe how proud of yourself you will be when you get a job using these methods. It is an exciting endeavor. If you follow your schedule and listen to your SUCCESS IMAGERY script you will create an exciting opportunity to change your life. It's all up to you and how much effort you are willing to invest. Go for it!

How Long Does It Take?

Clients always want to know how long it will take before they feel totally confident as a result of using SUCCESS IMAGERY. I'm not sure that any of us will ever feel totally, 100% confident, 100% of the time. I see confidence building as an ongoing process, not as a one time end result. Therefore the length of time it will take for you to feel confident, as a result of using SUCCESS IMAGERY, will vary. It depends on how confident you already are. It also depends on the task you select. You can experience an increase in confidence as soon as you start using SUCCESS IMAGERY. However, this feeling may dissipate if you do not use SUCCESS IMAGERY every day. It's important to keep sending new messages to your subconscious mind until you spontaneously experience the behavior you are seeking.

Six years ago I wanted to raise my resume rates to $45 an hour, but deep inside I didn't feel I was worth that much. I knew my resume writing skills were excellent so it was more a matter of feeling worthwhile as a person. Being told and believing negative things about myself all my life, my self-image just didn't match my image of someone who could charge $45 an hour. To overcome these feelings I developed a SUCCESS IMAGERY script and listened to it every day. At the end of three weeks I became discouraged. I still felt nervous and anxious whenever I considered raising my rates so I stopped listening to my script. Three days later a client asked about my rates and $45 an hour just popped out of my mouth. I quoted that figure spontaneously. I didn't argue with myself or question what I said, it just came out. When SUCCESS IMAGERY replaces old thoughts you'll also experience new, positive thoughts spontaneously.

Thoughts and Behaviors Change Spontaneously

Be sure to use SUCCESS IMAGERY until your thoughts and behaviors change spontaneously. As a guide, give yourself a months' time before you expect to feel confident and able to achieve maximum performance. If you are experiencing a lot of self-doubt you will need to bombard your subconscious mind with more repetition throughout the day. Listen to your script in the morning, while driving, at lunch and dinner time, and at bedtime. You may have millions of negative memories stored in your subconscious that you need to re-program, and repetition of positive thoughts is the key to replacing them.

Are You Worth More Money?

As you change jobs, you may experience some of the same feelings I felt when I wanted to raise my rates. If you want a higher paying job you may feel you're not worth more money, or you may worry that you won't be able to convince employers of your worth. When I recommend to many clients that they apply for jobs with higher pay they often say, *"Gee, I can't apply for that job, it pays $200 (or whatever amount) more a month than I'm making."* Many of my clients have admitted that they don't even answer want ads for jobs with higher pay. It doesn't matter to them that they have all the skills listed in the ad. The idea of being paid more money scares them and makes them feel that they aren't qualified for the job. Because of these fears many of my clients have passed up excellent advancement opportunities. When we develop SUCCESS IMAGERY scripts for them they are then able to apply and be hired for these jobs. As they begin to believe they are worth more money their thoughts also change spontaneously. Without effort they feel excited and confident about their ability to get a better paying job.

Select Only One Goal at a Time

Select one goal at a time to maximize your success. It is very tempting to tackle several goals once you experience the positive effects of SUCCESS IMAGERY. You might get so excited that you decide to change jobs and lose weight simultaneously. Since each of these goals is very different, each one demands a lot of attention. Working on both goals can diffuse your energy and motivation and it can take longer to reach each goal. You also won't experience changes as dramatic as you would if you were focusing on only one goal at a time. It's much better to select one goal you are really excited about achieving. Stick with it until you are satisfied with the results and then use SUCCESS IMAGERY to tackle your next goal.

Make Suggestions Believable and Personal

I tried using a pre-made imagery tape which focused on achieving financial success. It made me feel tense because I was to imagine doubling and tripling my income which put me so far out of my comfort zone that I couldn't relax. This meant that the tape was communicating with my conscious mind rather with my subconscious mind. The script gave me no steps for achieving these goals, so I had no reason to believe I could double or triple my income. If the script had suggested I achieve a smaller increase in my rates and find additional services to offer, thus making more money, I could have believed the statements. Tripling my income sounded like too much to me and I automatically experienced negative thoughts. This is one of the most important keys to using SUCCESS IMAGERY. You must feel challenged yet fairly comfortable with what you are imagining. SUCCESS IMAGERY suggestions should motivate you and cause you to look forward to achieving your goal, not be intimidated by it.

When you write SUCCESS IMAGERY statements that soothe and resolve your anxious feelings, you'll know you've succeeded in creating imagery which will work for you. As you write your suggestions be aware of subtle differences in how you feel when you use certain words and phrases. Use words and images that feel right to you, that you find challenging yet obtainable and motivating. For example, if you are having a hard time writing a resume, then break it into smaller steps:

"See yourself writing your resume, identifying and describing your skills. Remind yourself that many people have succeeded using the techniques in this book and you will too. Remember all the things you've done well on your past jobs that have shown you're a success. Remember things you are proud of. Imagine holding your completed resume and feeling proud of your accomplishments. All of these things motivate you to work on your resume."

Some of the sentences above may have worked for you and felt motivating while others didn't seem quite right. Those that didn't would need to be re-written to match your feelings. For example, while working with Roger, a master carpenter, I came up with the following sentences for his SUCCESS IMAGERY script:

"You know that your design skills are <u>excellent</u> and have resulted in extensive client referrals and a reputation for outstanding workmanship. These skills are also the foundation for you to start your own business."

These sentences seemed great to me. Roger had told me he had won three national awards and several of the homes he had remodeled were featured in *Sunset Magazine*. However, Roger didn't feel comfortable with the word - *"excellent."* He wanted to change the sentence to read:

"You know that your design skills are <u>good</u> and have resulted in extensive client referrals and a reputation for outstanding workmanship. These skills are also the foundation for you to start your own business."

As you can see, these sentences don't have nearly the same impact as the first ones. I knew that Roger had to feel comfortable with his SUCCESS IMAGERY script, but I also felt that the word *good* presented too weak of an image. We must have spent ten minutes trying to replace that one word. Here's what we came up with:

"You know that your design skills are <u>unique and innovative</u> and have resulted in extensive client referrals and a reputation for outstanding workmanship. These skills are also the foundation for you to start your own business."

Roger felt completely at ease with these sentences. He didn't view his skills as *excellent*, yet he felt totally comfortable with *unique and innovative*. This is the type of difference you can make in your own script. Although subtle, these differences can have a big impact on how relaxed, comfortable and motivated you will feel while using SUCCESS IMAGERY.

237 ◆

Focus On The Positive

As you write your SUCCESS IMAGERY suggestions keep them focused on the positive and on what you want to accomplish. You must avoid reinforcing negative feelings and thoughts. For example, if I tell you not to think of Zebras, what do you think of? Zebras. If I tell you not to think of being nervous in an interview, what do you think of? Being nervous in an interview. Therefore, if your suggestion is, *"I won't get nervous just before an interview,"* you automatically conjure up an image or feeling of being nervous. This statement reinforces exactly what you want to avoid. To write a script that focuses on improving your interviewing skills and boosting your confidence you could ask yourself the questions below. This list can give you ideas of similar questions to ask yourself about any activity in order to create a script.

♦ How do you want to feel during your interview?
♦ How can you increase your confidence before your interview?
♦ Have you done well in the past at expressing yourself? Can you use these memories to help yourself feel more confident about interviewing?
♦ How will you feel when you are offered the job?
♦ What will you hear as the employer offers you the job?
♦ What will you be wearing? Will you carry a leather portfolio and be able to smell that new leather smell?
♦ How will you hold your body? Attentive yet relaxed?
♦ How will your voice sound as you speak?

Just as Roger was more comfortable with *unique and innovative* than *excellent*, be sure to search for words and images that make you feel comfortable. Take the time to write and polish your sentences until you feel satisfied with them.

Be Descriptive and Repeat Key Words

It is very important that all of your SUCCESS IMAGERY suggestions be in the present tense. They must be written as if they are happening to you at that very moment. When you listen to or read your suggestions focus your full attention and imagination on them, and vividly experience each feeling, thought, or task. As you write your SUCCESS IMAGERY suggestions describe how you feel, what you see, and what you hear. This will help you experience the suggestions more fully. The paragraph below describes writing a resume. Notice how details and descriptions help to paint a vivid picture:

"See yourself sitting at your desk working on your resume. You are holding a pen in your hand and feel the pressure of the pen against the paper as you write your resume. Notice how confident and totally relaxed you feel. As you notice these things you are very pleased to find writing your resume is so enjoyable, fun, and exciting."

The Length of Your Script

When you write your SUCCESS IMAGERY script keep in mind the length of time you have available each day to listen to it. For example, if you have a 15 minute bus ride to and from work then record a 10 minute script. This will allow you enough time to get on the bus, get settled and begin your cassette tape. If you have more time available record your SUCCESS IMAGERY script for up to 20 minutes. Remember that listening to a shorter script three to five times a day will be more powerful than listening to a longer script only once a day. I usually prepare scripts that are about 15 minutes long. When I type the script I end up with three to four single spaced pages. I like to record my script in a relatively calm voice and at a moderate pace. You may find that you like to speak in an excited and enthusiastic way. Do whatever makes you feel the most motivated when you listen to your SUCCESS IMAGERY tape.

Use Your Learning Preference

It is well known that we each have a particular learning style. In teaching gifted as well as remedial students it is important that these styles be utilized to maximize absorption and retention of educational materials. Our primary learning styles are auditory, visual, and kinesthetic; or any combination of the three. You may have noticed by my writing style that my preference is visual and kinesthetic. To tap into my visual learning preference I describe how things look to me. To tap into my kinesthetic learning style I describe how I feel or the sensations I experience when handling or touching things. In a job situation it is important for me to read and see what I am supposed to do, as well as doing it, especially if it is a hands-on project. Others find that they are primarily auditory learners because they focus on what they hear. They may describe how an instructor's voice sounds or describe the noises a computer makes as they use it.

Take a moment and remember one of the happiest times in your childhood. Now replay the memory. Do you tend to see, hear or feel things? Randy recalled playing with her first puppy. She remembered how much fun it was to hug the puppy and roll around on the grass with the puppy licking her in the face. She loved to see the expressions of excitement and bewilderment on her puppy's face as it explored the yard with her. In recalling this memory, Randy felt her primary learning styles were visual and kinesthetic. She relied heavily on these styles when she wrote her SUCCESS IMAGERY suggestions. A friend of mine remembers playing the flute. He recalls how vibrations traveled through his flute as the flute pads opened and closed. He also talks about how the music he played moved him emotionally. He feels his primary learning styles are kinesthetic and auditory.

Once you've identified your learning style you can rely on that style to increase the vividness of your suggestions. Describe in detail the sights, sounds, touch of things, and feelings you want to have. You'll find as you do this, it increases your motivation and excitement about SUCCESS IMAGERY. Tapping into your natural learning style will also speed the re-programming of your subconscious memories.

Vividly Experience Success Imagery

To create vivid memories, you must deeply experience your SUCCESS IMAGERY suggestions. Most of the memories we recall were originally very exciting, boring, pleasant, scary or painful. These events stand out in our minds because of the intensity of the emotion, whether it was negative or positive, that we felt at that time. Normally we don't remember unimportant or trivial events as vividly, nor with as much detail or emotion. Such memories don't have the same impact on our feelings as strong and vivid memories do. Therefore, SUCCESS IMAGERY statements must be emotionally packed and vivid to increase our recall and strong experience of them. To create vivid memories you must emotionalize them. To do so, deeply feel, hear, see, and touch what you wish to experience. For example, as you listen to a description of how confident you feel, really imagine feeling that confident. If you describe a scene where you are holding a pen, piece of paper, or a book then really imagine holding them. Actually feel them in your hands. If you enjoy using a particular pen when writing then imagine how it feels to write with that pen and feel the point rolling against the paper smoothly and easily.

If you hear others compliment you then imagine how good you will feel when this really happens. Imagine that your heart is filled to the brim with happiness. See your friends smiling at you and patting you on the back. You can hear them say, *"I knew you could do this. I'm so proud of you and all that you've accomplished."* If you read novels notice how your favorite author describes people, places and things. Pay attention to the adjectives and descriptions of sights and sounds as well as feelings that get your attention. It's a wonderful learning process to read a novel and discover how vividly we use our imaginations. By harnessing this same power you can use SUCCESS IMAGERY to change your life.

Use Existing Skills

Include the skills you possess or past experiences you've had that make you feel more confident in undertaking your goal. Teaching resume classes gave me an opportunity to get feedback from large groups of clients at one time. Having a large group compliment me on my resume techniques and teaching style boosted my confidence. I used memories of teaching as a building block in my SUCCESS IMAGERY for writing this book. I continue to recall those memories by listening to the SUCCESS IMAGERY script below:

"Remember standing in front of your students, and how the room smelled musty on that rainy day at the U.W. campus. Remember Mary telling you that your class was the best class she had ever taken at the Experimental College. Remember how many of the students were eager to go to lunch with you to discuss their background and see how you could help them. Remember how confident, relieved and happy you felt when you realized the class was a success. Remember all these things and know that you are merely writing down the information in this book that you presented in those classes. Since those classes were so successful you know that your book will be too. Think of all the people who already want to buy your book."

Ways You Can Use Success Imagery

The most effective way to use SUCCESS IMAGERY is to write out a script and record it on a cassette tape. Set a goal of listening to the tape at least three times a day. As you listen to your tape over and over you may find that your attention wanders. Even though you may not always experience every suggestion as vividly as you did when you first listened to it, your subconscious mind is still aware of everything it's hearing on the tape. The same principle works here as when you drive home safely, but don't remember doing so.

NOTE: Never record or listen to any suggestions, such as closing your eyes or sleeping, that would be dangerous or result in injury while driving, operating equipment or performing any other activity.

Flashcards

If you can't record your SUCCESS IMAGERY script on a cassette tape, you can make flashcards and then read them at least three times a day. Read a statement then close your eyes and visualize, as strongly as possible, that your suggestion is really happening to you. A successful corporate trainer told me this story about using flashcards:

> *"I supported myself through college with door to door selling. The Saturday before I started my first sales job my imagination ran wild. I was terrified. I had never sold anything in my life and worried that people would be rude to me and slam their doors in my face. Worrying about these things caused me to feel sick to my stomach. By Sunday, I knew I had to do something to feel differently about my job so I wrote down all the things that worried me about door to door selling. Then I wrote sentences that turned each of my negative thoughts into a positive one. I then spent Sunday night reviewing them. What a difference it made. By Monday morning I was relaxed while making my sales calls and people were very friendly to me. At the end of my first day I had the highest sales out of 20 salespeople."*

In Summary

SUCCESS IMAGERY is the most effective tool I've found to change my self-image. It's inexpensive, easy to do, and can be a whole lot of fun - especially when you reap the financial and psychological rewards it can provide. I've included step by step worksheets that will help you write your own SUCCESS IMAGERY script. Each step provides a short explanation of what to do. Don't feel you have to write a "perfect" script. After you listen to your first script a few times you'll discover several ways you want to improve it. When you're ready to conquer a new activity write and record a new script. I've included a sample script on page 247 that focuses on conducting a successful job search.

Good luck. I think you'll be both amazed and pleased with the results you achieve by using SUCCESS IMAGERY. Let me know about your journey.

1) What is your career goal or job objective?

_____

_____

_____

_____

_____

_____

_____

_____

2) What intangible desires do you wish to fulfill by completing this goal?

If you list something that is tangible, something you can see or touch, ask yourself what desire lies beneath it that you wish to fulfill. For example, if you list a garage because that's one of the things you will be able to buy with the increased income from your new job, ask yourself why you want a garage. Is it because working in a garage will be relaxing, or make you feel competent because you can organize all your tools? Being relaxed and feeling competent are intangible desires and they are what will really motivate you to achieve your goal. When you describe your intangible desires be descriptive and use words and phrases that you find motivating.

_____

_____

_____

_____

_____

_____

_____

_____

_____

_____

_____

_____

_____

_____

_____

_____

3) What are the fears or de-motivators you experience when considering this goal?

You may worry that your next job will be worse than your current one. You may worry that your lack of an educational requirement will keep you from getting a better job. You may fear you'll fail if you take on a more responsible job or one with higher pay. You might also have the feeling that this job search stuff is just too much work.

_____
_____
_____
_____
_____
_____
_____
_____
_____
_____

4) Turn each de-motivator you listed into a motivator.

For example, if you listed the lack of an educational requirement as a de-motivator, but know of someone who has gotten a job like you want, you might write: *"Sally's education is just like mine. She used her skills to sell herself into that job. My skills are just as good as hers. If she can do it, I can too."* Remember to focus on how you want to feel and what you want to achieve. Don't include descriptions of what you want to avoid.

_____
_____
_____
_____
_____
_____
_____
_____
_____
_____
_____
_____
_____

5) Describe how you will feel when you reach your goal and fulfill your intangible desires.

For example, when I receive the first bound copy of this book I will feel proud, excited and very content. I will celebrate with a very special dinner. Holding my book will make me feel that I'm capable of much more than I ever realized. I will feel able to set and achieve any goal I desire. My self-esteem will go up. Imagining these things makes me feel very motivated.

_____

_____

_____

_____

_____

_____

_____

_____

_____

_____

6) Make a list of activities that you need to complete to achieve your goal.

Decide how long it will take you to reach your goal. Write down what you will do each day, week and month to achieve your goal. Break your goal into small steps and activities that seem challenging yet obtainable to you. As you write, remember to tap into your visual, auditory or kinesthetic learning styles. Describe how it feels to hold the pen as you write your resume, what you see as you gather your job search materials together, or how it sounds to hear an employer offer you a job. Describe in detail how you will feel as these things happen.

_____

_____

_____

_____

_____

_____

_____

_____

_____

_____

7) **Make a list of the skills you already possess that will assist you in reaching this goal.**

Have you accomplished something that is similar to this goal? Does a past accomplishment give you confidence in achieving it? I used my success in teaching career classes to help me believe the information in this book was worthwhile and to help me convince myself that I was worthwhile.

_____

_____

_____

_____

_____

_____

_____

_____

_____

_____

8) **Combine your entries from Sections 1 and 2 with your entries from Sections 4 through 7 to create your SUCCESS IMAGERY script.**

_____

_____

_____

_____

_____

_____

_____

_____

_____

_____

_____

_____

_____

_____

_____

_____

245 ♦ _____

A Sample SUCCESS IMAGERY Script

Picture yourself sitting at your desk working on your resume. You are holding a pen in your hand and feel the pressure of the pen against the paper as you write your resume. Notice how confident and totally relaxed you feel. As you notice these things you are very pleased to find writing your resume is so enjoyable, fun, and exciting.

See yourself holding this book and reading it, applying the information in it, and using the resume samples to write your resume. You are pleased at how easy writing your resume is. You understand how to describe your skills, write good sentences, select the right format, and design a resume that gets attention. Understanding these things makes you confident of your writing skills and of your ability to produce an excellent resume. You know that your success is ensured because this book is based on proven, successful results.

Imagine holding your completed resume. You feel very confident reading it and very proud of your background and qualifications as others read it. Your resume is very convincing and demonstrates how you can contribute in a significant and positive way to a company. Knowing and feeling these things makes you feel confident when applying for jobs and makes you feel proud to hand your resume to employers.

You've decided you would like to have a new job within a month. You are committed to complete several job search activities each day to reach your goal. The intangible desires that motivate you are feeling more competent on a new job, feeling proud of yourself because you are in control of your job search, and feeling excited about the prospect of making more money. You know that by making more money you will feel relaxed and in control of your financial situation. It's very empowering and motivating to look for a job that will help you achieve these things.

You see yourself going to the library and conducting research on employers. Notice how relaxed and comfortable you feel as you gather this information. You feel excited to call employers and submit your resume to them. You've already had several people compliment you on your resume. You look forward to talking with employers on the phone. Because you have rehearsed how you will sell your skills when talking on the phone, you feel confident about using the phone in your job search. You know that your voice sounds good over the phone and projects a very professional image.

You have practiced answering all the interview questions in this book and you know you can market yourself effectively as a result of answering these questions. You are pleased and proud of yourself because you have so many skills and qualifications.

Imagine going into an interview. You see the interviewer smile as he reads your resume. He says he's impressed with not only your skills but with your personality and self-motivation. He says he needs someone just like you on his team. Standing, he reaches across his desk to shake your hand and says, *"You're the best candidate I've interviewed out of 30 people. When can you start?"* You are excited and pleased to say, *"I accept the job."* You can't wait to share your happiness with your friends and family.

Naming A Specific Position

- Seek an _____ position utilizing my _____,

  _____, and _____ skills.

  <u>or:</u>

- Seek an _____ position utilizing over _____ years

  _____ experience.

Naming Skills

- Seek a position utilizing my _____,

  _____, and _____ skills.

Combining Objective & Qualifications

_____**OBJECTIVE & QUALIFICATIONS**_____

Seek an _____ position utilizing the following background:

- _____

- _____

- _____

- _____

Job Search Planner

Month _____   Year _____

Sunday	Monday	Tuesday	Wednesday	Thursday	Friday	Saturday

Suggested Reading

♦ ♦ ♦

Career Satisfaction and Success (A Guide To Job and Personal Freedom), Bernard Haldane, PhD., JIST Works, Inc.

> The best career counseling book I've found. Helps you identify skills which give you the most job satisfaction. Also helps you understand how to transfer these skills into other occupations.

♦ ♦ ♦

Wishcraft (How to Get What You Really Want), Barbara Sher with Annie Gottlieb, Ballantine Books.

> Recommended as a motivational guide for career changers. Gives excellent examples of people who have made career changes.

♦ ♦ ♦

The New Success: Redefining, Creating, and Surviving Your Own Success, Pamela A. Murray. Thanks to Pam Murray for providing an excerpt from her book. You may contact her at TLPO Box 8073, Kirkland, WA 98034 to request her newsletter and catalogue.

> Excellent guide on achieving success. Great tips and recommendations for networking. A workbook which results in self-learning and goal achievement.

♦ ♦ ♦

Molloy's Live for Success, John T. Molloy, Perigord Press.

> Excellent guide to corporate dress. Also explores the affects clothing has upon hiring and advancement. A must read for anyone seeking promotion in corporate environments.

♦ ♦ ♦

Storms of Perfection (In Their Own Words), Andy Andrews, Lightning Crown Publishers, P.O. Box 17321, Nashville, TN 37217.

> A motivating and often heartwarming collection of letters written by fifty celebrities. Recommended reading when you feel down and out. Shows how these celebrities have dealt with and overcome failure.

♦ ♦ ♦

Choices (Discover Your 100 Most Important Life Choices), Shad Helmstetter, Pocket Books.

> An excellent guide on how to make daily choices that lead to satisfaction and fulfillment. Also explores the destructiveness of negative thoughts and how to reprogram your subconscious mind.

Index

Additional Products

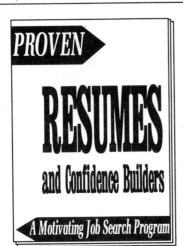

Instructor & Student Workbook

12 chapters on confidence building, resumes, cover letters, job search and interviewing. Retail $19.95.

> The only book that addresses self-confidence and its impact on resume writing and job search. Critical when dealing with college students and career changers.
> •••
> Every time I teach a class and require this book I hear success stories like this: "My old resume didn't get any response. I sent out 10 new ones and got 7 interviews!"

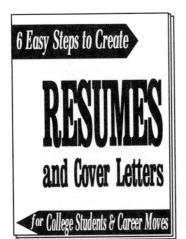

Booklet For A Mix of Students

Contains the best of the 256 page book at $8.95. Includes scanned and internet resumes. 56 pages.

Self-Confidence and Your Job Search
Before and After Resumes
Before and After Cover Letters
Before and After Thank You Letters
6 Steps to Create A Great Resume
Worksheets for the 6 Steps
Skill Lists and Sample Sentences
Transferable Skills
12 Questions To Describe Your Skills

Strategies That Blow Away Your Competition
Marketing The 10 Hottest Skills
Selling The Benefits of Your Skills
Solving Employer's Hidden Needs
Using PowerBase Statements
How To Create Targeted Resumes
Before and After Targeted Resume Examples
Easy To Use Resume Templates
Scanned and Internet Resumes

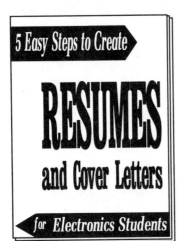

Targeted Booklets for College Programs

Call for list of completed booklets for over 70 college programs. Minimum purchase 5 booklets, $6.95.

> The booklet for accounting students made writing my resume very easy.
> •••
> The functional headings and sample sentences showed me how to describe my past experience to match a customer service position.
> •••
> I sent out 2 resumes, landed 2 interviews and accepted a $30,000 position using the strategies in the electronics booklet. And, I'm a recent graduate.
> Dawn Mitchell, Systems Technician

Order By Phone or Complete Form on Page 255

To order the 256 page book, *Proven Resumes and Confidence Builders*, complete the order form on page 255. Or call 1-800-957-1209 to charge by VISA or MasterCard. Orders for other products must be placed by calling 1-800-957-1209.

Instructor Transparency Set

Each transparency contains an instructor box which includes all the stories, thoughts and questions to ask students. Instructors love the transparencies because a great presentation can be given with only a few minutes preparation. Notebooks are priced individually or as a set for $169.95 (includes video).

As a State Employment Specialist, I achieved a 57% increase in placements over the state average by using the book and instructor set.

•••

I finally feel confident teaching resume and job search workshops and I've been teaching career classes for over 10 years!

•••

We purchased 27 instructor sets and now have 40 instructors using them. My staff loves the book and transparencies!

3 Notebooks of 94 Transparencies

Use this set to teach Resumes and Cover Letters, Tapping the Hidden Job Market and Interviewing.

Resumes & Cover Letter Notebook
Design Must Direct and Control the Reader's Eye Path
Design Must Sell Your Top Job Titles or Skill Headings in 5-10 Seconds
Content Must Make An Employer Want To Interview You
Strong Content Generates More Interviews - Weak Content Generates Fewer Interviews
12 Questions To Create Strong Content
Proven Resume and Cover Letter Examples
How To Create a Strong Objective Statement
Identifying Your Audience, What Your Audience Wants To Hear, and Hooking The Audience's Self-Interest
How to Write With Impact Checklist
Functional Skill Heading List
Skill Lists and Sample Sentences
How To Write Cover Letters That Land Interviews

Job Search Notebook
Understanding and Expanding Your Comfort Zone
Top Methods To Tap the Hidden Job Market
Becoming a Cherry Picker
New School Method of Sales
Doing Effective Library Research
Creating an Effective Phone Script
Informational Phone Script
Contacting Employers Directly by Phone Script
Leading With Your Strengths
Understanding and Expanding Your Comfort Zone

Interviewing Notebook
Marketing Your Top 5 Skills
10 Hottest Skills Employers Look For
10 Most Common Questions
De-Emphasize Your Weaknesses
Answer Questions You're Afraid Of
Ask Questions You Can Sell Yourself Into
Learn to Explain and Demonstrate Your Knowledge
Use Power Words and Quantify
Close Your Interview and Call For Action
Writing Effective Thank You Letters

Order Form

for

"Proven Resumes and Confidence Builders"

To Order by Credit Card
Call Now:
1-800-957-1209

To order a copy by <u>check or money order</u> complete the following:

Proven Resumes and Confidence Builders	$19.95	$	<u>19.95</u>
For Book Rate Mail Add	$ 2.50	$	<u>2.50</u>
For Express Mail	or $12.00		_____
If Washington Resident Add @ 8.6%	$ 1.72	$	<u>1.72</u>
Total (U.S. Dollars Only)			_____

Send check or money order to:

Abrams & Smith Publishing
P.O. Box 52901
Bellevue, WA 98015-2901

Your Name:_____

Mailing Address:_____

City:_____ State:_____ Zip:_____

Phone: (_____)_____

Please Send Complete Information For Prompt Processing

Your Notes